ENDING POVERTY

Changing Behavior, Guaranteeing Income, and Transforming Government

JOSEPH V. KENNEDY

ROWMAN & LITTLEFIELD PUBLISHERS, INC.
Lanham • Boulder • New York • Toronto • Plymouth, UK

ROWMAN & LITTLEFIELD PUBLISHERS, INC.

Published in the United States of America
by Rowman & Littlefield Publishers, Inc.
A wholly owned subsidiary of The Rowman & Littlefield Publishing Group, Inc.
4501 Forbes Boulevard, Suite 200, Lanham, Maryland 20706
www.rowmanlittlefield.com

Estover Road
Plymouth PL6 7PY
United Kingdom

British Library Cataloguing in Publication Information Available

Library of Congress Cataloging-in-Publication Data:

Kennedy, Joseph V.
    Ending poverty : changing behavior, guaranteeing income, and transforming
government / Joseph V. Kennedy.
        p. cm.
    Includes bibliographical references and index.
    ISBN-13: 978-0-7425-5872-4 (cloth : alk. paper)
    ISBN-10: 0-7425-5872-X (cloth : alk. paper)
    ISBN-13: 978-0-7425-6563-0 (electronic)
    ISBN-10: 0-7425-6563-7 (electronic)
    1. Poverty—United States. 2. United States—Economic policy—2001-
I. Title.
HC110.P6K46 2008
362.5'5610973—dc22   2008016336

Printed in the United States of America

∞™ The paper used in this publication meets the minimum requirements of
American National Standard for Information Sciences—Permanence of Paper for
Printed Library Materials, ANSI/NISO Z39.48-1992.

CONTENTS

PREFACE

The purpose of this book is not to identify those policy changes that might be implemented quickly in order to make marginal improvements in the relationship between the federal government and individual Americans, especially those people at the margins. Those types of changes are most appropriate if the basic structure of government is essentially sound and capable of achieving the purposes for which it exists. This book argues that government is becoming increasingly incapable of realizing its basic goals, and thus, a more radical reform is necessary.

If we had the luxury of starting over and designing new public policies capable of realizing our goals in the type of economic and social environment we expect to face, what programs would we design? This book suggests the answer to that question. In doing so it points out the general direction in which we should go and when we get the chance to reexamine existing policy.

The idea of this book started several years ago out of a fascination with organizational structure and a conviction that proper program design played an important role in shaping individual behavior and, hence, social outcomes. Many of our most important programs devote large amounts of resources to social problems. But, because they provide the wrong incentives, they make very little long-term progress. They seem merely to hold back forces that would make the problem worse, rather than eliminating it altogether.

Several years ago I began to transform my own life. First, I learned to dance. Eventually, I adopted a teenager, Gary, and married a wonderful woman, Jeanette. Both have made significant accommodations in order to allow me to write this book. I am extremely grateful to them and to my parents, William and Marla Kennedy; my siblings, Tim, William, Kristin, and Dan, who made my childhood challenging and fun; and to my many nieces and nephews who represent the next generation, which always holds the promise of a fresh outlook and renewed energy.

Finally, I wish to thank Rob Atkinson and my editor Christopher Anzalone, both of whom helped me find a way to finally transform these ideas into the book you have now.

INTRODUCTION:
THE VALUE OF A
CONSISTENT ALTERNATIVE
TO CURRENT POLICIES

This book argues in some detail for a new and consistent approach to how the government intervenes in economic markets in order to foster social goals. This new approach is built on three main principles. The first is that government policy is far more effective when it channels market forces than when it tries to override them. Economic motives do not explain all individual behavior, but they explain a lot. Whenever the government tries to implement a policy, however fair, that frustrates the economic interest of a large minority of individuals, it will almost always fail. Either individuals will defeat the policy by finding a number of ways to circumvent it or the government will be forced to spend inordinate resources to enforce it.

The second principle is that individuals should have far more control over the resources that government spends on their behalf. In most cases, such as primary education, housing support, and Medicaid, government programs are primarily meant to help individuals as individuals. While the benefits of some government programs, such as defense and transportation infrastructure, mainly go to general society, the purpose of most social spending is to help specific persons. Money spent and benefit delivered can be attached to a particular recipient. The fact that helping individuals can have social benefits is an extra bonus. But if the purpose of government spending is primarily to help individuals, then there ought to be a strong presumption that the individual, rather than the government, has the best sense of how that spending can further their interest.

A corollary is that many government policies actually benefit the middle and upper classes, often making it harder for the poor to climb the economic ladder. Determining who bears the ultimate burden of government policy can be extremely difficult because good data is often lacking and its analysis requires several assumptions about how government policy affects economic decisions. So the assertion just made is more of a hunch than a proven fact. But I believe it is likely that many government policies are counterproductive to society's effort to help those who most deserve and need it. The distribution of their benefits and costs reflects the political power of various interests rather than policy makers' expressed wishes.

The third principle is that access to a decent life free of poverty should be seen as a conditional right in American society. This right would not rise to the constitutional level, for the right to a material standard of living cannot be innate in each individual. It can only exist within a society that is capable of providing the transfers of wealth needed to ensure it. For example, we can meaningfully insist that North Koreans have the basic human rights of free speech and the right to assembly that their government currently denies them. But it would be meaningless to talk about their right to a middle-class lifestyle because there is no possible means by which any government could deliver it within the foreseeable future. Such a right, if it ever were to exist, would require the prior establishment of an advanced economy. The right to political freedom merely requires a constraint on a government's ability to actively interfere with it. But the right to certain economic goods implies the presence of an entity capable of providing them if they are missing. If no such entity exists, then the right is meaningless. Such a right is also not inherent. It should be conditioned on a basic level of contribution to society.

The purpose of this book is twofold. The first purpose is to lay out a policy for eliminating most poverty within twenty to thirty years. On one level this should be relatively easy. The United States is an extremely wealthy society. In 2007 Americans spent $41.2 billion on their pets,[1] $9.5 billion on computer games,[2] $87.4 billion on alcohol and cigarettes,[3] and $23 billion on high-definition televisions.[4] All of these expenditures may bring great satisfaction to the consumers that make them, but they are not nearly as important as spending for the basic necessities of life. A society in which so much is spent on items like these can easily ensure a decent living standard to the minority that needs its help, especially if payments are conditioned on an acceptance of socially accepted obligations. One could even argue that, in the absence of such a social support, there is something immoral about the current demand for ten thousand-dollar John Lobb shoes and ex-CEOs multimillion-dollar retirement packages.

The purpose of this program is not to eliminate all domestic poverty. The biblical observation that the poor will always be with us is likely to prove true. But poverty is caused by many different factors, and a wealthy society can eliminate many of those factors through well-designed programs that provide individuals with the proper incentives to do those things that experience shows are strongly correlated with personal success. Other factors, such as drug addiction, crime, teenage pregnancy, and the arrival of new immigrants with little education and few skills, will continue to cause a base level of poverty that is more resistant to social policy.

Much of life is governed by the eighty/twenty rule. According to this rule, if one looks at the total effort required to solve a given problem, roughly 20 percent of the effort is needed to solve 80 percent of the problem. The vast majority of the effort is needed to solve the minority of very difficult cases. Applied to poverty, the rule would lead one to believe that a large portion of poverty can be eliminated by relatively straightforward programs that provide income to people who would otherwise do well on their own. For these recipients, poverty is largely an income problem: provide the income and they can become successful members of society. This is the central purpose of the book. A critical assumption is that most poor individuals will willingly comply with the program requirements in exchange for government payments.

A minority of cases will continue to require more intervention. In some cases, an individual may be engaging in behaviors that continue to impoverish her or him despite the government's assistance. These may include criminals and addicts whose actions continue to estrange them from society. Teenage parents and high school dropouts present a slightly different problem in which actions taken at an early age impose burdens and responsibilities that make it more difficult to undertake the educational and other investments needed to advance economically as one grows older. In each of these cases, the mere transfer of a certain sum of money may not solve the underlying problem. But even so, the existence of the social contract proposed in this book offers an incentive to the individual and a point of leverage to the government to encourage a change of paths. It provides the route by which prodigal sons and daughters can return to a productive place in society and we can welcome them back.

Finally, there will always be individuals who, because of one handicap or another, will need continuous government support in order to be properly housed, fed, and cared for. Some of these individuals may need significantly greater resources, in both time and income, than the proposed contract calls for. But the hope is that, by placing the large majority of easier cases on the path toward self-sufficiency, the government will have both more resources and more attention to devote to the minority of individuals who truly need intensive intervention. By managing by exception, government can do a much better job of prioritizing its scarce resources.

A central principle motivating the book is that government assistance is much more effective when the income needed to purchase necessary goods and services is channeled directly though recipients rather then given in a form that leaves individuals no choice. The former approach allows individuals to make those tradeoffs at the margin that are in their best interest, and it gives them purchasing power to choose between more than one potential supplier. The latter approach often results in a service that is unresponsive to recipients' needs and subject to capture by special interest groups. Switching to a client-based system would not result in the dramatic overhaul of housing, education, or other sectors, but it would gradually lead to markets that show a great deal more continuous improvement and diversity than the current top-down system.

During the last two decades, most of the private sector has implemented management and technology reforms that have dramatically improved quality while reducing costs in real terms. The main reason these same advances have not occurred in the public sector is that the structural incentives for this type of innovation are largely absent. There is little pressure to do better over time, either in terms of quality or cost. In fact, the belief that over time quality should increase while costs fall is regarded as unrealistic, even though it has regularly been achieved in broad areas of manufacturing and private services. Unless the structural reforms needed to achieve similar progress in the public sector are put in place, government will increasingly lose the ability to provide economic security to its citizens.

ORGANIZATION

Chapter 1 explains how events of the last two decades have limited the federal government's power to control private markets. The causes include technological innovation, the rise of competing economies including China and India, globalization, deregulation, and a growing skepticism of the government's ability to efficiently pursue social goals. Yet the world within which government must operate has become much more complex. Thus, while the challenge of intervening in the economy has become more difficult, the government's power to do so has diminished. The government would have more success if it selected a few key social goals and crafted policies that are narrowly designed to achieve them, instead of trying to solve all problems in all markets. Following this advice requires the government to pull back from some efforts in order to concentrate on those that truly matter. Concentrating only on those goals that are most important and most achievable frees up resources and creates additional degrees of freedom within which individuals can act. Officials must then be content to let the market evolve as it will, hopeful that, however it evolves, the achievement of their primary goals will hold.

Ensuring a decent income for all responsible Americans should be one of the priority goals that government seeks to achieve. To do this it must act transparently so that it can verify what its efforts are accomplishing. For many poor individuals poverty simply stems from a lack of income. Therefore, the simplest way to solve it is by transferring income. Yet more often than not, government has tried to solve poverty by intervening in a diverse set of markets including housing, health care, education, and agriculture. The rationale for doing so is not clear. Each market, although complex, is capable of producing a diverse supply of products and services to anyone with sufficient income. The problem is usually not with the market; it is with the lack of income. Rather than try to change the market to compensate for the problem, officials should address the problem directly. Doing so would be easier and more efficient.

In some cases, market problems do exist. Often government itself introduces these problems. In such cases the simplest solution is for government to withdraw its intervention and let the market work unimpeded. In other cases, such as health care, problems are inherent in the particular sector. Even here, rather than impose complex regulations designed to overcome normal market forces, the best policy is to try to impose simple rules that address the specific market failures and then to allow the natural forces of choice and competition to operate as freely as possible.

The book proposes to accomplish this channeling through two main avenues. The first is a bilateral, annual, and voluntary contract between the federal government and any citizen above the age of twenty-one who wishes to participate. The government would hopefully guarantee the individual a minimum income of at least $20,000. The exact amount would be determined by the resources made available by the spending reductions discussed in chapter 10 and would increase with GDP. For comparison purposes, in 2006 the official poverty threshold for a single person was $10,488, and for a family of four it was $20,444. If a husband and wife both signed the contract they would receive a total income of at least $40,000, well above the poverty level.

Chapter 2 explains why the federal government should make this commitment. It also explains why the type of contract proposed above is the simplest, most direct way to achieve this goal, not just for the current poor, but also for future generations. The chapter reviews some of the current literature on the nature and causes of poverty. Finally, it argues for major changes in a number of existing programs in order to free up the resources needed to fund the program. Many of these existing programs fund activities that are of minor national importance. Others were originally justified as efforts to help make certain goods or services more affordable. The benefits seldom went to the poor, however. If instead we concentrate on making sure that people possess sufficient income, the rationale for these programs is severely diminished.

In exchange for the government's commitment, the individual would commit to doing a limited number of qualifying actions. These actions are chosen because they are relatively easy to verify, they are strongly linked to personal success, and there is a broad public consensus that individuals ought to engage in these behaviors irrespective of any government commitment. The requirements are as follows:

1. Work at least forty hours per week.
2. Do not take illegal drugs or become an alcoholic.
3. Do not commit any crimes.
4. Complete high school and at least two years of additional school or training.
5. Do not have children before the age of twenty-one.
6. Save at least 15 percent of income.
7. Pay taxes.

Chapter 3 explains what these requirements would entail and why each is both necessary and reasonable in exchange for the government's reciprocal obligation to guarantee the promised level of income. The chapter also discusses how violations of the contract might be handled. Briefly, some violations would not necessarily disqualify an individual from receiving support, but they would provide leverage by which the government could intervene to encourage or require a return to the path of self-sufficiency.

The proposal also advocates an active role for social assistance, albeit in a much different form than traditionally. Guaranteeing income to workers creates demand for a wide variety of services including job training, financial advice, and counseling of various types. These services may be provided by traditional businesses. But they could also be provided by a vast array of nonprofit groups and government agencies at the local, state, and federal level. By changing the dynamic from centralized bureaucracies handing out assistance in accordance with specific government policy to much more decentralized efforts focused on serving clients who pay for at least part of the cost of service, this reform should lead to more responsive assistance that meets the true needs of the poor.

The first part of the book therefore lays out a program in which the federal government can provide each working individual with an economic floor that must be regarded as generous given current policies. But income is not the whole side of the equation. To be fully self-sufficient individuals must also have access to essential goods and services. In some markets, such as agriculture, there is little reason to think that, once a person has an adequate income, they will have difficulty finding the goods that they need. Despite tens of billions of dollars in wasteful and counterproductive federal subsidies each year, agricultural producers reliably supply a diverse variety of affordable food and efficiently deliver it to every neighborhood in the country.

Other industries are more problematical, however. Education, health care, housing, and savings markets all perform less reliably, especially for those with the least income. Each is important to public policy because an individual's decision to purchase these services has important social effects. Each also suffers from market imperfections of different kinds that cast some doubt on the private sector's ability and willingness to provide the type of services that the public needs at an affordable price. These failures have been used to justify government involvement. However, this involvement has brought failures of its own, often making the lack of affordable supply worse rather than better. The result has been that, despite large expenditures of public resources, each of these industries remains unable to provide sufficient affordable services to those at the bottom of the economic ladder.

The rest of the book argues that the government should pursue a much different approach to each industry. Instead of directly intervening in the markets, it should use refundable tax credits to give individuals both the means and the incentive to purchase these services on their own. Government should then rely on normal market forces to respond appropriately to demand. Doing so would produce more variety, higher levels of service, and greater efficiency. The greatest improvement would come at the bottom of the market where most of the new purchasing power would be created. Where gaps in the provision of services still exist, the government should set up independent nonprofits with a specific charter to close them. Provided that the government can credibly do this, it can play a powerful role in supplementing normal market forces without many of the perverse incentives that normally accompany government efforts.

In arguing that the government should rely largely on transfers of purchasing power rather than the direct provision of services, the book places heavy reliance on the private sector to provide services like housing, education, and health care at affordable prices. It is possible that most parts of the reputable private market will continue to concentrate on middle- and upper-income consumers who are able and willing to pay higher profit margins for slightly better service. People with low incomes and little education may continue to face a dearth of good alternatives. Although this outcome is unlikely, chapter 4 addresses how it can be addressed by a growing nonprofit sector.

Once the government has transferred sufficient purchasing power, it should be possible for a variety of nonprofits to provide needed services at cost and remain financially stable. In fact, governments at all levels could create new nonprofits specifically chartered to serve any viable markets that the private sector overlooks. Provided that the government required the new organizations to stand on their own without public assistance, it could have a reasonable hope that they would work hard to serve the needs of their intended customers. But by participating in their formation and chartering, government could ensure that they focused on parts of the market that might otherwise be neglected.

Chapter 5 looks at education. Education, or more specifically marketable skills, is increasingly a prerequisite for finding a middle-class job. Yet our current system does a poor job of providing the most appropriate training for the least amount of money, the normal function of a market. Many primary schools, especially in the poorest neighborhoods, fail to teach children the basics skills of reading, writing, and arithmetic. High schools also suffer from poor performance, even as some of the brightest students spend their junior and senior years in a holding pattern waiting for college. The college system also exhibits serious market failures. A large portion of government assistance simply funds tuition increases, rather than increasing affordability. Universities possess a poor understanding of the private sector markets in which most of their graduates will have to find employment. College accreditation and professional standards often protect existing institutions and professionals against competition from innovations that might make training more accessible and relevant while reducing its cost. The book argues that a greater reliance on vouchers and tax credits would give parents, students, and workers more flexibility and power in making the best choices for their long-term future. Opening up alternative paths for obtaining and demonstrating the competence needed to perform specific jobs would make education more accessible to those who have the hardest time affording it now.

Chapter 6 looks at housing policy. There is little risk that individuals will not seek affordable housing on their own. In this case the problems occur on the supply side. Overly restrictive zoning laws severely limit the ability to create affordable housing units. Current government policy often produces high-priced, low-quality units that isolate people in pockets of high crime. At the same time, the tax deduction for mortgage interest provides a large subsidy to the housing industry, but in a way that encourages overinvestment, raising housing costs even higher for those who cannot take advantage of the tax benefit. The benefits of the deduction go mainly to the middle and upper classes, who of course can afford adequate housing without assistance. Very few of those most in need of help benefit. A flat tax credit that could be applied to either mortgage payments or rent would provide more broad-based help. Rolling back government regulation and restricting the ability of local governments to engage in social planning through zoning laws would make it easier to build attractive low-cost housing in safe neighborhoods.

Chapter 7 argues that the main problem with the health care sector is excessive government involvement. Through government programs and the exclusion of employer-provided health insurance from income, the government continues to deliver large subsidies to the health care industry that are poorly linked to either quality or need. In doing so it has severely limited the employment flexibility of workers, made health care too expensive for many Americans, and reduced the incentives for continuous improvement that normally exist in competitive markets. A single-payer system of health insurance would only make these problems worse. Yet, like other insurance markets, health insurance suffers from problems of adverse selection and moral hazard. To address these problems the government should provide each individual with a refundable tax credit equal to 100 percent of the cost of an average standard health care plan, provided that the individual purchases a qualified insurance plan. It should fund this by eliminating the tax exclusion for employer-paid insurance and both Medicare and Medicaid. The government should also remove barriers to competition that make it difficult for new providers to enter the market with low-cost, high-quality services.

Chapter 8 looks at retirement policy and Social Security. The income supplement contract calls for individuals to save a significant part of their income. This might seem onerous, until one remembers that Social Security already takes a comparable portion of each worker's paycheck, without guaranteeing an equivalent return. It would be much better to allow low-paid workers to divert this amount into their own private accounts. Workers should also have the option of placing an even greater portion of their pay into a tax-deferred savings account. Under certain assumptions, these accounts might increase the net present value of the taxes that government can expect to collect. Even if they do not, taxing income when it is consumed rather than earned makes it easier for the average worker to save enough to become self-sufficient at retirement.

Chapters 9 and 10 look at broader reform of taxes and spending, respectively. In order for the above programs to work, a great deal of restructuring will be needed in other parts of the federal government. In addition to freeing up financial resources, tax and entitlement reform can spur economic growth, creating even more resources to devote toward those programs that the government must operate. By simplifying the government's role in the economy, reform can also make it easier to identify and affect those areas where continued federal intervention is truly needed.

Social growth does not stop once a country is rich enough to fulfill all of its basic needs. For all of the recent emphasis on economic growth, rising incomes cannot be the end objective that society seeks to maximize. It must be something else, perhaps happiness or a different kind of personal productivity. Recent research demonstrates that individuals do not become appreciably happier above a certain low level of income. Instead, their focus shifts to a higher level on a hierarchy of needs. The conclusion discusses the need for a broader social dialogue on what individuals should seek and what they should be encouraged to find.

Given the current political climate, it would be impossible and probably unwise to enact all of the book's recommendations at once. But that does not lessen their value. Social growth is a voyage and therefore requires at least a tentative destination. In order to achieve any long-range goal we need some criteria for evaluating whether changes in the status quo take us closer or further away from our destination. We can then have some confidence that reforms that get us closer to our ultimate goal are worth supporting. Changes that move us further away from our goal should be opposed. I believe that economic and political events will drive us in the direction advocated in this book. As we come to believe more in the ability and right of each citizen to control resources spent on their behalf we will adopt many of these reforms. And as changes in the world continue to limit government's power to control markets, these policies will be the only ones that let government ensure that each individual possesses the resources needed to succeed.

Both parties should welcome reform in this direction. In the current terms of debate, the programs here might initially appeal to Republicans more than Democrats. But much of the current political division between the two parties is due to the influence of the interest groups each party is currently allied with, rather than the product of a consistent political philosophy. For example, at one time the Democratic Party was the champion of free trade largely because it benefited the South, which was then a Democratic stronghold. Republicans favored tariffs in order to protect industry from its European competitors. Now Democrats oppose trade deals in order to protect unions from competition while Republicans argue the need to give businesses access to growing global markets. Yet a dispassionate view of trade shows that it always increases national wealth over time, even though some domestic groups suffer severe losses.

It is not too much of a stretch to imagine that Republicans could favor creating a generous income guarantee in order to bring the benefits of the market to all Americans and to encourage the type of personal behavior that is linked to both individual success and social stability—nor is it impossible to believe that Democrats might insist on vouchers and tax credits as the surest way to get around entrenched bureaucracies and empower those individuals that society might otherwise ignore. The values enshrined in these recommendations are ones that both parties truly espouse. An argument is made here that these programs offer the greatest promise of promoting those values.

One is then left with the question of will it work? Unfortunately, social institutions and human behavior are much more complex than the hard sciences. As a result, economic evidence about what works is often subject to a great deal of legitimate debate. Even the best data is often ill suited to measure the specific questions being asked. There can be valid disagreements about causation and the model that should be tested. It is very difficult and expensive to run the type of randomized experiments that are common in other sciences. Finally, policy makers and the public too often seem uninterested in understanding the issues, preferring instead to latch on to bombast and ridicule that confirms their preexisting prejudices.

But many experiments along the lines advocated in this book do show success. Unfortunately, that success is usually mixed and subject to a large number of complicating influences. It is impossible to prove that this approach will work. Yet current programs clearly spend large sums of money without accomplishing reasonable progress. With government's traditional powers waning and the practical and moral arguments for increasing individual choice growing, the burden of proof should be on those who would argue that individuals are incapable of making intelligent choices if given greater freedom or that markets are incapable of serving all Americans.

1

HOW THE MODERN WORLD
DIMINISHES GOVERNMENT POWER

A major premise of this book is that policy changes are necessary because the complexity of the current economic, social, and political
environment severely limits government's ability to shape it by conscious
policy. Social goals that government might have accomplished a few
decades ago are increasingly difficult today and will be impossible tomorrow. Although in developed countries the national government retains its
monopoly on legitimate force within its borders, its economic, political,
and even physical powers are weaker than they previously were. Since this
trend is likely to continue, governments must change their tactics. They
must concentrate on a narrower set of goals. They must pursue those
goals with focused policies that co-opt rather than challenge the forces
operating in the private sector. Finally, they must abandon many attempts
to engage in the detailed regulation of markets, instead finding ways to
align market forces to operate on their own within broader government
parameters.

This chapter will look at the main forces acting on government and
their effects. These forces produce a wealthier society with greater latitude
for individual action. On the other hand, each imposes costs on those who
benefit from the existing status quo. Because these costs tend to be con-
centrated on a narrower section of society, they tend to be more visible than
the benefits of change, which are often spread out over the broader population. In addition, by reducing the relative power of government to control society, these forces also reduce its power to accomplish many social
goals. The future becomes shaped by the collective impact of billions of individual decisions rather than by a few collective decisions by society acting
as one.

INHERENT LIMITATIONS ON
GOVERNMENT'S ABILITY TO ACT

Government policy has always suffered from a number of inherent problems. These include the collective choice problem, principal/agent issues, information costs, rent-seeking, and cost-shifting. Although these problems are interrelated, each presents a unique source of difficulty that complicates the implementation of any government policy.

Even if we assume that government is capable of implementing policies that efficiently achieve their goal, there remains the problem of how these goals are selected. In a modern society with a wide diversity of citizens, there is likely to be a great deal of disagreement regarding the goals that government should pursue. It is possible that individuals will largely agree on the desirability of many general goals such as social equality and economic growth. But when policy requires weighing the relative priority of these conflicting goals, which it usually does, differences are likely to emerge. These differences may stem from personal interest, moral or philosophical differences, or different opinions on future events and the way in which government policy affects the economy.

The lack of unanimity complicates decision making but normally does not prevent it. Every government has procedures for making a decision in the face of conflict. The most common in democratic societies is majority voting. But such procedures do not permanently solve the problem. When there are more than two possible policies it is quite possible that none will be the preferred policy of a majority of citizens. In this case no matter what policy is currently being pursued, there will always be a majority in favor of changing it. Economist Kenneth Arrow demonstrated that, under quite reasonable assumptions, no voting system is capable of producing a unique ranking of policy preferences.[1]

The difficulty of developing a clear and consistent consensus behind public policy is likely to increase as the policy becomes more complicated and as it conflicts with other policy goals that also enjoy widespread support. This book argues that guaranteeing an adequate income to each working person who complies with certain limited behaviors should be a primary goal of government; that it should not be attached to other goals; and that, when it conflicts with other possible goals, those other goals should give way. It also presupposes that such a goal, if implemented in a manner similar to the suggestions of this book, can receive strong and consistent public support. The difficulty will be in getting from our current policies to the recommended one.

Simplicity is important because the government also has a great deal of difficulty implementing any policy once it is agreed on. The primary problem is that the public has imperfect control over its agents in the government. Policy makers often pursue their own agendas rather than the public interest. Bureaucracies, such as teachers unions, frequently try to protect their jobs by resisting reforms, such as merit pay, that might reduce the cost of government or improve the delivery of services. And special interests try to influence the government to act for their benefit, rather than in the general interest. It is difficult for people on one level of government to verify that those at lower levels are doing their best to fulfill their duties. In complex markets, this difficulty is especially challenging because Congress and the president cannot draft laws that will take into account every contingency that might arise. Officials therefore must be given a great deal of discretion in how to apply general principles to specific cases. But the interests of these officials are not identical to those of either national policy makers or the public in general. This opens the way for opportunistic behavior in which those who actually implement policy do so in ways that Congress did not intend and that do not further the public interest.

It is not safe to assume that a clear intention at the national level can be reliably implemented in actual practice. The federal government may have a strong desire to see all children achieve a given level of education in high school. But articulating this desire into specific legislation, agreeing on the best policy to achieve it, and then ensuring that schools consistently follow this policy would be exceedingly difficult even if the federal government controlled all high schools, which it does not. Instead what we find is that the interest of teachers and administrators often trumps that of the children they are supposed to serve because the former control the resources and the latter do not. This divergence of interests explains how, in the fall of 2006, the teachers union in Detroit could shut down the city's school system while claiming to act in the best interests of the city's children.[2]

A third source of difficulty lies with information costs. In order to implement a program with any consistency, government needs good information about its application in thousands of specific cases. But this information is often unavailable and usually costly when it does exist. Yet without good information, it is increasingly impossible for government to enact policies that accomplish specific purposes. Several factors conspire to make this so.

Several decades ago, economist Friedrich Hayek asserted that centralized planning systems were doomed to fail because they lacked access to the private information of individuals.[3] Although government experts could know a great deal more about general economic and technological conditions than the average citizen, each citizen has a store of private knowledge about the specific conditions in his or her immediate world. Since any detailed policy would actually play out in these local markets, the government has an inherent difficulty in crafting policy that will actually work as intended. A policy that applies an identical broad-brush approach to all cases does not need much private information, but it is likely to result in a great deal of inappropriate responses. Conversely, a detailed policy that depends on the specific facts of each application may work well in theory, but because the government lacks the required information, it will fail in practice.

Of course, the government can try to acquire the necessary information. There is an inherent lag in the information-gathering process, however. Even the lowest government official generally has relatively broad responsibilities and therefore faces a limit on his or her ability to gather the necessary information. At higher levels, individual commissioners of the Federal Communications Commission are responsible for policies covering the entire communications industry. It is impossible for them to know all of the relevant details about how a proposed decision will affect the private sector. There is a natural decrease in knowledge as information flows between the substantive experts within a company, the company lobbyists in Washington who try to convey this knowledge to Congress and administration officials, and the ultimate policy makers themselves. Not only is information lost, but also the process takes a great deal of time to produce a decision. The result is a system in which those making the broadest decisions have the least amount of information and where the procedural delays in making a decision produce policies that quickly lose their relevance because the world has changed. As a result, government often has difficulty acting in an informed and timely manner.

This problem is exacerbated if an issue is complex or changing rapidly, as most markets increasingly are. Complexity adds to the information load policy makers must bear. In recent years many interest groups have pushed for legislation to preserve the "net neutrality" of the Internet. On its surface, the concept of treating all data streams alike has a certain appeal. But even a brief inquiry into the issue shows that Internet companies frequently discriminate among different data streams and that many of these practices are highly beneficial. The task of understanding exactly how this is done, which forms of discrimination are valuable and which should be discouraged, and what form of legislation would distinguish between the two without giving rise to a great deal of litigation is extremely difficult. The problem may be impossible in the face of rapid changes in technology, business practices, and market structure. For example, government mandates that are prohibitively expensive may become much more affordable later. Or telephone companies that seem to have a monopoly over local calls may suddenly find a substantial portion of their business migrating to cellular and Internet phones.

A fourth problem derives from the source of most knowledge. Because government lacks the funds, time, and expertise to understand the specifics of given markets, it necessarily relies on private parties for a large portion of the knowledge it does have. These parties have their own interests, and the information they convey carries a range of conscious and unconscious biases. Liberal think tanks tend to see economic facts in a different light than their conservative counterparts, partly because they attract like-minded researchers in the first place. More explicitly, the National Association of Broadcasters exists to further the economic interest of its member television and radio stations, not the general interest and certainly not that of competitors such as cable television or satellite radio. The information it provides to policy makers will reflect this purpose.

This leads to yet another problem that policy makers face. The environment in which they operate is filled with private interests that seek to use government to pursue their own welfare. Steelmakers lobby for protection from cheap imports. Airline companies seek laws that would limit the ability of foreign carriers to offer flights in the United States. As discussed above, even if there is broad agreement that all legislation should further the national interest, it is not very clear exactly how this interest should be determined. To the extent that existing laws reflect the product of a multitude of economic actors battling it out in the political process, one could claim that by definition they represent the national interest. But it is doubtful that such a process would produce those laws that, above all others, further any objective measurements of national welfare. There is a difference between a random agglomeration of private interests and the true public welfare.

Finally, in a complex economy, the great degree of economic freedom that each person enjoys gives her or him a greater ability to find ways to pass the costs of any government regulation on to others. Under current law taxes for Social Security and Medicare are collected from both the employer and the employee with each paying half. Yet economic studies clearly show that over time employers have been able to pass almost their entire portion of the tax on to their employees in the form of lower take-home pay. The same is generally true of private employment benefits such as pensions and health care. Thus, instead of paying 7.65 percent of their salary in payroll taxes, employees are in fact paying twice that. In general, one party's ability to pass costs on to another increases as the latter's market power and range of alternatives falls. In other words, those with the fewest choices and the least ability to bargain are likely to find that a greater portion of the costs of regulation end up on their shoulders. Although we may not always be able to trace the flow of funds exactly, we should not be surprised if most of the cost of government eventually is paid by the poor and least powerful groups, since they have the least discretion and the fewest alternatives.

Each of these five sources of difficulty in determining and implementing the right policy is likely to become more serious as markets become more complex and as the speed of social and technological change increases. As a result, government will become increasingly unable to implement specific policies that fine tune different parts of the economy. In addition, it is likely to face increased social resistance to any attempts to do so.

THE LINK BETWEEN NATIONAL INCOME AND GOVERNMENT POWER

One of the primary forces acting on society is the general link between rising national incomes and both a reduced need to rely on government as a source of security and a reduced willingness to accept government limitations on personal choice. As economies develop, the government's role shifts from being a creator of wealth to being either an enabler or impeder of wealth creation. In a primitive economy government may be equally or better placed to handle the task of coordinating diverse economic functions into a product that exceeds the value of its components. In a modern economy characterized by great complexity and rapid change, only the diversity and freedom of the private sector can discover sufficient methods of continuous improvement. Government policy still has a large impact on the degree to which this process occurs but it is mainly in helping to create and enforce the social and legal environment within which private initiatives either flourish or fail. As such, its ability to impact variables like national wealth is once removed. Its main impact is on the conditions it helps create rather than on activities that directly add value. Even if the government's budget as a percent of gross domestic product (GDP) remains the same, its relative power is likely to decline as national income grows because a larger portion of government activity will be concerned with income transfers that have little effect on productivity, rather than on activities that directly add to the wealth of its people.

Richer societies are obviously able to pay more in taxes. As a result the government usually gains absolute power as an economy develops. It is able to hire more regulators, build a larger police force and army, and increase its spending on a variety of programs. Richer societies also need government participation in a wider range of activities. As industries and social relations become more complex, government policy must extend to new areas such as communications regulation, environmental protection, and energy policy. However, the relative power of government declines, largely because it is less relevant in meeting the most important needs of its people.

The psychologist Abraham Maslow theorized that individuals have a hierarchy of needs.[4] In most individuals, needs at one level are only expressed once lower-level needs are satisfied. At the bottom of the hierarchy are those needs essential for physical survival. These physiological needs include food, shelter, and sleep. Individuals who have to struggle to fulfill these needs operate in a very basic state of subsistence and are highly dependent on others. At the next level are safety needs such as social order and physical safety, which satisfy a longing for physical security in an uncertain world. Here an individual might prefer the harsh rule of a strong state to the freedom that is inherent in anarchy. It is only at the third level of belonging and love needs that individuals begin to think of others and their role in society. But most individuals cannot devote energy to meeting these needs until want and aggression no longer demand their constant attention. Maslow felt that individuals have a need for a place in society and connection to others. At a higher level, individuals can concentrate on building esteem, both the esteem of others and their own self-esteem. Finally, at the highest level, individuals seek self-actualization, the desire as Maslow says, for people to "become actualized in what they are potentially . . . to become everything that one is capable of becoming."[5]

In a modern economy physiological needs become easily satisfied, allowing individuals to feel and express their higher-level needs. Within developed countries, safety needs are also usually met, otherwise the economy quickly relapses into a more primitive state. The presence of a stable government and high personal incomes reduces the risk of crime and poverty. Although there may be continued anxiety about economic and social dislocation, these fears are often mitigated by personal savings and government support programs. Thus, individuals have both the income and the security to focus on the higher-level needs, including their own self-actualization. As they reach this level they become both less dependent on government and less willing to comply with policies that might hinder their own personal expression. It is possible, however, to confuse levels of need. Therefore, an individual may try to satisfy the need for belongingness or esteem by eating more or by trying to accumulate material possessions. Such a strategy is unlikely to produce the desired satisfaction.

Maslow's theory can be applied to the need for a stronger social contract in three ways. First, we are unlikely to see a general rise in higher capacities among individuals until society guarantees that their basic needs will be met. Of course, this assumes that the society is wealthy enough to make such as guarantee meaningful. It also assumes that the policies put in place are effective in meeting these basic needs, something that should never be taken for granted. Second, it may be impossible for even the wealthier members of society to meet their goals of self-actualization until and unless they have put into place policies that create a fair distribution of resources among all who contribute to society's well-being. Failure to do so may indicate that rather than transcending the lower levels of need, individuals are merely fixated on them. Finally, as society becomes wealthier, the polices governments pursue may have to give greater scope to individual choice and expression as individuals become increasingly willing to leave the security of the state to pursue their own path to growth.

Richard Posner points out that education, strongly correlated with rising income, also can reduce the individual's willingness to abide by collective norms.[6] By teaching individuals to think for themselves and instilling tools such as rationalization, casuistic reasoning, and moral skepticism, education may increase their tendency to question authority whenever it frustrates their individual goals. Thus, a wealthier society may exhibit less inclination to defer to government policy that pursues collective goals, even when the goals are popular and the policies are well designed for achieving them.

The government's relative power also declines as an economy becomes wealthier and more complex. In a traditional agricultural or manufacturing economy the government exercises great power over macroeconomic variables like the exchange and interest rates. Because trade volumes and financial flows are relatively small, the government, by intervening in financial markets, can have a disproportionate marginal effect on market prices. However, as financial markets become more complex, the volume of private transactions can quickly overwhelm the resources the government commands. Moreover, the increased sophistication of financial markets over the last three decades has given the private sector a large supply of instruments with which to arbitrage or counter government policy. For example, the U.S. government's decision to move to flexible exchange rates was strongly influenced by the rapid growth of U.S. liabilities to foreign entities, which could be used to speculate against the dollar. The deregulation of banks was largely forced by the rapid growth of money market funds in the 1970s, which promised savers higher returns. And the decision to allow banks and securities firms to merge was preceded by the growth of private security offerings in which private companies increasingly borrowed money by issuing their own bonds rather than taking out a loan from banks. Over the past few decades, exponential growth in both the volume and variety of derivative instruments has given the private sector a large range of new tools to hedge risk and arbitrage disparities between individual markets. Electronic commerce has further reduced government's ability to separate one market from others and ensures that billions of dollars in private wealth and investment can flow across markets and borders within seconds.

As the economy has become more diverse, it is also more difficult for government to assist one sector of the economy without hurting others. When companies were vertically integrated and few engaged in international trade, tariffs to protect one sector had little impact on others. Even if other countries retaliated, the overall impact on the entire economy would be small. But when supply chains cross a number of borders, when U.S. companies depend on imported components to remain competitive, and when many companies rely on foreign markets for a large portion of their sales, any attempt to protect one industry, especially one that produces a widely used commodity, is likely to cause net harm, even if other countries do not retaliate. In 2002, the United States imposed temporary tariffs on steel imports from a number of countries in order to protect the domestic steel industry. This benefited a number of struggling steel companies, giving them time to restructure and save a number of jobs. However, domestic steel prices rose, increasing production costs for other industries that are heavily dependent on steel inputs. Some of these industries found that they could no longer compete against foreign companies for international sales. Others, such as the auto industry, found that higher production costs only added to their existing financial difficulties. The net result was a loss of U.S. exports of higher value products and a net reduction in the pace of job creation.

GLOBALIZATION

Recent trends in technology and business practices have increased America's reliance on events beyond its borders, over which Congress and the president have much less influence. Some companies have always operated abroad, but until recently most of these operated as traditional multinationals. Foreign operations were usually separately managed, much of the production was intended for nearby markets, and whatever trade did occur was usually one way. Increasingly, companies now operate as truly global enterprises. Production is sourced where it makes the most economic sense in flexible factories that can expand or contract in response to labor and input prices. Management is more international, with individual businesses often reporting across country borders and fully integrated into a central strategic plan. And trade flows both ways, often more than once in the journey from raw materials to final product and then aftermarket use.[7]

Aside from the competition between nations, which will be discussed below, globalization implies a much greater degree of integration with, and therefore dependence on, activity overseas. This integration has been facilitated by a number of technological and management developments, which are unlikely to be reversed except in the face of heavy government pressure. Because global integration strongly benefits the national economy, any attempt to stop it is likely to cause far more harm than good.

One of the most influential factors has been the steady drop in both communications and computing power. The price of an international call dropped by over 80 percent between 1993 and 2003. Since then the threat of Internet calling has only put further pressure on prices. Global data networks not only allow companies to place a large portion of their support staff in countries like Ireland and India, but they also allow American engineers to actively collaborate on projects with colleagues halfway around the globe.

Cheap computing power has made it easier to collect, analyze, and distribute information. One of the first significant developments was the growth of international capital markets capable of transferring trillions of dollars each day across borders and offering investors an increasing diversity of opportunities to seek the best combination of financial return and risk. This mobility limits government control of markets.

Rapidly declining transportation costs have also facilitated global integration. The advent of containerization changed transportation in two major ways.[8] First, the movement toward a standardized container created efficiencies in the way goods were moved within a single mode of transport. Shipping capacity could now be sold as a commodity. The time and cost associated with loading and unloading cargo fell dramatically, and the opportunity to use machinery rather than labor increased. This placed pressure on port unions to increase efficiency and reduce labor costs in order to maintain their competitiveness. Containers could also be transferred from one mode of transport to another more efficiently, opening up a second source of cost reduction. Different modes of transport such as ships, trains, trucks, and even planes increasingly found themselves competing for the same loads. For high-value or time sensitive cargo, air transport is increasingly cost effective: green beans picked yesterday in Kenya end up in British restaurants today.[9] The resulting competition forced governments to deregulate transportation industries in order to give them a chance to compete in this new world.

The rapid decline in information costs also transforms the relationship between citizens and large institutions, including government. The full effect of the information age should arrive within the next two or three decades. Economic and social interactions will increasingly be integrated through a high-speed information network consisting of sensors, transmission lines, data storage and processing capabilities, and output devices. Technological progress in each component has been marked by a form of Moore's Law, with both the quality and affordability of a component improving at exponential rates. The continuation of these trends should make information ubiquitous over the next few decades.

Although many governments have tried hard to limit access to satellite dishes and Internet websites, none is likely to be able to enjoy both significant control over information flows and a competitive economy. Even democratic governments are experiencing a decline in relative power. Citizens are increasingly able to communicate directly with each other across international borders. Electronic communications let ordinary people record music, produce film, and publish books without depending upon established producers to create and distribute their content. Blogs and websites like youtube.com allow individuals to bypass the traditional media and reach large audiences directly. Media markets are increasingly being led by technological abilities and consumer behavior rather than the wishes of traditional record companies and movie studios. This limits the government's power to regulate traditional media because any policy that adds to production costs without delivering a corresponding increase in consumer value simply puts these companies at a further disadvantage against competitors that the government cannot control.

Regulation has also been inhibited by the convergence between previously separate industries. This convergence has occurred most rapidly in the financial, transportation, and communications sectors. The rapid growth of modern financial markets blurred the distinction between the banking, securities, and insurance industries. Companies began to purchase investments that exhibited features of all three industries. As mentioned above, the widespread use of standardized containers made it easier for manufacturers to use more than one shipper, forcing intermodal competition. Finally, within the media sector, cable, satellite, and telephone companies now compete with each other to deliver broadband Internet access and high-value content to homes. Content producers increasingly use movies, video sales, television promotions, and merchandise sales to leverage the same product platform. All of these developments have forced government to deregulate markets, which in turn has led to more differentiation and further complexity.

DEMOGRAPHIC FACTORS

Demographic factors have also forced government's hand. For several decades after World War II, heavily unionized industries purchased labor peace and consumer satisfaction by promising their workers large pension and health care benefits when they retired. They also committed themselves to large, highly paid workforces with little flexibility. Since companies did not fully fund their retirement promises, they began to experience large legacy fixed costs that were not associated with current production. This created an opening for not only foreign competition but also domestic entrants such as Nucor, Southwest Airlines, and Toyota plants in West Virginia, Alabama, Indiana, and Texas, which, because they had younger and more flexible workforces, could offer customers lower costs. The government was put in the awkward position of either discouraging new entrants who promised to create jobs in states that needed them and save customers money or protecting established industries that were generally responsive to government policies but were increasingly unable to compete in open markets. The process of restructuring traditional companies so that they can better compete in the modern economy is still continuing.

Unless federal entitlement programs are significantly reformed, demographic factors will also begin to impinge on the finances of state and federal government. The retirement benefits of many state and local governments are severely underfunded, meaning that jurisdictions will face the prospect of raising taxes, cutting benefits, or declaring bankruptcy.[10] Without reform, Medicare, Medicaid, and Social Security will account for 18 percent of GDP by 2050.[11] Since federal revenues are unlikely to rise much above their historic average of 18 percent of GDP, spending on other programs will face increasing pressure, further limiting the government's freedom of action.[12]

Governments that overregulate or overtax increasingly risk seeing economic activity move to other places. Not too long ago, land and labor were the major determinants of economic value. Land of course was immobile. No matter how highly it was taxed, the owner's only alternative was to let it lie unused, and even then taxes could be imposed. Labor is mobile, and large waves of immigration have occasionally had a significant effect on national economies. But even then, it usually took a large difference in prospective earnings to induce individuals to leave their family and friends.

Increasingly, the inputs that matter in today's economy can easily move across borders. Financial flows are extremely mobile and move within a fraction of a second. Capital equipment is also highly mobile due to falling transportation costs. In many industries, the most valuable assets take the form of intangible knowledge residing in software or the heads of highly skilled and increasingly mobile employees. These assets can be easily withdrawn in response to government disincentives. Just as important, the productive life of many capital inputs is relatively short. A constant inflow of replacement capital is usually needed in order to remain competitive. If this flow is interrupted in response to government policy it does not take long for the effects to show up in reduced economic growth and increased unemployment.

States have always faced competition from each other. The growth of economies in the South and Southwest was partially at the expense of traditional industries in the Northeast and Midwest who had allowed the cost of labor in some industries to rise above the value of its productivity. But competition between nations has also intensified. For much of the Cold War period, large parts of the developing world pursued policies such as centralized planning and import substitution that were antithetical to economic growth. Over the last few years more governments have pursued policies that encourage investment and productive activity. The result is that companies now have many more choices about where to base their plants. This allows them to evade countries that impose high costs and encourages competition between states and countries to attract the most valuable investments.

It is extremely important to remember that on a net basis this development helps the United States. A recent study estimates that globalization has increased household income by at least ten thousand dollars, or 21.6 percent of the median household income in 2005.[13] America is far better off with a wealthier, more diverse China and India with large middle classes and high levels of consumer consumption than it is otherwise. Not only is there a moral imperative to assist the elimination of massive poverty and inequality, but the entry of these nations into the global economy should promote better political and social relations as well. On the economic side, growth overseas opens vast new markets to American companies. To the extent that American companies are able to export to these markets, jobs will be created here. But even if companies have to go abroad to compete effectively, American shareholders will still benefit. Finally, American consumers benefit from the availability of imports. Domestic politics often demonstrates an unfortunate lack of appreciation for consumer benefits, preferring instead to focus on the needs of producers and the jobs that they create. But the two are ultimately inseparable. Workers cannot get paid unless someone ultimately purchases what they make, and a main motivation to work is to earn enough income to buy products and services. A deeper appreciation of the importance of keeping prices low for the average consumer would strengthen the support for free trade.

America's interest then is in seeing that countries like China, India, Brazil, and Argentina continue to develop into modern economies. On their part, this requires a significant transition from top-heavy centralized national systems to more democratic, decentralized economies. In each country there is a strong imperative to maintain a certain amount of busy work to manage the large migration of workers from unproductive state-sponsored or protected enterprises to companies that are capable of generating enough true value to cover all of their costs, including worker salaries. Any transition of this magnitude engenders significant social unrest. The United States has a large strategic interest in helping developing countries get the process right and in moving them to the stage where increased incomes begin to generate large internal consumer demand. Although in the short run it may be frustrating to see jobs migrating to China and watch its export capacity grow faster than its internal markets, we would be much worse off if this process was halted or reversed.

But international competition further limits the government's power to intervene in markets. Now that other countries are serious about attracting investment and production to their shores, companies have more options about where to base their facilities and the jobs that they entail. National governments must be more attuned to macroeconomic indicators like exchange rate stability, inflation, and labor availability. In addition, they must worry about factors such as physical infrastructure, corporate tax rates, and government corruption. Policies that burden the private sector with fixed costs or that limit its flexibility to respond to changes in the business environment threaten the competitiveness of domestic industries. Just as important, they put the nation at a relative disadvantage in attracting new companies. Within the United States, individual states often directly compete against each other to attract new plants. On a national level, companies continually make decisions about whether to source production here, in Europe, or Asia. Call centers, software developers, and even lawyers find themselves in direct competition with individuals half a world away.

Even individuals are increasingly mobile. For decades developing countries suffered from the migration of their most talented people to Europe and North America. This migration was only partially motivated by better opportunities in the developed world. At least as important has been the paucity of opportunity for all but the most privileged in their home country. However, even developed countries now compete for talent. Over the last decades Germany and France have lost many of their most talented young students, driven abroad in search of better opportunities.[14] Even within the United States an increasing number of wealthy individuals give up their American citizenship each year in order to avoid paying tax on their accumulated wealth.[15] If several developing nations made a concerted effort to establish safe, stable, low-tax but prosperous areas in order to attract middle-class Americans in their retirement years, much larger sources of wealth could escape taxation.[16]

Increased economic and social flexibility in the private sector improves the ability of both individuals and companies to evade the effect of costly national laws and search out more welcoming jurisdictions. Although most governments still retain an effective monopoly on the legitimate use of force, individuals' ability to evade this force by moving their money and even themselves to other jurisdictions is expanding. Companies can decide not only where to place their plants but also within relatively quick time frames whether to shift production volume between existing plants in different countries. The complexity of modern supply chains also gives them a greater ability to avoid paying high taxes by deciding where to realize profits.

MAKING GOVERNMENT POLICY IN AN INCREASINGLY UNCERTAIN WORLD

In the face of greater fluidity, governments need to be much more precise about how they intervene in markets. Governments still have enormous power, but often the most effective uses of this power are counterproductive. The most effective regimes at exerting force, such as North Korea and Burma, suffer from stagnant economies precisely because the government is so powerful. On a lesser scale, both Venezuela and Iran are gradually becoming more politically coercive. This has been successful in allowing the government to change the economy but only at the cost of economic stagnation and decline. If these policies are pursued consistently, their nations will be substantially poorer a decade from now. Although destroying wealth is relatively easy, creating it is much more difficult. Government attempts to increase national wealth must often be limited to creating a climate inductive to private efforts to invest and generate economic growth. Such a passive role depends on factors outside the government's direct control and can be frustrating to policy makers who feel direct action is called for. Despite this frustration, lawmakers need to remember that, in order to effectively influence a fluid economy, government action needs to be much more limited, prioritized, focused, and direct.

The first step is limiting the goals of public policy. Government should be concerned with economic growth, but as we have seen, it can best do this by creating a favorable climate in which growth can occur. Government should also be concerned with certain noneconomic goals. To the extent that the pursuit of these goals harms economic growth, both goals are best achieved by targeting the social goal directly and leaving the economy free to adapt to and work around it. If the policy is well targeted, the social goal should be achieved and the negative effect on growth should be minimized. The economy's ability to work around government constraints will increase if the constraints are relatively few and the economy has more degrees of freedom within which to adapt. The more that government tries to regulate the economy, especially when it regulates the means of achieving a goal as well as the goal itself, the greater the constraints and the fewer the private degrees of freedom. Therefore, government should pursue only a limited number of social goals that it deems essential to the public welfare.

It also helps if government policies are well targeted toward achieving its goals. Economist Jan Tinbergen argued that a government with multiple policy objectives needs multiple tools in order to accomplish each.[17] Ideally, the government should have at least one tool for each policy objective, thus minimizing compromises that threaten each objective. Social Security has long suffered from having two conflicting objectives. On the one hand, it is often justified as a program that ensures each worker saves a sufficient amount of her or his income for retirement. It thus taxes each individual a uniform percentage of their wages up to a cap, beyond which the individual presumably has enough set aside to maintain a fair standard of living. However, the program is also intended to redistribute income, both from high-income to low-income individuals and from current workers to previous generations. These two goals often conflict. As a result, the program is unable to pay even the lowest-paid workers entering the workforce today an amount equivalent to what they would earn if they invested the funds themselves. It also does a very poor job of redistributing income to those who need it most. In fact, using reasonable assumptions it is possible to argue that the program is actually becoming regressive, the opposite of what was intended.[18]

If government is going to pursue a more limited set of objectives, it needs to ensure that the ones it does pursue are the most important to society and to let less important objectives fall by the wayside. Government cannot shape the markets to its suiting, but it can determine the broad parameters within which they operate. In the next chapter, this book argues that one of the most important goals is the guarantee of a fair income to all Americans who comply with certain basic obligations of citizenship. If the government attempts to achieve this goal by heavily regulating individual markets, it will fail. If, however, it puts its energy into a well-defined program that attacks the basic problem at its source—the lack of money—then it has a good chance of succeeding. If it also changes its regulation of certain markets to remove the existing bias that disproportionately benefits higher-income workers and discourages private markets from providing the goods and services that low-income individuals want, it can also reduce inequality and increase the effectiveness of the demand thus created.

Government efforts should therefore focus directly on the specific problem it seeks to address. Government should withdraw from the market in all other respects in order to increase the degrees of freedom that people have to find the best solutions for meeting their individual needs.

Finally, government assistance should be targeted directly to those it is meant to help. Channeling assistance through government agencies and private companies, even those in the nonprofit sector, only introduces a middle agent whose goals and objectives are not those of the people who deserve the assistance. These middlemen are likely to address their attention to the government that is funding them, rather than the clients who depend on them. It is very possible that new sources of supply will be needed in order to meet social demands for new housing, better education, and affordable health care. But private markets are unlikely to deliver value unless their revenues come from their customers rather than directly from the government.

In order to make a positive difference, then, government policy must increasingly follow certain basic principles. It must delink the important from the unimportant and concentrate on ensuring that the former is accomplished. If the government accomplishes its important goals, does it really care about the less important details of how the markets respond? Second, the government should act to increase the degrees of freedom within which the market can adapt to changes and find better outcomes. It can best do this by creating a climate that is hospitable to innovation and competition and by regulating as few aspects of the market as possible. The more freedom that markets have, the more likely they are to meet individuals' needs.

Another important principle is that government policy should work to align incentives. To the extent that health care professionals, teachers, and landlords look to the government for resources, they will not have as their primary mission the patients, students, and tenants that they should be serving. The best way to align incentives is to give purchasing power directly to the latter groups and to ensure that markets are kept open to new providers that promise to do a better job for less money. If the goal of public policy is to help each individual attain the basics of a comfortable life, then by far the best strategy is to ensure that those individuals have enough income to purchase what they need. If markets are slow to supply appropriate goods and services, there is a role for government to create new providers, but even these providers are unlikely to have the right incentives unless they have to compete on their own for customers.

Another principle is that the government increasingly must seek to rule by exception.[19] Returning to the eighty/twenty rule, government lacks the resources to give each person a great deal of time and effort. Public policy needs to be structured so that one simple program works to allow the great majority of people to be independent. The program needs to be transparent and simple so that recipients, government, and the general public all understand what it can and cannot do. There will be exceptions in which individuals need more assistance. By keeping the main program simple, the government will be better able to distinguish those cases that need more intensive intervention from those that do not. It will also have more resources to devote to the former.

Finally, there is a strong role for subsidiarity and federalism in government policy. Issues such as health care, education policy, and income support need to be treated at the national level in order to ensure consistency and eliminate discrepancies caused by regional variations in wealth. Yet state and local governments are often best placed to identify and care for those citizens within their borders that need extra assistance. It would be a serious mistake to have the federal government run a complex national health care or education program. It lacks the capacity to do that well. Yet having the federal government act more aggressively to administer a simple national income guarantee program and to ensure that markets are kept open to new entrants should give state and local governments an increased opportunity to set up independent service providers that focus specifically on those parts of society that continue to need help.

2

WHY SOCIETY SHOULD GUARANTEE A MINIMUM INCOME

The proposals in this book reflect two central arguments. The first is that government should drastically reduce its involvement in individual markets so that the private sector can do a better job of responding to the needs of individuals. Doing so will also remove the opportunity for powerful interests to capture wealth at the expense of the poor. The second argument is that government policy should include an explicit commitment to redistribute income so that every citizen has a clear path to a life without poverty. It can best do this through a combination of refundable tax credits and a bilateral income guarantee contract that is offered to every adult citizen.

THE JUSTIFICATION FOR A SIGNIFICANT INCOME GUARANTEE

Why should government use the force of law to take money away from some people in order to give it to others? Given the large amount of taxation and social spending that government already engages in, it might seem that Americans already agree on the answer to this question, otherwise they would not tolerate current policy. In fact, a great deal of government policy is totally devoid of any intellectual justification, and any careful comparison of whatever justification does exist with the actual effects of spending would cast serious doubt on the wisdom of current spending, let alone new programs. Agricultural crop support programs are an excellent example. They are usually justified as ensuring a secure supply of cheap food and preserving the family farm. But despite costing society tens of billions of dollars each year, they actually do very little toward the first goal and speed the decline of family farms by encouraging high-volume farming.[1]

There is a good economic justification for government spending on public goods: those things such as defense, transportation infrastructure, and a legal system that benefit society as a whole. Private markets have difficulty providing these services because their benefits are difficult to allocate to specific consumers and because, once they are provided, it is usually most efficient to extend them to all people, whether or not they pay for them. It is not that private companies could not offer these services. Indeed, things like lighthouses and roads have been privately supplied. But in order to be successful, private markets in these goods require that the government enforce well-defined rules. And for many public goods it is most efficient for the government to simply supply the good itself.

But economists have little to say about the wisdom of purely interpersonal transfers such as the kind normally associated with income support programs. Because economics lacks objective criteria for making interpersonal comparisons of utility, it cannot tell policy makers whether taking money from one person and giving it to another makes society as a whole better off, even if the former is rich and the recipient is poor. These decisions are political, ethical, and social in nature.

From a purely economic point of view, interpersonal transfers of wealth can have both good and bad consequences for society as a whole. Although conservative economists are not opposed to redistributive policies, they would caution lawmakers to study and accept the effect of such transfers on individual incentives and longer-term social welfare. Seventy years of communism proved conclusively the dangers of pursuing equality as the only social goal. Yet in Venezuela, Hugo Chavez is rapidly instituting a number of policies that have the explicit goal of redistributing income to the poor. No one would dispute that many of the recipients live in desperate poverty. Nevertheless, these particular policies have been tried before and always lead to the same results: centralized power, rapid inflation, reduced investment, higher unemployment, and falling national income. History will repeat itself in this case. If redistribution is to be done, how it is done is just as important as how much is done.

A clearer justification of redistribution policy is helpful for several reasons. First, because economics is silent about the degree to which involuntary transfers of income can make society better off, another source of justification is clearly needed. If a clearer rationale leads to stronger public support for redistribution, policy makers might enact better programs. At present, many social programs suffer from one of two problems. For some, such as Social Security, legislators' reluctance to acknowledge a redistributive goal leads them to combine it with other goals, creating unnecessary complexity that ultimately jeopardizes all goals, undermines the program's effectiveness, and jeopardizes its long-run solvency. In other programs, imprecision with regard to who should benefit from redistribution allows lawmakers to pursue policies that would fail to get public support if their true effects were known. Finally, a stronger justification would help separate those cases that deserve redistribution from those that do not. This also would lead to greater public support for the redistribution that does occur and produce more effective policy.

Redistribution can be justified first because in at least some circumstances it is the right thing to do. Most major religions contain some formulation of the Golden Rule: do unto others as you would have them do unto you. Each citizen seeks the support of the community when they are in need, and each would ask the community to care for their spouse and children were they to die suddenly. Therefore, each can be called on to answer the same desire when it comes from others.

Within Christianity the call is explicit: "Tell them to do good, to be rich in good works, to be generous, ready to share, thus accumulating as treasure a good foundation for the future, so as to win the life that is true."[2] In the parable of the dishonest steward, Christ points approvingly to the practice of giving some of one's wealth to others so that they will care for you in times of need.[3] But the command to charity is not based solely on self-interest. Christ also commended the woman who donated some of the little she had to the temple.[4] The Bible contains numerous other injunctions commending charity and warning against the temptations of wealth.[5] Those who seek to follow Christ might reflect on the morality of a society that glamorizes Louis Vuitton handbags and $240 jeans from a company called True Religion at the same time that many working parents lack adequate housing and health care.

Some people might argue that charity and altruism should be individual choices and not the subject of government policy that, because it is based on majority voting, neglects the wishes of the minority that might oppose coerced redistribution. The fact that much of the support for redistribution might stem from religious motivations could cause further unease. Yet, the political process is continually used to enact large subsidies that do little for or even harm the public interest and that are strenuously objected to by a minority of voters. Any theory of politics that admits the propriety of current farm subsidies, federal backing of government-sponsored enterprises, and tax breaks for oil exploration must also admit the propriety of programs that explicitly seek to help the poor. The fact that income transfers are morally motivated as opposed to being the product of raw interest politics can hardly be an objection.

One might argue that, because the government should not provide the subsidies listed above, it should also not run programs explicitly designed to help the poor. Yet, public policy frequently reflects moral beliefs with regard to crime, immigration, abortion, and a host of other issues. Even if there were no broad public benefit from a program that provided a better safety net to those who live in poverty, it would still be the right thing to do.

But there are many reasons to think that a well-designed income support program would benefit society as a whole, not just the recipients. One reason is that it might increase social peace. In his *History of Early Rome*, Livy spends a great deal of time detailing how the long-running animosity between the patricians and the plebes distorted politics and weakened the Roman state. Social inequality leading to political perversity is a recurrent theme in history. France under Louis XVI and Robespierre and Argentina under Peron are just two more examples. Persistent poverty breeds discontent, and discontent threatens the social stability upon which the wealth of the middle and upper classes depends. This discontent is not inevitable, however. The continued popularity of ineffective but polarizing politicians such as former mayor Marion Barry in Washington and Rev. Al Sharpton in New York should probably be taken as a clear sign of the vacuum created by the inability or unwillingness of other leaders to address some of the legitimate issues connected to inequality rather than as an inevitable desire on the part of their followers to eliminate all forms of inequality or privilege.

Of course, social inequality in the United States cannot fairly be compared with that of ancient Rome or even current South America. In fact, one could make a good case that America currently offers more opportunity and social mobility than any other society in history and that even its poor enjoy life spans and living standards that would have been envied by most Americans only fifty years ago. But if today's inequality does not compare with the past, there are still ample signs that it unnecessarily contributes to political unrest and reduces social welfare.

First, there can be little doubt that the debate over inequality drives much of the division between political parties. Democrats have seized on issues like the minimum wage, unequal education, and homelessness as examples of the failing of unregulated markets. Their refusal to accept responsibility for actually alleviating these problems and the fact that their remedies would make the problems worse does not detract from the effectiveness of these issues in rallying opposition to policies designed to increase economic growth. Arriving at a consensus on a fairer distribution of the fruits of collective action could reduce the amount of social friction and hopefully eliminate one of the main rationales for harmful social policy.

On the other hand, some Republicans are quick to support any policy that disproportionately favors the wealthy in the cause of increasing economic growth without being very concerned with either evidence that the policies do indeed increase growth or whether the resulting higher incomes will be shared by the majority of people.

Economics does in general say that public welfare is increased when individuals receive the full benefit of their work, but it also holds that most people will continue working as long as the portion of benefits that they are allowed to keep exceeds their cost of working, largely in terms of lost leisure. So taxing them more may or may not have a large impact on growth. Even if it were true that the efforts of richer Americans deliver disproportionate benefits to society, there are arguments against attributing all of that increase in welfare solely to them.

In a modern economy, the worth of any individual effort depends a great deal on the entire economic and social environment in which it occurs. New York stockbrokers may create great gains for society by raising capital for business to invest. But the value they create would be substantially diminished if there did not exist a well-functioning judicial system to uphold contracts, intricate communication and transportation networks to facilitate commerce, and integrated distribution systems for dealing with the food, waste, energy, and other needs of the metropolis in which they work. High-value production depends upon a reliable base of more plebian services. Although the average worker does not create enough economic welfare to justify a high salary, in the aggregate his or her activity is a prerequisite to the efforts of those who do.

The system of property that protects the wealth of the rich cannot be justified as an absolute right, superior to all other rights. No society can exist without laws, but the moral obligation to obey those laws depends upon their derivation and effect. Society cannot reasonably ask the poor to respect the wealth of others unless it also ensures a certain fairness in the origin and distribution of that wealth. Public appeals that one "ought" not engage in theft or destruction can easily be met with responses that one "ought" not allow significant discrepancies in income or power. And appeals that massive redistribution would discourage economic growth and leave all worse off in the long run may legitimately be discounted by low-income individuals who would prefer a certain benefit now to an uncertain one later. Neither argument advances the social debate very much. Respect for laws has to depend on the legitimacy of the process that led to them and the results they produce. Concern for economic growth must be tempered by the realization that increased wealth is not an end in itself and is only desirable to the extent that it leads to a better society, of which income is only one aspect.

In addition, many industries depend upon access to one or more sources of common property in order to function. This is most true of extractive industries that exploit resources such as oil or gold on public lands. But it is also true of any industry that imposes external costs such as air and water pollution. In many cases these are currently made freely available to everyone, and from an economic viewpoint they probably should continue to be. But their existence underlies the fact that the creation of any private value occurs in a context of common rights and institutions that are collectively owned and, for the use of which, no payment is made. Even where government does require explicit approval to drill public oil fields or pollute, the benefits conferred by granting these public rights may not be equally shared. At least one author has raised the idea of formalizing such rights by transferring a broad definition of common properties to public trusts that would be owned by all citizens.[6] One need not agree with such a formal restructuring of property rights to admit that the large benefits that private investments derive from the common social and political framework should entail some sort of reciprocal obligation toward those citizens most in need.

Redistribution can also be justified by self-interest. Several years ago economists James Buchanan and Gordon Tullock wrote that uncertainty in how one might fare in the future could lead to support for redistribution as an insurance against poor outcomes.[7] Philosopher John Rawls agreed with this basic premise, arguing that individuals who were deciding social rules behind a "veil of ignorance" about their own futures would accept inequality of opportunity only if it enhances the opportunities of those at the bottom.[8] According to this reasoning, income support programs are a form of social insurance. Individuals are motivated to support them now because someday either they or a family member may benefit from them. There is no question that many workers benefit in direct ways from the pensions and health care that Social Security and Medicare provide to their parents. But again, this benefit varies in proportion to the worker's income. Those with relatively high incomes might benefit dollar for dollar from such government spending, either in the form of reduced payments to parents or higher inheritances when their parent dies. Those with low incomes probably are not in the position to help their parents as much, even if government support is cut.

But the argument for a fair social contract does not depend solely on an expectation of reciprocity. Buchanan also argued that redistribution could be justified by foreseeing that a potentially dissident minority that found itself disadvantaged under future laws could withdraw the support without which the legal order could not survive.[9] In a modern society the economic damage that a small group can inflict by actively sabotaging a critical part of the infrastructure or even by actively withdrawing their participation is increased. Defensive efforts to prevent such losses may limit potential damage but represent a net cost to society because they do not increase total wealth.[10] To the extent that disaffection of this type is caused by discontent over the distribution of income or by institutions that seem biased in favor of the rich, a different arrangement might reduce the cost of civil strife and crime on society. These costs include not only the direct cost borne by victims of the acts but also the much larger expense of protecting against such acts and administering a justice system to deal with them.

The social effects of poverty and inequality affect society even apart from the deliberate acts of those subject to it. In recent years public health officials have become increasingly worried about the possibility of a global pandemic originating from impoverished areas of Southeast Asia or Africa. Urban blight holds down property values in large areas of America's cities. Poor education and health care reduce productivity and transform a large number of workers from potential contributors of social value to dependents on public generosity. Well-designed programs could reduce these costs.

Smart redistribution can also be justified as an investment both in individuals and in the society of which they are a part. Continued economic growth is an important social goal for many reasons. Growth depends upon productive investment. One of the rationales for government is the need for collective action in cases where individuals lack the incentive or ability to act on their own. Most businesses would invest in an opportunity that promised a real expected rate of return of 30 percent per year. Well-designed investments in proper child care, education, basic health care, and poverty alleviation all offer social rates of return above this threshold. The problem is that poorly designed government programs often do not achieve them. And, because these benefits go to society as a whole rather than the individual investor, the private market lacks the incentive to enter the market.

Apart from this, individuals deserve the opportunity to maximize their own potential. This can only be done if they receive a certain level of the basic requirements. All of us begin life helpless and dependent. In most cases parents and a supportive community provide the building blocks upon which individual initiative can build. But where these are not available an alternative foundation is needed. Setting a better safety net could also encourage individuals to take more risks and invest in themselves, which would increase their long-term productivity.

Greater personal security might also reduce public resistance to growth-enhancing policies that might threaten an individual's immediate welfare, such as trade and deregulation. Economists can point to many policies that would clearly boost national income if implemented. Political opposition comes mainly from the minority of interests that benefit from the status quo and that might suffer as the result of increased competition or change. The difficulties of collective action often mean that this determined minority is able to frustrate the broader interests of the majority.[11] By reducing the costs of change and by linking the amount of individual assistance to national income, public support for more efficient policies should be strengthened.

Finally, redistribution toward the poor and the powerless can be justified as a rebalancing of the effects of normal political and economic forces. If markets were perfectly fair and the political system was unbiased, the need for redistribution probably would not be as strong as it is and the ability to advance on one's own would be greater. However, markets tend to reflect purchasing power, which is skewed toward the well-to-do. In addition, more powerful groups frequently lobby for and obtain laws that impose artificial barriers to protect themselves from competition by low-income Americans. Thus, the poor are often excluded from neighborhoods by zoning laws, shuttled into the worst-equipped schools within a district, and faced with unnecessary education requirements in order to enter a profession. All of this is usually done in the name of a paternalistic desire to protect the average American from unscrupulous fraud. Yet, strangely, this paternalism seldom results in the provision of better services, leaving the impression that the main concern is to control the political process by which services are delivered and to protect the middle and upper classes from the competitive efforts of the poor. While some regulation of markets is necessary, much government regulation simply protects the economic interest of a narrow constituency.[12] Even if these laws imposed equal costs on everyone, they would place the poor at a relative disadvantage because they have the fewest resources to bear them.

The strength of these arguments is not diminished by the fact that the problems of poverty and inequality are often exaggerated by many Democratic leaders. Even poor Americans live lives that are far better off in terms of nutrition, life expectancy, health, housing, and material possessions than all but the wealthiest citizens enjoyed fifty years ago. The *Economist* notes that poverty describes two quite different phenomena: utter penury, experienced by the roughly one billion people who today live on a dollar or less a day, and the situation of people in the rich nations who have less than their neighbors.[13]

Although poverty remains a serious problem, its incidence is often distorted by poor statistics and a tendency to concentrate only on aggregate numbers at a snapshot in time. For instance, poverty data tend to concentrate on pretax income, rather than actual living standards. Yet the two approaches give much different pictures. In 2003, reported annual income for the poorest one-fifth of American households was $8,201, but their reported expenditures were $18,492. Although official poverty numbers have not declined much in recent decades, life has gotten better. Poor people live longer, are better educated, and are more likely to have jobs. Fewer live in substandard housing, while more have cars, refrigerators, electronics, and other necessities that were luxuries a generation or two ago.[14]

In addition, poor individuals can and do advance out of poverty much more often than is commonly believed. Between 1996 and 1999, only 2 percent of Americans were poor every month over the full four-year period.[15] Most remaining in poverty for long periods of time suffer from either serious physical and mental handicaps or preventable conditions such as poor education, drug dependency, and criminal activity, which are widely known to reduce earning power.

But if the picture is not as bleak as some people would portray it, it can still be made better. We cannot achieve the goal of ensuring that no person is poor regardless of what actions they take or how short a period they have been in the country. We can probably ensure that every American who works at it does not have to worry about being hungry, homeless, or without health care. But in order to achieve this goal, programs need to be much more transparent and focused than they are now.

Public policy should concentrate on ensuring that Americans have ready access to the investments, such as education, that they need in order to compete in the workplace. It should reward them for doing those things that are consistent with individual and civic responsibility. And it should give them maximum flexibility to structure the mixture and timing of consumption to suit their individual circumstances.

MEETING WANTS NOT NEEDS

If one accepts the need for some sort of redistribution of income in order to create a social contract encompassing all Americans, the question remains how this policy should be structured and what guarantees it should fulfill. Turning to the second question first, people can genuinely disagree on how generous an income support program should be. Most policy makers now agree that "from each according to his ability, to each according to his needs" is a poor principle for organizing a modern economy. Some financial incentive is needed in order to motivate most individuals to engage in productive activity. In addition, a decentralized mechanism of prices and profit has proven to be much better than centralized planning at coordinating economic activity within a society.[16]

In order to be sensible an income supplement program must distinguish between an individual's needs and wants. In today's consumer society wants are endless and are continually fed by an organized advertising industry. While materialism has weaknesses as a guiding philosophy, it does underpin the national economy, for consumer purchases are the necessary complement to productive jobs. There is nothing inherently wrong in the pursuit of better things. But society cannot guarantee everyone everything—nor can it ensure that each person has what everyone else has. The difficulty of using wants as a guidepost is that few people are ever satisfied.

Also, it would not be good to try to provide too much. Recent research shows that an increase in income above ten thousand dollars in developed countries is not correlated with an increase in perceived happiness.[17] Individuals are spending most of this extra income on material goods, but it seems not to bring them any lasting satisfaction. Instead, research indicates that individuals tend toward a constant level of internal happiness. Increases or decreases in wealth cause temporary changes in perceived happiness, but the effect eventually wears off as individuals adapt to their new circumstances, causing them to return to their prior equilibrium.

Because wants tend to be infinite, a society cannot meet them and should not try. Needs, on the other hand, are fairly limited. Referring to Abraham Maslow's hierarchy, most individuals in developed countries already have their basic physiological needs met. In countries where these needs are not met for a large portion of the population, the reason is usually due to war, state mismanagement, or natural disaster rather than any inherent failure of the people or inability of a market economy to form and grow. Looking forward, the needs for love and belonging, esteem, and self-actualization tend not to depend on material wealth. Although government may have a role in helping to meet them, providing income is not likely to play a big part in any successful efforts. It is the lower physiological and safety needs then that are most responsive to increases in income within a well-ordered society. These needs are relatively few: providing people with a basic level of physical comfort and guaranteeing economic and physical security.

The main target of any redistribution program should be to ensure that basic needs are met. Officials should be much less concerned with addressing inequality per se. There are several reasons for this. First, the "problem" of inequality, both its nature and causes, is extremely controversial. Some inequality benefits society by providing proper incentives and giving markets a signal about what goods and services are most in demand. For instance, higher education levels benefit society, but it is hard to see why students would spend several more years in school unless they could expect to earn significantly higher incomes during their careers. Because inequality can be measured many different ways and over different time periods, its exact magnitude is difficult to determine. Finally, since much inequality is caused by technology and, to a lesser extent, trade, it is difficult to see what policies would address the root causes of the problem without making society as a whole worse off. While it is not free of controversy, ascertaining a basic level of income that allows the average individual to satisfy basic needs is a much easier and more objective task than trying to ensure that all inequality is justified by some broader social policy.

The two problems are related to some extent, however. The exact level of needs deemed to be basic should of course depend upon the general wealth of society. A fair social contract needs to reflect national income for several reasons. First, as income rises, the nation is able to afford more support to a given segment of its population. Conversely, countries with low average incomes and large populations in poverty are simply not able to match the level of even low-income workers in the West. Second, price levels tend to rise as a nation gets richer, reflecting higher opportunity costs. Thus, a higher level of support is necessary in order to afford basic needs like housing and food. Third, for most individuals even the higher needs such as esteem and self-actualization will depend to some extent on one's relative position in society. So, concepts like relative poverty do matter. Income transfers that leave too large a gap in relative consumption are not likely to be regarded as fair. Finally, as national income increases, the amount of wealth that depends on social peace—which in turn rests on an implicit agreement about the fairness of the rules and distribution of income—also increases and with it the losses that can come from a breakdown in social peace. To the extent that this wealth depends upon the general social and institutional environment, those whose labor is not highly valued by the marketplace have just as much right to an equal share as anyone else.

The remarkable thing is that for most people meeting the basic safety needs simplifies to a question of money. In developed countries families above a certain income threshold almost never go without having these needs met. For those few who cannot afford a decent lifestyle, the government's role can largely be limited to establishing an income guarantee program conditioned on behavior. The vast majority of recipients will then have the resources necessary to satisfy their needs themselves. Economists admit that markets do not reflect the needs of individuals who lack effective purchasing power. However, once this power exists, markets tend to work very well within the boundaries set by government policy.

Accepting inequality as a rationale for government policy raises distinct dangers. Because inequality is integral to a modern economy, it serves as a constant justification for continued government regulation of specific markets. Thus, policy makers have used the "digital divide" to justify costly programs such as the Universal Service Fund, which does more to subsidize inefficient incumbents than to extend broadband service to poor and rural neighborhoods.[18] The rationale of a divide has also been used to prevent new entrants from improving service in just one area of a city as opposed to everywhere, thereby protecting existing monopolies and aborting the incremental process that underlies the spread of all technologies.

Concentrating too much on inequality can easily lead to bad policy. The markets for housing, food, health care, and clothing could all be judged unfair, since poorer individuals tend to spend a higher portion of their income on each than do their richer neighbors. But this is not the relevant question, nor is it whether consumers with more money can afford certain things such as cable service or Lasik surgery that others cannot. Instead, policy makers should determine what general basket of goods and services represents a fair minimum for society at the current time and then what income level is required for the average individual to afford that standard of living.

POVERTY IN AMERICA

Studies of poverty and income inequality raise difficult issues of both definition and analysis. On the one hand, in the vast majority of cases the determination of who is poor is extremely subjective. Individuals living at the poverty level in the United States enjoy standards of living that are much higher than a large fraction of the population of developing countries. As indicated above, the standard of living associated with some poverty measures tends to rise over time as society becomes richer. The implication of poverty statistics can also depend upon whether one studies wages, total income including employer benefits, income after taxes and government benefits, or consumption levels.

The causes of poverty are also the subject of fierce debate. Even when the cause of individual poverty can be traced to concrete actions such as drug addiction or teenage pregnancy, many would argue that these factors stem largely from an environment of poverty and inequality that discourages individual initiative and makes it difficult for people to complete an education, find a job, and accumulate wealth.

The government should not be very concerned with addressing inequality in society, except to the extent that it helps lift individuals out of poverty. In other words, what matters is that some people lack what is necessary, not that some people have a great deal more than others. Although inequality has increased during the past few decades, its increase is often exaggerated. Many commonly cited income figures omit health care and retirement benefits, which benefit workers just as much as wages do and which have risen much faster than wages. They also omit the net effect of government policy such as progressive taxation, Food Stamps, Medicaid, and welfare payments. In addition, government figures show that consumption varies much less than income.[19]

Second, inequality plays a positive role in society. It provides the necessary incentives for individuals to work hard. As Adam Smith showed, most of this hard work is beneficial to society even if the worker does not intend it to be.[20] Inequality and even elitism serve the valuable purpose of providing sufficient rewards for winning and support for ideas that benefit society as a whole. Such distinctions are only objectionable to the extent that otherwise deserving people are precluded from having an opportunity to compete or when the forces of competition are allowed to impoverish those whose efforts the market does not value highly.[21] Trying to eliminate all forms of elitism would be both futile and destructive. The important question is what criteria determine membership in the elite and whether all individuals are given a chance to meet those criteria. Ideally, membership in the elite would be reserved for those who make great contributions to society, who sacrifice for its welfare, or who live according to standards that increase overall welfare. Although this has never been totally true, competitive markets are usually a better judge of merit than government.

Yet leadership and privilege imply responsibility toward others. Lately, this has been lacking. An analysis of the Enron collapse concluded,

> The larger message was that the wealth and power enjoyed by those at the top of the heap in corporate America . . . demand no sense of broader responsibility. To accept these arguments is to embrace the notion that ethical behavior requires nothing more than avoiding the explicitly illegal, that refusing to see the bad things happening in front of you makes you innocent, and that telling the truth is the same thing as making sure that no one can prove you lied.[22]

A study by the Brookings Institution concluded that markets are not always even. Lower-income families often pay more for exactly the same product as families with higher incomes, differences that added up to hundreds, sometimes thousands, of dollars per family per year.[23] The study found that reducing the costs of living by just 1 percent would add up to over $6.5 billion in new spending power for poor families. Not all of these higher prices could be explained by the higher risks and costs associated with serving poorer populations. It is important to acknowledge and try to address these market failures, many of which stem from government policies and anticompetitive behavior. Similarly, U.S. tariffs tend to hurt low-income Americans more than others because tariffs tend to be higher on the goods that they purchase relatively more of.[24] Rather than seeking to limit inequality directly through higher taxes on the rich, the government should eliminate many of the public policies and market imperfections that selectively disadvantage the poor by limiting competition.

A third reason for concentrating on absolute poverty rather than inequality is that common statistics of the latter are often deceiving because they reflect only a snapshot in time and do not show the degree of movement between income brackets. Even within a typical middle-class life, individual income varies dramatically as students emerge from college, possibly with debt, get their first career job, rise slowly in experience and pay, get married, pay for their children's education, and eventually retire and spend down their savings. A nation of overlapping generations of identical middle-class individuals would show a significant degree of income inequality at any one point in time.

There is also a significant amount of movement between income classes due to variations in fortune. Immigrant parents arrive here poor but see their children or grandchildren graduate from professional school. At the same time, individuals born to wealthy families make personal choices involving drugs and crime that cause them to fall to the bottom of society.

A final reason for treading with care is that income inequality does not have major effects on either growth or poverty, but government efforts to combat it may have strong negative effects. A recent study found that the distribution of income might not have a large impact on children's lives unless other factors change at the same time.[25] The main reason disposable income is more unequal in the United States than in Europe is due, not to market forces, but rather to the fact that U.S. taxes and payments do less to reduce inequality. Although pay was more unequal in the United States, more people lacked any job at all in Europe.[26] The effects of inequality on economic growth, health, and equality of opportunity are modest and uncertain in developed countries.[27]

As to the causes of increased inequality, most economists believe that the best explanation is a shift in the demand for labor toward relatively more skilled workers in response to new production technology; economists found little evidence that trade is a major explanation for growing wage disparities.[28] Few people would argue that technological advancement is bad for society or that its pace should be significantly slowed so that workers have more time to adjust. As a result, anything government does to stop the real cause of inequality is likely to hurt society, not help it.

Immigration presents a more difficult issue. Most studies show that immigration has little effect on overall wages and that it increases economic growth.[29] However, it does skew inequality statistics because many immigrants arrive here very poor. Despite the fact that they are earning more than they could in their home countries, their negative impact on income distribution could contribute to the impression that private markets are not providing opportunity to the poor. Immigration probably increases domestic inequality even as it decreases global inequality.[30] Again, policies that might appear to reduce income inequality, such as slowing technological change, globalization, or immigration, would have the net effect of reducing per capita income. The best policies for reducing inequality focus on improving the health, education, and job readiness of low-income children and young adults.[31] This book argues for similar solutions, first by ensuring that working individuals have an adequate income to afford a decent lifestyle and, second, by reforming government policy in critical sectors in order to increase access to the basic components of a successful life.

Reducing inequality is an imprecise and dangerous goal. Government can never achieve enough of it to quiet all critics. Its elevation to public policy encourages jealousy and discounts the type of individual contributions that have produced the economic growth and social progress we enjoy today. It is true that the definition of an adequate income supplement can also lead to prolonged disagreement. But the policies designed to implement it need not call into question the basic mechanism that underlies a free economy and may even bolster it. Moreover, once the proper goal is agreed on, its achievement is much easier and less intrusive.

REDUCING POVERTY

If the government resists setting itself up for failure by trying to significantly reduce inequality and instead limits itself to the more achievable goal of lifting up the bottom of the income distribution, it needs to define what the minimum standard should be. Such a judgment is inherently subjective, especially in a wealthy economy in which biological needs are already met. The official poverty numbers, although widely used, are poorly suited to this purpose. Unfortunately, there is no widely used measure that tracks the basic income needed to purchase "decent" levels of nutrition, housing, education, transportation, and health care. The current measure basically takes the price of a nutritionally adequate diet in the early 1960s, adjusts for inflation since then, and multiplies by three. Yet, over three hundred billion dollars in annual federal assistance is linked to it.[32]

Agreeing on a minimum income standard may be much easier than reducing poverty. In fact, no poverty program, including the one advocated in this book, is likely to eliminate poverty. New immigrants will always arrive at our doorstep, fleeing absolute poverty in their native land for the opportunity to do better in ours. More significantly, poverty is not solely a matter of income. As long as drug addiction, crime, and other vices exist, some individuals will pursue them into poverty. Unless medicine advances far beyond where it is now, physical and mental illness and handicaps will place other individuals in a state of permanent dependence. What income supplements can do is lift the majority out of poverty and ensure society that no person of average abilities is poor due to a lack of their own effort. This in itself would be a great advancement.

It is clear that both personal choices and social conditions play a role in individual cases. While most experts would admit that both play a role, the question of which predominates has been the subject of much debate. The answer matters for two reasons. If poverty is due mainly to environmental factors such as poor schools, crime-ridden neighborhoods, and widespread discrimination, then urging poor people to work harder will have little effect. Significant decreases in poverty will require broad-ranging changes in society. Second, to the extent that environmental factors predominate, individuals are less complicit in their own poverty, and both the practical and moral arguments for assistance are strengthened—nor are these arguments diminished by a lack of program success. If social programs do not reduce poverty, the fault lies in society and not in the recipients.

Although virtually everyone would admit that environmental factors play some role, over the last two decades researchers have formed a consensus that individual choices are a key determinant of poverty and that government programs both influence behavior and should be conditioned on behavior. When Charles Murray wrote *Losing Ground* two decades ago, such views were a direct challenge to the existing welfare system.[33] By now liberal academics acknowledge the role that personal decisions play in determining individual futures. In a review of the literature on family poverty, Isabel Sawhill concludes that "children of school age whose mothers delay childbearing until they have finished high school, get married, and are at least twenty years old are one-tenth as likely to be poor as those whose mothers have not done these three things."[34] Earlier, she summarizes that

> Public and private efforts to promote a different set of behaviors may have modest direct effects, at best. However, because even small changes in behavior may be socially contagious and lead eventually to a shift in norms and attitudes, such efforts are worth pursuing.[35]

Another study finds that changes in family structure explain roughly half of the increase in income inequality between 1971 and 1989.[36] The poor are disproportionately comprised of single parents, mostly women, with children.[37] Hilary Hoynes, Marianne Page, and Ann Huff Stevens find that changes in family structure should have increased poverty rates from 13.3 percent in 1967 to 17 percent in 2003. However, this effect was largely offset by higher earnings stemming from increased education and greater participation by women in the workforce.[38]

Education also matters. In 2003, 31.3 percent of individuals living in a family where the head of household had less than a high school education were poor. The poverty rate for families whose head had completed high school was only 9.6 percent.[39] In contrast, only 4.2 percent of people who completed college had incomes below the poverty line.[40]

For this reason, researchers have increasingly come to accept that at least that portion of public assistance designed to take people beyond the bare threshold of survival should be attached to conditions on recipients that are both greater and more explicit than those that existed in the past. A recent news article quotes Isabel Sawhill as saying, "Perhaps it should . . . include such things as finishing high school; perhaps it should include delaying child-bearing until you're old enough to support a child, or at least make a good effort at supporting a child—then maybe we link some new benefits to those new kinds of responsibility."[41] Indeed, society does have a strong common sense of general moral propriety that is ingrained in human nature.[42] Sawhill summarizes the public sentiment well:

> Most Americans embrace neither the liberal nor conservative positions in full. Most do not want to turn back the clock to a time when divorce was highly stigmatized and women were restricted to domestic roles. They want to preserve a safety net for single-parent families and provide extra help to poor children. But they believe that parents are ultimately responsible for their children's well-being, see merit in increasing the proportion of children being raised by two married parents, and are open to public or private initiatives that promise to achieve these objectives. The real question is whether effective interventions exist.[43]

Programs that reflect and reinforce this sense are likely to have an easier time obtaining public support and resources.

PRIOR ATTEMPTS TO ELIMINATE POVERTY

Over the past century public welfare has experienced great changes.[44] Originally, most public support was provided by private efforts, which often stressed personal self-help.[45] Public descriptions of poverty periodically led to significant demands for greater government involvement, most notably in post-Depression New Deal programs and later in President Lyndon Johnson's War on Poverty. By the 1980s, there was very little connection between government assistance and personal responsibility. In fact, the structure of welfare often encouraged perverse individual behavior.[46]

Some of the first significant reforms surrounded the Negative Income experiments proposed by President Richard Nixon and supported by a group of academics that included conservative Milton Friedman and liberal James Tobin. Although no legislation was passed on the federal level, a series of randomized experiments were done in a few states. These experiments provided families with income supplements that gradually fell as income rose. Although initial evaluations indicated that such programs had a significant negative effect on family structure, later study showed that these effects were small and inconsistent in most families.[47] In addition, the four experiments studied show that guaranteed incomes reduced work incentives to a minor extent.[48] In general, these programs failed to generate strong interest for two reasons.[49] First, the welfare profession and welfare rights groups opposed it as not being generous enough. Criticisms included the fact that the guaranteed income was too low, did not cover all people, and required recipients to work. On the other hand, there was broad public opposition to any type of guaranteed income. Whereas social workers and many economists at the time viewed poverty as basically a lack of money, the public tended to believe that poverty stemmed from the lack of a job, as well as the discipline and self-respect that go with it. According to this view, income transfers, unless they are linked to a work requirement, ignore the real problem and might even exacerbate it by instilling a sense of dependency. For this reason, there was broad public support for providing goods and services and even for guaranteeing work rather than money.

A broader reform movement began in the early 1990s when a number of states were granted waivers to the federal Aid for Families with Dependent Children (AFDC) program, which traditionally provided very little assistance to working families. These waivers allowed the states to experiment with program innovations such as welfare-to-work training, time limits, family caps, and sanctions. As a condition to obtaining a waiver, states were required to conduct evaluations of the new programs' success, producing a body of literature for researchers to analyze.

This momentum for reform eventually led to the replacement of AFDC in 1996 by the Temporary Assistance for Needy Families (TANF) bloc grant. TANF required states to link a greater portion of assistance to work requirements but gave them much greater flexibility in structuring their programs. During this time period other programs such as the minimum wage, the Earned Income Tax Credit (EITC), and health care for children were also expanded. Adjusted for inflation, federal dollars available to support working low-income families rose from $11 billion to $66.7 billion between 1988 and 1999. At the same time, cash support for nonworking families headed by nonelderly, nondisabled adults fell from $24 billion to $13 billion.[50] These changes were accompanied by dramatic declines in the number of families receiving assistance and increases in the proportion of single women with children who participated in the workforce.

While the decline in caseloads was helped by the strong economy of the 1990s, studies show that the policy changes enacted during the decade were even more important. These policy changes, including the expansion in the EITC, were also important in moving individuals to work. Although the evidence is somewhat weaker, the income of single mothers also rose, even after the decline in government assistance.[51]

Sawhill cites a growing body of work that not only points to the importance of personal behavior but also recognizes that it is influenced by the behavior of others. Once one recognizes that peer influence matters, then government programs that change individual incentives might also have large secondary effects by changing the environment within which each person acts. These effects would be likely to grow over time, even if traditional economic studies were unable to measure them.

3

ATTACKING THE
SOURCE OF POVERTY

This chapter describes the basic structure of a new income guarantee conditioned on personal behavior. Unlike past and current policy, the income guarantee would not require complex legislation to guide it. Congress would only need to authorize public officials to enter into the necessary contracts according to general guidelines set out in the statute and appropriate the necessary funds.

The heart of the income support program is a simple bilateral, annual contract available to any U.S. citizen over the age of twenty-one. The contract need be no longer than one or two pages in regular-sized font. It need state only the individual's identifying information, the few terms agreed to by the individual, and the promised level of government support. Since most of the behavior requirements are simple, little detail is needed except to the extent that special circumstances arise. The parties could agree to settle any disputes under the contract by taking them to informal arbitration similar to small claims court. This would give workers the opportunity to tell their side of the dispute without hiring a lawyer or incurring large costs. It would also keep the government's administrative costs very low. Disputes at this level should be solved quickly. Giving each side the right to appeal would allow the establishment of a body of precedent to settle more complex questions and guide expectations. But because the terms of the contract are relatively simple, few of these more expensive cases should arise.

The contract should be bilateral, involving only the individual worker and the government. Although only the federal government needs to participate, it would be preferable to have multiple levels of government involved. A federal role is necessary because the national government has the largest amount of resources and can help set a common national contract. However, states could also participate by providing matching funds in order to give their citizens a higher level of minimum support. Finally, the involvement of local government may be important to help enforce the terms of the contract and operate various services to deal with special circumstances. Whether state or local governments are involved, the actual contracting party should be either the federal Department of Health and Human Services or the state social services agency, representing all levels of government.

The contract would have a term of one year. The government's support payments would be paid in equal installments throughout the year on either a monthly or biweekly basis. After the end of the year, the individuals would have the option of signing another contract. Individuals could participate for some years but not for others and also participate for part of the year but not the whole year.

The contract would be available to any U.S. citizen over twenty-one years of age. Since the contract requires individuals to complete high school and two years of additional schooling, few individuals would be eligible before their twentieth birthday. In any case, most children are supported by their parents until then. Despite the age requirement, we should expect a significant income guarantee to have a major prospective impact on younger children who see both greater assurance of a decent place in society and the expectations that go with it.

There are several reasons for limiting the contract to citizens. First, if the contract is to promise a significant increase in lower-paid workers' incomes, it must have broad public support. Public support for maintaining even legal immigrants is lukewarm. The 1996 welfare reform reflected this by eliminating most forms of federal assistance for new immigrants. Public support is also likely to be higher if total costs can be kept down, which is easier if there are fewer eligible workers. Second, there is a clear difference in the equity arguments for helping citizens and immigrants. Citizens owe their primary loyalty to the United States. They are required to pay U.S. tax on their full income and are subject to all of the obligations, both actual and prospective, that the federal government may impose. Conversely, immigrants voluntarily came here, presumably because their life is better here than it is in their home country. In doing so, they are not obliged to reduce their loyalty to their home country, nor should there be a presumption that they have done so prior to being naturalized. Illegal immigrants have an even weaker case for public assistance. Providing the type of support called for in this proposal would only encourage greater illegal flows.

Limiting assistance to citizens also serves the cause of immigration, however. Despite the claims of some, there is little question that a significant amount of legal immigration is beneficial to both the United States and to the individuals who come here. This is true at both the higher end of the skill level, where we benefit from the knowledge and experience of some of the world's best scientists and engineers, and at the lower end, where low wage labor fills many jobs in the agricultural and service sectors that would otherwise go unfilled. Although there is some evidence that low-skilled immigration depresses the wages of poorer Americans, these effects are minor when compared to the impact of technological change and are outweighed by the benefits to the rest of society. But significant levels of legal immigration cannot happen without public support. That support will be harder to get if Americans believe that immigrants come here mainly in order to take advantage of government assistance or if they see immigrants as a public burden. The cause of immigration and of immigrants is better enhanced by allowing increased numbers of legal immigrants and by encouraging naturalization once immigrants arrive. Americans at the bottom of the pay scale are also more likely to support additional immigration if an income guarantee ensures that their incomes will not fall below a given amount.

Structuring the federal assistance involves a number of difficult questions. The first is whether assistance should be given as a lump sum irrespective of how much an individual earns in the private sector or whether the amount of aid should be reduced as income rises. There are problems with both approaches. A lump sum provides individuals with the maximum benefit from any raise that they receive in the private sector, but because the full amount is paid to anyone who participates, total program costs will be very high unless either the lump sum amount is kept low or some way is found to limit the number of individuals who participate to those who truly need assistance. A benefit that is phased out as income rises reduces government expenditures but exposes recipients to high marginal "tax" rates. Under current law, poor workers can already face extremely high marginal rates: In 2006, for every additional $100 that a two-worker family making between $16,850 and $38,348 earned, they had to pay $7.65 in taxes for Social Security and Medicare (as did their employer). In addition, they lost $21.06 in benefits from the Earned Income Tax Credit (EITC). If they received housing assistance, as much as one-third of the additional income might have to go toward rent, replacing government aid. The tax code contains a number of other benefits that phase out at various levels, although some only at incomes well above the poverty line. For middle- and upper-class individuals these provisions merely add needless complexity to the tax laws, without changing behavior a great deal. For the poor, they defeat much of the purpose of rising up the income ladder. The argument for progressive taxation is not a very strong one, especially when marginal tax rates approach 40 percent or more. Yet when benefit reduction rates and Social Security taxes are included in the analysis, the poor often pay much higher marginal rates than do the rich. This is wrong.

With a work requirement, the government presumably does not have to worry that high benefit reduction rates would discourage individuals from entering the job market. But they might discourage individuals from investing in the training and experience needed to progress to the middle class, by either making it harder for them to afford these investments or making it less worthwhile.

Linking benefits explicitly to income earned also imposes administrative burdens on the government. Underreporting of income is a serious problem with low-income workers.[1] Although the poor account for only a small portion of the estimated $345 billion in taxes that went uncollected in 2001, the EITC program has had a history of fraud. Verification problems like these reduce the program's effectiveness and jeopardize public support. These problems would only be magnified if support payments were paid monthly.

The EITC is primarily meant to reduce poverty and is explicitly linked to an individual's income. In contrast, payments made under the income support contract can be viewed as being earned in return for the promised behaviors. This reduces the need to link payments to income. According to this view, the private income of the individual is no more relevant to determining the government's obligation than is the total profitability of a company that contracts with the government to perform a specific service. This fulfills the often stated goal of ensuring that those who work and play by the rules should not have to scrape by on the barest margins or feel that events beyond their control could easily push them into poverty. It also builds on the idea of reciprocal obligations, sending a signal to individuals that their actions are valued by the community and that they are expected to live up to those obligations. One of the persistent themes of poverty is the accompanying lack of self-confidence and self-respect. Changing the assistance relationship from one of dependence to one of mutual benefits and expectations could have a significant motivational effect on those at the very bottom. A belief in the transforming potential of the human spirit argues in favor of exchanging benefit reduction rates for a fixed lump sum commitment to each participant that is not reduced just because she or he does better.

On the whole, it would be much better to specify the government's obligation as being a specific sum of money, paid out in regular installments over the year. This gives the individual maximum certainty regarding the level of support and preserves for him or her the full benefit of individual initiative. The problem again is that, if the terms and conditions are too generous, every person may decide to participate, in which case either the cost will be too high or the level of support will be so low as to be meaningless. The discussion below suggests ways to reduce the level of participation to an acceptable level.

The total amount of money appropriated for the program should be linked to the gross domestic product (GDP). A measure of the nation's income, GDP specifies how much money is available to fulfill its wants and needs. Linking the program's size to GDP has two advantages. First, it signals a commitment to set aside a specific fraction of national income to ensure that every contributing member of society shares in any increased wealth. Second, it gives contract participants a stake in policies, such as trade, deregulation, and immigration, that would raise national income over time. This stake could alter the political calculus of domestic policies and help create an environment that would increase productivity and national wealth at a faster rate.

THE CONDITIONS FOR
FULFILLING THE CONTRACT

A recent article on New York's Rheedlen Centers for Children and Families examines the approach to poverty of its president, Geoffrey Canada.[2] The center sidesteps the traditional conservative/liberal debate by operating under the premise that both are correct. Poverty is caused by the culture and behavior of its victims who frequently engage in bad parenting, out-of-wedlock births, crime, drugs, early dropouts, and a poor understanding of the skills and actions needed to succeed in a permanent job. At the same time, the hurdles any one person faces are formidable: bad schools, dangerous neighborhoods, high prices for many basic goods, a lack of well-paying jobs for those with few skills, and an atmosphere of low expectations and social discrimination.

Efforts on both fronts are needed. The income contract addresses the first by explicitly linking government support to specific individual behaviors. Recipients must perform their obligations in order to receive payment, just as they would in any other contract. These obligations are widely recognized as being closely linked to personal success and have broad public support as components of the informal social contract spelling out the type of behavior citizens should expect from each other. They are limited in number and well within the reach of virtually every young person. Although older individuals may have already disqualified themselves or have a hard time going back to meet the educational requirements, transitional rules should make it possible to extend the contract to them while still preserving its basic purpose and effect going forward. Finally, with few exceptions, the government should have a fairly easy time observing whether each requirement has been met in substance.

In setting the requirements it is important to keep them relatively simple and few in numbers. There will be a continuing temptation to attach a variety of other conditions to the contract, such as community service, parenting lessons, job training, and counseling, on the theory that the government should get more for its money. The temptation is likely to be especially strong for politicians seeking to gain popular support. These efforts should be resisted. The conditions are part of a broader social contract about what is fair and due in a society as rich as ours in which a large portion of the population still underachieves its potential. Making the contract more complex without also increasing the level of support devalues the contribution of participants, adds unnecessary complexity, and by returning the program to the bureaucracy, risks the broad popular support and understanding that is needed to sustain it.

The support program does not seek to transform individuals' lives beyond the basics. The view for doing otherwise is stated by Martin Anderson:

> The provision of an adequate income may eliminate poverty in the official sense, but it does not guarantee that those who receive welfare will spend that income in a manner that also eliminates the characteristics that many people associate with poverty . . . if they personally value nice cars, good liquor, and gambling, they may not have much money left for housing, clothing and food.[3]

This analysis correctly points out that recipients may not make optimal use of government payments. But to a large extent this should be their choice. We usually rely on individuals' self-interest to ensure that they obtain adequate clothing and food. Given the spread of obesity among lower-income children, the most pressing problem is often the nutritional value of the food consumed rather than its cost. Housing is a different matter, but only slightly. Few individuals are likely to forgo adequate housing for frivolous expenditures, provided that reasonable housing exists at an affordable price and that government policy does not subsidize living in substandard housing. The government has a stronger interest in making sure individuals get adequate health insurance and save for their old age, but these can be dealt with by rather simple government policies. Beyond that, the money should be the recipients' to do with what they please. If government believes that certain decisions would be wiser, it can make its case directly to people through education and social outreach, relying on the wisdom of its message and their own self-interest, rather than by directly controlling their lives.

Because individuals may continue to spend money unwisely, the program is set up as an annual contract with a regular stream of income. Some policy makers have called for transferring wealth to individuals, either at birth or at other stages in life.[4] The problem with this approach is that, if individuals run through the money because of unwise decisions or bad luck, the government is again faced with the moral obligation of supporting them. Onetime transfers of wealth may fail to create any permanent improvement in an individual's life, yet it would be hard to draft regulations that would allow people to use the wealth to their best advantage while also preventing them from making decisions that in retrospect look unwise. The advantage of a regular income stream is that if an individual spends all of it, the next year new payments are made.

Individuals could still overcommit by borrowing. It would be ironic if one of the major beneficiaries of higher income was the credit card industry, which might enjoy greater recoveries from distressed borrowers. But to a certain extent, this is an inevitable risk. The best solution to excessive debt levels is not to restrict poor peoples' access to credit but rather to enter the market directly to provide them with financial education and cheaper forms of credit. The income contract should make the market for serving low-income borrowers more attractive.

The elimination of poverty also requires efforts to address the environmental factors that reduce the gains from individual initiative. The majority of this book addresses some of the most important of these. Its basic premise is that past efforts to address these problems have failed mainly because they followed a top-down bureaucratic approach that was incapable of delivering continuous improvement in the services that the poor received. Devoting more time and energy to the current approach is unlikely to be more successful than past efforts. Instead, government needs to pursue a radically different approach that deregulates major sectors of the economy while at the same time increasing both the resources handed directly to citizens and the number of interested providers offering services and products of value.

In exchange for a guaranteed income, each person would agree to abide by certain behaviors.

Work

The first requirement it that individuals work for a living. This general requirement has broad public support. As Dennis Coyle and Aaron Wildavsky note in their analysis of the income maintenance experiments of the Nixon period,

> The public's attitude toward poverty is that giving money to those who cannot handle it is futile. Better to follow a paternalistic policy of giving the poor what is good for them—such as food and clothing—and requiring and guaranteeing work, which will give them the moral character to be self-reliant. Then (and only then) should they receive the reward—the freedom to spend their earnings as they please. Rewards should flow from taking advantage of opportunities, not from getting rewards in order to seek opportunities.[5]

The contract follows this preference by requiring work but also requires that the public accept the premise of a much larger income supplement in return for the requirements placed on the individual. The welfare reforms of 1996 have already linked assistance to work for a large proportion of those receiving government help. The contract would go further by requiring it of everyone who receives government funds.

Some difficulty exists in defining what the work requirement should be and in verifying that individuals are meeting it. Both are much easier if the work is defined as being part of a normal employer-employee relationship, which it will be in most cases. For these jobs, a requirement of forty-five hours per week would be relatively easy to verify and enforce.

In some cases it may be difficult to distinguish true work opportunities from arrangements that are meant only to satisfy the letter of the requirement without requiring any effort from the participant. In a significant number of cases, the best opportunity for advancement might lie in self-employment or employment with a very small business. Under present law, workers lose their benefits if they start their own business. Yet this is often one of the best routes out of poverty for people who have little capital but know their own communities very well. Although these options open up the possibility for fraud, they should be allowed. To ensure that the work requirement is meaningful, workers could be required to seek preapproval for employment in business with fewer than ten employees. The government could also audit business receipts to ensure that the enterprise had economic value and was not just a front for avoiding work. For farmers and some other occupations, the work requirement might be defined by an objective metric such as acres planted.

In difficult cases, some combination of rule-making and case-by-case adjudication will be necessary. As one of the contracting parties, the government social agency could set a policy that proposals will be accepted as meeting the work requirement if they satisfy certain criteria or are overseen by a case worker. Participants should have the right to challenge a denial of coverage by going to a neutral fact-finder. In doing so, they would gradually build up a series of cases that should help guide workers and agencies. The general test should be, not whether there is a formal employer-employee relationship, but whether what the individual is engaged in demands equivalent effort from her or him and offers a good opportunity for economic advancement. Another criterion should be whether the activity makes a positive contribution to society that reflects the abilities of the worker. For workers of very few abilities, the activity may be relatively simple and low paying.

If the government is going to require all recipients to work, it has an interest in ensuring that even the lowest skilled can find some employment. It is important that both parties know participants cannot credibly claim that they cannot find work, despite trying. This creates a strong argument for doing away with the minimum wage. For some reason liberals have remained fiercely loyal to this concept despite evidence that it does little to advance the cause of the poor, especially when compared to alternatives such as the EITC. This strong support probably stems from three causes. First, there is still a residual belief in the lump supply of jobs theory that assumes there are only so many jobs in the economy and adding workers to the pool will only increase unemployment. By the same logic, raising wages will not reduce the number of jobs available to workers; it will only increase their incomes at the cost of employers or consumers.

Second, unions continue to have a strong influence in Democratic circles, due in large part to the heavy contributions they make during elections. Since unions represent relatively few of the people on the bottom of the ladder, they tend to be more concerned about the threat that those people will compete with their members by working for lower wages and less concerned about whether jobs are available at the bottom. Finally, raising the minimum wage gives the appearance of helping the poor without requiring an increase in government spending. Because the cost is borne mainly by employers, consumers, and the workers themselves, politicians get credit for something that costs them very little.

Although the federal minimum wage has not kept pace with inflation, a number of state and local jurisdictions have set their own, higher minimum wages. This has produced a wealth of statistics for researchers to analyze. A recent review of the literature concludes that no consensus exists about the overall effects that an increase in the minimum wage has on low-skilled employment.[6] In other words, even if the minimum wage does result in an overall loss of jobs, the effect is likely to be very small. But the researchers also found that, among the least-skilled workers, there is overwhelming evidence that an increase in the minimum wage produces strong disemployment. Yet these are the people that supporters of the minimum wage claim to be most concerned about.

There are several reasons an increase in the minimum wage is an inefficient way to help the poor. First, much of the benefit of any minimum wage increase goes to teenagers, many of whom are in middle- and upper-class families. While higher wages help these individuals, it is not clear that they should be the primary beneficiaries of government efforts to help the poor. Second, even if a higher wage does not reduce employment, it still must be borne by either employers or consumers. If employers face heavy competition, they will be forced to pass the costs on to consumers, and if the businesses are primarily local, most of these customers will themselves be poor. Higher income is therefore at least partially offset by higher prices on the things low-income workers buy. Most important, the current structure of tax and benefit law exposes poor workers to high income reduction rates in the form of taxes and reduced benefits. As much as half the benefit therefore goes back to government, rather than staying with the worker.

If, in return for a more generous social contract, liberals can be induced to drop their support for the minimum wage, then it does become more difficult for anyone to assert that they are unable to find a job at any wage. Of course, much of the problem is not in getting the job but rather in keeping it. One option for ensuring that individuals get the confidence, discipline, and social skills needed to keep a job is to allow designated agencies to hire workers for two dollars an hour for a limited time for the primary purpose of giving them the basic skills needed to succeed in the job market. This option would ensure that workers perform some type of service and would serve as a staging area for the acquisition of the skills needed to move to a better job.

The work requirements of the Temporary Assistance for Needy Families (TANF) have already taught us something about the benefits of working. First, getting individuals into work quickly matters. Studies comparing programs that stress labor force attachment with those that focus on human capital development show that the former increased earnings and decreased dependence more quickly, while the latter cost more without achieving superior results.[7] These results held even three years out, suggesting that the experience of working is more important than additional training or education outside the workforce. The best outcomes have been achieved in programs that combined financial incentives to work with a strong work mandate. Although programs like this have been tried in only a few states, they have been effective in increasing employment and reducing poverty.[8] Evidence also shows that permanent jobs are better than temporary ones; a rush to put people into the first job available may make it impossible for them to search for a better job with greater stability.[9]

The contract does not make special provisions for anyone; however, the government would have flexibility in defining work. The premise is that all but the most incapacitated are capable of making a positive contribution to society. This includes individuals over sixty-five. The modern concept of retirement arose by accident as the result of artificially imposed age requirements and Social Security's age of eligibility (the program's original retirement age of sixty-five reflected the prevailing life expectancy at the time so that individuals reaching that age were truly viewed as being near the end of their life); rising incomes in the middle class that freed them from having to work after a certain age; and the lump sum of labor fallacy that believed that encouraging older individuals to retire would free up jobs for younger workers. Unfortunately, it instilled a cultural expectation that an individual's obligation to make a productive contribution to society ends at sixty-five. This is morally harmful to both older Americans and society, which still needs their talents. Those with sufficient savings can do with them what they like, but workers who seek continued government assistance should be compelled to contribute to the society that supports them no matter what age they are.

Work requirements should, however, reflect the abilities of the participant. Individuals whose abilities are impaired by old age or handicap may need assistance in finding meaningful ways to contribute to society. The purpose of the work requirement for these individuals is less about finding remunerative employment and more about creating a place of value in society. Creative ways exist for doing this. For example, the government could require the residents of a nursing home to connect with school children as their obligation. Experiments show that such connections lead to meaningful interactions on both sides.[10] Finding such solutions will be one of the new demands on nonprofits and government agencies.

Another example of creative interpretation of the work requirement would be an option allowing mothers of children under five years old to satisfy the work requirement by staying at home with their infant and participating in nursing and educational classes aimed at ensuring that the child enters kindergarten healthy and educationally prepared. Studies show that parental behavior plays a large role in the health and well-being of children. In fact, one expert has written that the success of poverty programs may depend on the parent-child relationship:

> Existing government programs that provide more income or other supports to families and children are costly and are fighting demographic trends so strong that even substantial amounts of aid will do little to improve children's prospects unless changes in norms and values lead their parents to behave differently.[11]

It would therefore be of great benefit to help parents improve the effect they have on their child's development. The opportunity cost of doing so is relatively low. If mothers return to the workforce the child must be placed in day care, an expense that either the parents or the government must bear. The marginal benefit of having both parents working is therefore reduced, at least until the child is ready to enter school. Properly designed programs could give mothers an option that would benefit both families and society. Because participation would be voluntary, the program could be quite structured without adding to the complexity of the underlying contract.

Complete High School and Two Years of Additional Training

In September 2007, the unemployment rate for adults who had not graduated from high school was 7.4 percent.[12] For those with a college degree it was only 2 percent. Partly as a result, in 2006 the poverty rate among high school dropouts was 20.9 percent, compared with 3.9 percent for those who had completed college.[13]

Technological change has reduced the number of low-skilled jobs that earn a middle-class income. Pay strongly responds to productivity in the medium term, and innovation, including automation, has sharply reduced the productivity of workers with few skills. As a result, their incomes have fallen. This makes education more important than ever. At the same time there is a shortage of skilled workers in many occupations. A number of these, such as nursing and computer programming, require only a few years of training before a person qualifies for a good job.

Because the United States offers free K–12 education to all children, there are few excuses for someone not completing high school. Granted, many high schools are dysfunctional and therefore incapable of teaching all of the students that come to them. Chapter 5 discusses reforms, mainly centered on decentralization and parental choice, that would force these schools to either improve or give way to competitors. Giving purchasing power to parents rather than administrators would ensure that something from the private, nonprofit, or government level takes their place.

In addition to high school the contract calls for two additional years of training. This might require further specification by either the social agency or courts, but the line between reputable institutions and others is fairly sharp, so the task should be fairly straightforward. Courses from any college, university, junior college, or certified training school should qualify—so should military service. An agency could easily maintain a list of acceptable institutions in each state, and properly supervised accrediting bodies could be relied on for quality control.

As a contracting party, the government would have the right to waive this requirement in certain cases. Those cases should be extremely rare, applying to those few individuals whose mental and physical abilities preclude even a high school level education. The opportunity of a case-by-case exemption should be used to find an appropriate way in which these individuals can fulfill the work requirement. For while it may be appropriate to excuse them from repeatedly trying to pass courses that are beyond their abilities, it is virtually never appropriate to excuse them from working—not because work will advance them economically, but because each individual has value to society and this value can never be appreciated or experienced if nothing is asked or expected of them.

Avoid Drug Dependency

Drugs, both legal and illicit, have become a major social problem. In addition to destroying the lives of many users, they impose significant costs on the rest of society in the form of lost productivity, crime, and poor parenting. Yet, despite the expenditure of billions of dollars every year, federal policy has been largely ineffective in keeping illicit drugs off the streets. Meanwhile, the alcohol industry has become a powerful lobby in government and a major underwriter of advertising and sports events.

Part of the participant's obligation under this provision would be to refrain from taking any illegal drugs. As part of its rights the government would be allowed regular drug tests to ensure that the contract was being honored. Although testing can be expensive, certain policies can minimize the cost. First, the government should have broad discretion in who it tests and when. Some individuals are very unlikely to use drugs and therefore seldom need to be tested. Others with a history of abuse should be tested more often. Second, the government need not test every sample it takes. A practice of taking regular samples, but sending few to the lab, might be just as effective as if every sample was analyzed, since the participant would not know which samples would be selected.

With respect to alcohol and prescription drugs, which are legal, the contract should be interpreted to require the participant not to fraudulently obtain a prescription and to avoid undue dependence on liquor. Efforts like the Serial Inebriate Program in San Diego have had good success working with chronic alcoholics using the threat of incarceration in order to get them to participate. The bilateral nature of the income contract could serve as another lever for encouraging someone into treatment. If the government could prove that an individual had become a chronic alcoholic, then the contract would be void unless the individual entered treatment.

Civil liberties groups have opposed drug testing in the past, but it is difficult to take their arguments seriously. Few make the argument that individuals have a legal right to engage in illegal drug use. And given the bilateral nature of the income guarantee, the government should be able to condition its participation on reasonable requirements. Given its illegality and the clear harm caused by drug use, a requirement to refrain from drug use is reasonable. What is left then is the argument that, while the government has the right to require individuals not to use drugs, it has no right to verify whether they are abiding by their obligations and that doing so constitutes an invasion of privacy. This argument is rapidly losing favor even among liberals. Drug testing is increasingly becoming a part of employment in the private sector, especially for jobs that involve the public safety. Although an equally divided Federal Appeals Court has ruled that making "suspicionless" drug tests a condition of eligibility for welfare violates the Constitution,[14] the Supreme Court has not ruled on the issue. And the existing case should not be read as barring testing as part of a contractual relationship between the individual and government.

With this and certain other contract provisions, a violation need not completely void the contract or make the individual ineligible in future years. Instead, the government could offer to waive the violation if the individual participated in a drug program or counseling. Payments under the contract could be diverted to pay some or all of the cost. One of the problems with current drug policy is that there is a shortage of good centers for treating chemical dependency. By diverting payments to such centers the government could create more purchasing power behind the existing demand for treatment. However, the goal of any program should be to return individuals to regular compliance with all of the contract requirements, not to provide a long-term place for semicompliance. At some point, individuals who can or will not break their dependency should be cut off.

In this and other areas, a national rule should state what the government's general policy will be with respect to violations so that local officials cannot be completely arbitrary. Local officials should then apply this policy to the facts of individual cases, leaving the individual with a right to appeal. The goal should be to return individuals to full compliance and rights under the contract wherever that is possible within a reasonable period of time. But since compliance ultimately requires personal effort, in some cases it will not be possible. Because a violation is a breach of contract, conditional forbearance by the government does not waive the explicit terms of the contract but only sets out a policy stating how the government will enforce its rights. It can and should be changed to achieve the best results possible in individual cases, and any changes would not require the consent of the other contracting party any more than a credit card company's decision to moderate its collection policies diminishes the borrower's obligation to pay the full amount of existing debt according to its original terms.

Avoid Having Children until the Age of Twenty-one

The United States suffers from a much higher rate of teen births than do other industrialized countries. The rise in unwed mothers is one of the most significant demographic changes of the last several decades. Early, unintended children and lack of child support are major factors in the increase in child poverty and impose significant costs on the rest of society.[15] While society may feel obligated to help children caught in these situations, it also needs to deter young adults from behaving irresponsibly. The consequences of not deterring teen pregnancy are great.[16] Women who have a child before the age of twenty are likely to have more children, complete less education, and be more dependent on government support; also, they are less likely to marry than their peers. Their children are sicker, more likely to be abused and neglected, more likely to drop out of high school, more likely to be jailed, and more likely to become teenage parents themselves.

To prevent these consequences, the contract requires individuals of both sexes to avoid having children until they reach the age of twenty-one. There is no exception for married teenagers because it is unlikely that they possess the resources and maturity to adequately raise children. Of course, individuals are still free not to participate in the program, in which case neither they nor the government are bound by its provisions.

As with other provisions, a breach should not lead to immediate disqualification from all current and future benefits. But it should lead to significant intervention aimed at ensuring that the child is raised properly and that the parents continue with their personal development as far as possible. For fathers this should mean that some of the government payments are automatically diverted toward child support and payment for counseling services. For the mother it should require participation in a program aimed at ensuring the health and development of the child. Typical programs provide health screening, parenting classes, personal counseling, and continued education. Precedent exists for such a requirement. In the early 1990s some states obtained waivers from the Aid for Families with Dependent Children (AFDC) program allowing them to require teen mothers to stay in school and live at home with their parents or in another supervised setting.[17]

Violation of this requirement should therefore lead to a loss of freedom in the form of heavier intervention by the state to minimize the damage of an early pregnancy on both the development of the child and the advancement of the parent. By linking future assistance to successful participation in an intensive program, the requirement increases the likelihood of success while sending a clear message to teenagers. At the same time, the availability of good programs should reduce the incentive to obtain an abortion or to place the child up for adoption.

Do Not Commit Crimes

This requirement should be a no-brainer. However, additional detail is warranted. First, to justify it, a 1996 study estimated that crime and responses to it imposed an annual cost of $450 billion on the economy.[18] The cost is surely much larger today. Although this expenditure generates a large number of jobs, from a social viewpoint, it is a massive waste of resources. Efforts that could go into producing wealth are instead diverted to prevent the transfer or destruction of existing wealth. Society would be much richer if these costs were substantially reduced. Crime also dims the future of those engaged in it. Besides the threat of fines and prison time, a criminal conviction disqualifies a person from many careers and acts as a severe barrier to others.

Some definition of the requirement is needed. Clearly, parking and speeding tickets should not constitute violations of the contract—nor should misdemeanors that do not involve theft or physical violence. Although this is a closer question, the main purpose of the requirement is not to disqualify people for any violation of the law, no matter how technical the rule or how harmless the action. It is to strongly deter serious criminal activity and moral offenses by significantly raising the opportunity cost of engaging in them. The contract may, however, prove useful in providing those who plead guilty to misdemeanors with a steady stream of income that a court can tap for restitution to victims.

Commission of a felony is different and should disqualify an individual from participating in future contracts for the duration of his or her sentence, with perhaps a minimum disqualification of five years. Conviction or a plea of guilty should be sufficient to establish a breach of the contract. In cases that are difficult to prove, the government could be allowed to disqualify a person by showing with a preponderance of the evidence that a person has engaged in criminal activity. Preponderance of the evidence is the normal test for contract disputes. This would not be a formal conviction, but it would disqualify the individual from government support for a five-year period.

In applying the contract for the first time, it would be wise to offer it to past felons who have served their sentence. The main purpose of the income guarantee is to affect future behavior by altering incentives, not to punish past behavior. Extending it to past offenders may reduce recidivism rates.

Finally, it is worth stating the need for a much more rational and humane penal system. In 2006, over 3 percent of all adults were incarcerated, on probation, or on parole.[19] This included 11 percent of black males age twenty-five to thirty-four.[20] The United States has no clear policy for tapping the social contribution that prisoners are able to make or for integrating them back into society when they have served their time. Despite almost complete control over the conditions of incarceration, once an inmate is sentenced, the government has been unable to devise a system that is both humane and rational.

Ideally each prisoner, no matter what the term of his sentence, would face a constant choice between better or worse conditions depending upon his behavior. Good behavior and participation in education and volunteer activities should lead to gradations of greater freedom and trust. Belief in the redemptive abilities of each person should be instilled into the system both as a moral requirement and as a matter of practical public policy. It does the country little good to have such a large proportion of its population cast away without any clear option for making a productive contribution. One promising option would be to require the prisoners to develop a one-year plan setting out what they will accomplish and the improvements in their conditions that accomplishment would allow. A strict policy of separating out prisoners who create repeated problems would also create a better environment for those who want to improve themselves.

Upon parole, partial payments could be resumed to ensure that the ex-prisoner had some reasonable means of support as well as a growing incentive to stay clean. One of the conditions could be regular participation in support groups dedicated to helping clients deal with personal issues and to find productive roles in society. Since participants do not qualify for the regular contract until their complete sentences are served, the government would have great discretion in setting and overseeing the terms of any support.

Save 15 Percent of Income

For over a decade the low rate of personal savings has been a cause for concern among economists and policy makers. There are some reasons to believe that part of the problem lies in the way savings are defined and measured.[21] For example, although placing one thousand dollars in a mutual fund counts as savings, any increase in the value of the stocks in the fund does not—nor does the personal equity that homeowners accrue as their house appreciates. Investments in income-generating activities such as education also do not count, even though they increase an individual's financial well-being. On the demand side, individuals have far less need to save now than previously. Social Security has assured basic incomes to previous and current generations, and the rise in personal credit markets makes it unnecessary to save up most of the purchase price of an appliance, car, or home before buying it. Nevertheless, saving money is a wise activity for several reasons including the fact that it funds the investments that create economic growth.

For the poor, who are most in need of savings and the least able to set aside money, the accumulation of significant savings would make a dramatic difference. If the assurance of a steady income relieves one from the daily worry of poverty, significant savings give one a stake in the game. Suddenly it matters how the economy does, if government policy is unnecessarily holding down corporate profits, and if inflation is creating business uncertainty. The future looks different.

Participants would be required to set aside 15 percent of their income in a mutual fund run on the model of the Thrift Savings Plan that is available to government employees. There would be no matching funds and a small variety of index funds would be available, giving individuals some choice in the amount of risk they want to undertake. Proceeds could not be withdrawn until the age of seventy, although in certain cases such as terminal illness the government could purchase a viatical policy from the individual. Such a policy gives the recipient an amount close to the account value in exchange for the account reverting to the government when the individual dies. Over the last decade an active private market has arisen in these policies, mainly as a way for terminally ill patients to tap into the value of life insurance plans in order to pay for health care.

Some might argue that poor individuals cannot afford to save such a large portion of their income. Part of the purpose of the income guarantee contract is to set a minimum income floor that makes the requirement easier. But it should also be remembered that all workers are currently required to pay 12.4 percent of their income into Social Security's retirement system (half of this is paid by the employer on behalf of the individual); although 1.8 percentage points go toward disability insurance, the rest is solely for retirement programs. Of course, most of the money actually goes not to the worker but rather to current retirees to pay off the obligation that the federal government made to them. Under current law, which policy makers in both parties say is unsustainable because it does not collect enough in taxes to pay for future benefits, a low-income worker just beginning his career is promised a real rate of return on these payments of just over 3 percent.[22] Given that younger generations are going to have to pay for some of the obligations made to current retirees and older workers, it is fair to ask why any of this burden should fall on the poorest workers and how a savings program that provides a return of only 3 percent before future tax increases or benefit cuts can possibly be better than allowing low-income workers to create a private plan that would probably pay at least twice that.

Assuming that the contract value rose only with inflation, a worker who saved 15 percent of her income and earned a 5 percent real rate of return would enjoy financial security when she reached seventy. She could then take out an amount equivalent to the annual contract payment and still see her balance grow every year. At the end of her life, she could pass any balance on to her heirs.

This type of a growing stake in society is likely to change attitudes in important ways. It could also serve as an important gateway into the financial community. Presently, 23 percent of low-income households do not have a checking account, and another 64 percent lack a savings account. As a result, they often pay much higher rates for basic services such as money transfers and check cashing.[23]

Pay Taxes

Some conservatives oppose refundable tax credits because they think that, if the country drifts too far in the direction of having all taxes paid by a small minority of the population, and especially if a large portion of workers pay no taxes at all, then a new system of class warfare will emerge in which populists try to appease low-income voters by promising large social programs paid for by taxing the rich.[24] Tax and spend policies would cripple the economy but might generate popular support. Other countries have followed this general path to ruin, current examples being Venezuela and Iran, which in spite of their large oil revenues are having trouble sustaining populist policies. The predictable results—rising inflation, plummeting investment, and high unemployment—are already emerging.

Because government benefits all workers, most workers should bear some of its costs directly. It is important that average workers face a marginal tax of 10–15 percent and that any rise in taxes fall at least partially on them. The purpose is to give them some incentive to keep government limited and efficient. More importantly, they should have an ownership stake in how the government performs. For those with the lowest incomes, the marginal tax rate would actually represent a decrease in net payments under the income support program. They would still be receiving much more from the government than they paid in. The marginal rate would also be much lower than the effective rate many of them currently face once benefit phaseouts are taken into account. This compromise makes sense, since even groups like the Tax Foundation suggest that net taxes should not be levied on incomes under forty thousand dollars for a couple.[25] However, it is not unreasonable to insist that even the lowest-income individual face some marginal tax rate if the income support guarantee is set to accommodate it. It may seem inefficient to give income with one hand only to take part of it away with the other, but there is a benefit to having everyone explicitly pay something toward the governance of society.

The proposal is part of a larger bargain within society in which those who favor a stronger social net get it, but only according to terms that maximize the possibility of lasting change. In exchange, those concerned with economic growth and national competitiveness obtain the elimination of most of the programs that retard efficiency and the deregulation of important markets in ways that allow for an increase in both quality and efficiency. Both are necessary: dramatically increasing federal expenditures without at the same time achieving important reforms in existing programs would be destructive.

The vision set out in the chapters that follow is integral to the social bargain. It sets out a new role for government agencies on all levels and calls for much greater reliance on private markets, albeit markets in which agencies and nonprofits are much more active participants. If higher income alone is not enough to eliminate poverty, it at least creates a market that new organizations can enter in order to promote improvement.

It is important to acknowledge that such a simple program does not solve all social problems. An income guarantee contract can lift millions of individuals out of poverty and provide a clear path that reduces uncertainty for many more. But it will not eliminate poverty. There will always be individuals who, despite the best advice and help, make disastrous choices. Free will is a powerful force, and until these individuals decide to pursue a wiser course, it is often useless to try to head them off of one that they are bound and determined to pursue. The hopeful news is that programs such as the Serial Inebriates Program begun in San Diego, California, and Oxford House begun in Washington, D.C., have experienced great success working with those who do want help. Building government around the income support guarantee would not eliminate alcoholism, drug addiction, and crime, but it would help ensure that resources for treatment are available when they would do the most good.

Another source of continued poverty is immigration. America's immigration policy should be reformed to give greater preference to immigrants that have the skills and training the country needs. But there is no doubt that the American economy will continue to produce a large number of new low-skilled jobs every year. At the same time, the total number of native-born people entering the workforce is slowing and the proportion of these new entrants who have less than a high school degree continues to fall. America will continue to need a large number of new low-skilled immigrants each year. Because these workers enter at the bottom of the socioeconomic ladder, they artificially inflate the nation's poverty statistics. But rather than being a sign that the promise of continued advancement no longer works, immigration of the poor should be viewed as an affirmation of America's continued role as a source of economic promise and political acceptance. We should recognize that this source of poverty is temporary, as immigrant families with legal status demonstrate a strong ability to rise up the economic ladder and integrate into the broader framework of American society. In allowing them entry, America provides an opportunity to significantly improve their future and that of their children. However, it is important that the income support program should not be offered to immigrants until they become citizens, formally switching their full allegiance to this country. Otherwise, the cost of immigration will rise and its public support will fall.

4

THE NEED FOR A RENEWED
PRIVATE SECTOR

To the extent that poverty is caused by a lack of income, the contract discussed in chapters 2 and 3 should go a long way toward solving it. By ensuring that workers have sufficient income to express their needs in the form of market demand, the contract should trigger a response by the private sector to offer the appropriate goods and services. Although this is likely to happen much faster than most observers believe, two objections are possible.

First, poverty is not solely a matter of income. To some extent it is caused by the high crime rates, low property values, poor schools, and other factors that surround most poor neighborhoods. Although increased income should help ameliorate these factors over time, it does not suddenly make them go away. If markets and power relationships are tilted against the poor, higher income may merely result in rising prices as a series of unscrupulous dealers take advantage of workers with little experience and few alternatives. This objection can be overdone. Unregulated markets tend to be extremely responsive to new demand, and at some point, the poor have to be held responsible for their own choices if they keep purchasing inferior services even when better ones are available. Moreover, their ability to make smart decisions when given the chance is frequently underestimated. Nevertheless, concern about the persistence of environmental factors has some basis in reality.

This is related to a second objection that markets might not respond to the increased purchasing power of the poor. This concern is heightened by the fact that some of the services that poor individuals are most in need of, such as low-cost housing, financial advice, and job training, are not commonly provided by the private sector at prices they can afford. Later chapters will discuss the ways in which government regulation often makes this problem worse by flooding sectors with government money that is not linked to results, thereby crowding out private enterprises, or by imposing regulations that artificially raise the price of goods and services without creating corresponding value. This chapter examines the importance of a new effort by nonprofit organizations that are explicitly devoted to serving the poor. One of the benefits of the income contract is that it creates the market for such efforts to be self-sustaining, provided they are well run and provide value to clients. But if it is to take advantage of this opportunity to help the poor, the nonprofit sector first has to undergo significant reform.

The nonprofit sector has grown rapidly over the past two decades. Peter Drucker viewed nonprofits as "central to the quality of life in America" for having as their product changed human beings.[1] Their role in society has been boosted by a generous tax deduction for charitable contributions. At the federal level this subsidy totaled forty-seven billion dollars in 2006. Donations also enjoy similar exemptions from state and local income taxes. In addition, nonprofits are exempt from having to pay most taxes themselves. In exchange for this treatment, federal tax law generally limits them to religious, charitable, scientific, educational, or other purposes set out in the Tax Code.

It is not very clear what the government gets in return for this subsidy. The range of activities qualifying for tax exempt status is so broad that it includes many organizations that do little to improve the public welfare. Other organizations, such as the Metropolitan Opera in New York, largely serve the middle and upper classes, raising the question why the average worker should subsidize a service that its patrons could easily afford to pay the full cost of. It is not that these organizations do not have a place in society or that their place is unimportant. But if one of the primary purposes of government is to level the playing field between the classes in order to increase the effective opportunity of those born poor, it is not clear why large sums of money should go to underwriting activities that largely cater to the rich.

Another objection is that for too long nonprofits have constituted a quiet, but largely ineffective, sector that provided comfortable jobs for a number of people without insisting on the achievement of any measurable results. In fact, the demand for tangible results was often regarded as heresy, an attempt to apply the cold calculus of cost-benefit studies and efficiency analyses to human values that could not be measured. The nonprofit sector can often be divided into two groups: the talkers and the doers. Some, like the Children's Defense Fund and Americans for Tax Reform, limit their activities largely to lobbying government for different policies. These activities may have great social value because the quality of political decisions is likely to be enhanced if each viewpoint has an adequate voice. But one can question why private companies and individuals do not receive equal subsidies when they advocate directly for the policies that they prefer.

Although these groups are often very vocal about what they perceive to be the needs of the poor, they seldom engage in direct action to alleviate those needs directly. For instance, the Consumers Federation of America (CFA) often speaks about the government's responsibility to protect the poor. But it is not always clear that the policies it advocates are truly helping consumers. The federation recently spent a great deal of time arguing against legislation that would speed up the transition to digital television because it insisted that no consumer anywhere should have to pay the fifty- to one-hundred-dollar cost of the television converter needed to change digital signals into the analog signal used by their old television sets. The digital transition will free up a large amount of valuable spectrum that can be used to deliver a variety of new services to consumers and to reduce the price of old services. It is conceivable that the average consumer, when educated about the digital transition, would find that the cost of the converter is well worth the added capability of digital television. And delaying the transition by even one year probably imposes far greater costs on the consumer in terms of delayed new services than the converter box CFA cared so deeply about. The true consumer interest lay in accomplishing the conversion as quickly as possible and devoting the spectrum to more valuable uses.

A more direct example exists from CFA's approach to high-interest loans made to low-income consumers. Whether it is in the form of subprime mortgages, car loans, rent-to-own purchases, or payday loans, poorer consumers often pay much higher interest rates than do others. To some extent this reflects the higher cost associated with lending to individuals with few financial resources and poor credit histories. But it also reflects the fact that many lenders will not enter these markets because they think they are unprofitable. This limits competition and opens the way for others who are often unscrupulous. It is not clear what the right interest rate for serving this population should be, nor is it clear whether denying them existing forms of credit would on the whole hurt or help them. But CFA takes the clear position that such practices should be banned, even if it means that poor consumers have much less credit and far fewer choices. CFA spends far less effort on trying to arrange better credit for consumers. Doing so would require a calculation of what interest rate would lead to a sustainable business, how to distinguish good risks from bad, how to collect loans that are overdue, and how to convince customers to do business with you. These are much tougher problems, but they directly lead to improved services. While many advocacy groups shy away from these activities, they have no compunction about criticizing the practices of those who do try to provide services to the poor.

This marks the fundamental distinction between the two groups. The doers try to tackle perceived problems head on. They face difficult business conditions and competition from a variety of other companies good and bad. Habitat for Humanity is directly engaged in ordering materials, building houses, choosing buyers, and making mortgages. The Harlem Project in New York runs a number of schools targeted at those most in danger of dropping out. The Chicago Food Depository feeds the hungry and trains cooks. The success of these and other groups is vital to any national effort targeting poverty. These organizations cannot force individuals to act responsibly, but they can make a tremendous difference to those who do. The successful ones can also act as a focal point for private individuals who seek a way to contribute to society. Drucker pointed out the one common mission all nonprofits share: "to satisfy the need of the American people for self-realization, for living out our ideals, our beliefs, our best opinion of ourselves."[2] What this need most often lacks is a clear path for individuals to become actively involved in efforts that directly make a difference.

As explained above, for a growing portion of Americans, the most pressing needs are those associated not with materialism but rather with self-fulfillment. More and more young people are looking for meaningful ways to contribute to the world around them. The impersonal imperative of the average business to maximize the owners' return on capital by meeting consumers' demand for the vast variety of goods and services often does not fulfill this drive. Also, government cannot accomplish the dramatic social transformations that many once hoped for. But a third way exists. Private entities that supply their own capital can choose to put other ends above profits. As long as they can cover their costs, they have the freedom to address those needs they think are most important in whatever way they think best on a sustainable and replicable basis. And in doing so, they might attract talent and resources seeking more meaningful outlets. In this chapter we will look at some of the ways they might do this.

But before the social sector can make its maximum contribution, two things stand in its way. The first is the need for an increased emphasis on results. Over the last two decades, American businesses have undergone a revolution in management efficiency. Very little of this has affected the nonprofit sector. Too often nonprofits have acted as if good intentions were an adequate substitute for results. Accomplishments were not measured, management skills were discounted, and clear cost-benefit analysis was frowned upon. Organizations acted as if higher budgets should be an entitlement that society owed them for tackling social issues, rather than a use of scarce resources that needed to be justified by tangible progress. Over the last decade this has begun to change. A number of people have called for applying business principles directly to nonprofits.[3] One article estimated that foundations could realize an extra one hundred billion dollars a year by adopting some of the efficiency practices of the private sector.[4] And new economy philanthropists like Bill Gates have increasingly been requiring the charities they fund to commit to achieving specific objectives by a certain time and to measure results.[5] The opportunity for gains is there. In fact, increasingly, for-profit companies are seeking to provide social services directly.[6]

The second, and related, obstacle is the traditional focus on government or foundations as the primary sources of funding. This history has turned nonprofits away from the needs of their clients, while at the same time creating a permanent state of dependency. The average nonprofit leader now spends a great deal of her or his time fund-raising, and boards are often recruited primarily for their ability to help raise money. Nonprofits must continually cultivate existing sources of funding and seek out new ones. It is the needs of the funding sources, rather than those of the poor, that receive attention. Since funding sources often do not receive anything of direct value from the nonprofit, underfunding and the threat of budget cuts are constant worries. As a result, nonprofits seldom become self-sustaining.

There is no doubt that nonprofits account for a large portion of economic activity or that many of their employees and volunteers find a great deal of meaning in the work they do. It is also clear that the best nonprofits make a difference in the lives of at least some of the individuals whom they try to help. However, on the whole, it is not at all clear that the money used to sustain this effort would not achieve more good somewhere else, especially if it went directly into the hands of the people it is meant to help. Because nonprofits eschew the type of voluntary market transactions that characterize a successful business, we cannot know for certain whether the beneficiaries of their services receive enough benefit to justify the costs of providing it.

If the nonprofit sector is to achieve its full potential, it must therefore adopt a new business model focused on alleviating social problems by selling the necessary goods and services directly to those who need them. The income contract and other policies called for in this book are aimed at giving people enough purchasing power to create a desirable market for suppliers to offer better loans, safer housing, job training, and health care. But someone will have to step up and create the business model to actually deliver these services at an affordable cost. Social service organizations may not have the management skills to develop these models, but they often have knowledge of the community and an institutional devotion to the cause. And this is often the scarcest resource. Capital and management skills can easily be obtained either directly or by partnering with a private company.

Two reforms would help. The first would level the playing field between for-profit and nonprofit entities. The tax subsidies that the latter receive are presumably motivated by the charitable and educational activities they engage in. If for-profit companies increasingly choose to perform these same services, they should be welcomed, not discriminated against. Public policy has recently tried to level the playing field that religious organizations face by making them directly eligible for government funding. This is beneficial because of the large and positive role these organizations already play in delivering social services. Preventing them from receiving direct government assistance makes no sense given the historic role of religious institutions, the wide acceptance of their existing tax-exempt status, and the importance of ethical values and strong community backing in any personal safety net. Concerns about undue influence are best dealt with by ensuring that recipients of care have a variety of service providers to choose from.

For-profit organizations face similar distrust because of misperceptions of the role of profit. For economists, profit serves two functions, each of which is needed in the social service sector. First, it serves as reimbursement for the use of capital. Almost any organization requires capital in the form of land, buildings, office equipment, cash reserves, and so forth. In a for-profit business the owners provide the capital themselves, accepting in return the right to any residual excess between income and expenses. The alternative is to borrow the money, promising to pay it back over a set schedule. This is what most nonprofits do. Borrowing does not in any way reduce the need to pay a return on the use of capital. Although equity owners usually demand a higher rate of expected return, they also bear more risk if the return is less than expected. From an economic point, there is no reason to favor borrowing over maintaining equity as a way to raise capital.

In other words, nonprofits cannot escape the need to pay for the capital they use. Given this requirement, it may well be that adopting an equity framework similar to for-profit ventures is a more efficient means of raising capital, especially if the equity holders are willing to accept a lower rate of return in exchange for fulfilling the organization's social purposes. It is important to remember that even this lower rate of return has an opportunity cost because any foregone earnings could be used to expand services or to invest in other worthwhile activities.

The second function of profit is to serve as a signal to the rest of the market. In a competitive market, high profits typically mean either that an area is being underserved or that one particular business model is outperforming others. Either way, high profits allow for expansion, and therefore better supply, either by the business receiving them or by imitators. This market signal is just as important in the nonprofit sector where organizations struggle to determine the best use of their resources and the best business model for delivering a set of services. Without any price or profit signal, there are fewer methods for communicating the solutions to these problems and successful models have fewer ways of displacing failures.

Of course, the ability to earn profits does not mean the need to earn them. A social service organization run on a for-profit model could decide to limit its activities to meeting immediate social needs even if other needs offered a greater return. It could also decide to reduce its profit to the minimum needed in order to sustain its capital requirements and in doing so reduce the cost of its services to clients. Or it could maximize its profits in one area but use these profits to subsidize service in others. It could try to earn a greater profit in order to expand its service to new clients who would otherwise not be served. Finally, such an organization could solicit other sources of support, such as donations, with the promise that they would be used to further reduce the cost of services. Each of these is fully consistent with the moral purpose that drives the typical nonprofit and should be capable of inspiring the traditional enthusiasm of those who care about improving the world. A successful organization built around any of these models would be more deserving of public support than most of the traditional nonprofits currently receiving tax subsidies.

Removing both the tax deductibility of nonprofit contributions and the tax exemption that nonprofits currently enjoy would have several advantages. First, it would broaden the tax base, allowing a lower marginal tax rate for everyone while keeping tax revenues constant. It would also remove an artificial barrier that prevents for-profit organizations from competing with nonprofits. The artificial distinction between the two sectors has kept the majority of entrepreneurial talent from many of the economy's most important activities. It has also retarded the development of sustainable efforts to address social problems by encouraging the belief that normal business concepts such as return on investment and efficiency do not apply to some of society's most pressing problems. Instead of subsidizing the supply of services through organizations that are not economically efficient, the government should concentrate on subsidizing demand by directly boosting incomes.

The second reform would involve governments at all levels setting up independent organizations to address specific perceived social problems. There is, of course, no guarantee that existing organizations will step in to provide some of the services that low-income workers need. In some cases, such as low-cost housing, traditional builders might continue to find it more profitable to concentrate on medium- and high-end housing because the profit margins are greater. In such cases, government can and should set up enterprises to address these needs. These entities could be given specific charters that limit them to providing specific goods and services, and governments could retain the right to appoint a number of members to the board of directors. Setting up new organizations would free the government from depending totally on existing groups.

A POSSIBLE NEW ROLE FOR GOVERNMENT

The federal government already provides several services to its workers that could usefully be expanded to a broader audience. The Thrift Savings Plan (TSP) provides a choice of low-overhead diversified mutual funds into which employees can divert their income. Although in the past the TSP also provided far lower levels of client service, these concerns have largely been addressed. The Federal Employee Health Benefit Plan (FEHBP) offers federal workers a broad range of health plans. The FEHBP negotiates prices and coverage with numerous companies and presents them to workers. Employees who are denied coverage for a particular procedure can appeal to the government for a decision on whether the denial was unjust. Every year employees can elect to change plans. A number of commentators have advocated extending the FEHBP to other citizens.[7]

Any form of government sponsorship raises severe dangers, however. Politicians should not even consider it unless several precautions are taken first. The first danger is that the enterprises will become dependent on government instead of the intended beneficiaries. To prevent this, all funds except temporary start-up costs should come from clients, not the government. Even when this is the case, perverse results can occur. The worst examples of this happening are Freddie Mac and Fannie Mae. These organizations were originally created to help homeowners obtain low-cost mortgages when housing and financial markets were much less sophisticated. Financial innovations since then have produced a private sector that is fully capable of offering the same services as do these government-sponsored enterprises. Although Fannie and Freddie were "privatized" years ago, this only exacerbated the problem. The government still implicitly guarantees the debt of both organizations. Privatization therefore led to a situation where most of the gains from this implicit backing go to private shareholders, while much of the risk remains with the government. Both Alan Greenspan and Ben Bernanke have stated that this risk represents a systemic threat to financial markets.[8]

In order to protect their subsidy, both companies have made heavy investments in influencing Washington, with Fannie being the worst. It hired CEOs that were more prominent for their political connections than their financial knowledge or management skills, it actively recruited the family members of policy makers as employees, and it engaged in personal attacks against individuals who called for true privatization. These last efforts included personal ridicule in the press, the threat of lawsuits, and pressure on other clients of its critics.[9]

This lack of accountability has predictably resulted in large accounting scandals within each company, in which senior management deliberately violated accounting rules, misreported earnings, and collected millions of dollars in undeserved bonuses. An internal review conducted by former senator Warren Rudman (R–NH) concluded that "management's accounting practices in virtually all of the areas that we reviewed were not consistent with GAAP (Generally Accepted Accounting Principles), and in many instances, management was aware of the departures from GAAP";[10] "employees who occupied critical accounting, financial reporting, and audit functions at the Company were either unqualified for their positions, did not understand their roles, or failed to carry out their roles properly";[11] "the Company's accounting systems were grossly inadequate";[12] and "the actual corporate culture suffered from an attitude of arrogance (both internally and externally) and an absence of cross-enterprise teamwork (with a "siloing" of information), and discouraged dissenting views, criticism, and bad news."[13]

What has the government received in return? A preliminary study by the Federal Reserve Bank concluded that the government's implicit backing of Fannie Mae and Freddie Mac provided a subsidy of between $119 billion and $164 billion, most of which was retained by their shareholders, that this subsidy accounted for most of their combined market value, but that the subsidy does not appear to have substantially increased either home-ownership or the housing supply because the estimated effect on mortgage rates is small.[14] A study by the Congressional Budget Office using a much different methodology concluded that the federal subsidy to housing government-sponsored enterprises (including the Federal Home Loan Banks) amounted to only twenty-three billion dollars but concurred that a significant portion of the subsidy was not passed on to borrowers.[15] Some members of Congress, like representatives Barney Frank (D-MA) and Max-ine Waters (D-CA), strongly support Fannie and Freddie because they spon-sor affordable housing projects in their districts. But recent data show that affordable housing constitutes only a small share of the companies' total in-vestments.[16] Like other companies, Fannie and Freddie have learned how to buy goodwill cheap.

The last thing Congress should do is to create more government-backed entities in which all the gains from taking risk go to private owners and the government is stuck with either an explicit or contingent liability in case something goes wrong. New entities should be created with the ex-plicit understanding that they will be truly independent. In fact, a good test of whether lawmakers can be trusted to do this is whether they can finally sever the link between the federal treasury and Fannie and Freddie before moving to create new institutions. Until they do, the creation of new or-ganizations specifically chartered to fill market gaps should be left to state and local governments.

A more benign case of continued dependence is the Manufacturing Extension Program (MEP). The MEP funds separate nonprofit organiza-tions that provide small- and medium-sized businesses with scientific, engi-neering, and management information and that assist in the transfer of manufacturing technology and techniques. Large companies often have this capacity in-house or can obtain it from private consultants. There was a feeling that the private sector did not adequately serve smaller companies and so the federal government decided to support the creation of MEP centers to address this deficiency. There is little doubt that a good network of expertise that provided ordinary businessmen with sophisticated infor-mation about how to increase their profitability and learn about new tech-nology could significantly improve the vibrancy of the private sector.

As it was originally set up, MEP was to provide a declining amount of support for a maximum of six years. The recipients of MEP funding, pre-sumably relying on fees charged to the businesses they were helping, had to provide at least half the initial funding in the first few years. Government funding was then supposed to be phased out over a six-year period. This phaseout had two benefits. First, the individual MEP centers knew that they would have to be self-sufficient within a reasonable amount of time. This imposed discipline about controlling costs and focused the centers on delivering services that smaller businesses valued at a price they could afford. It also forced the centers to approach businesses and convince them that the services they offered were worth the cost of providing them. The centers were to clearly see private businesses as their ultimate source of support and focus on their needs, not the government's. Second, the phaseout freed up federal funds for the creation of new MEP centers or for other programs that might also benefit small companies. Having helped an individual center get started, the government could then move on to other problems. The MEP would serve as a revolving fund for financing an ongoing set of new initiatives.

Although MEP serves as an example of the way that government could act to spur the growth of underserved areas of the private sector, it is also an example of the inherent difficulty of imposing discipline on anything connected to government. In the end, the government has been unable to let go of the entities it created. They have continued to seek funding beyond the six-year period. Rather than cutting the centers loose to succeed or fail on their own, government has acquiesced to their lobbying efforts. Businesses have been complicit in this. Rather than wanting to bear the full cost of the MEP centers themselves, they have preferred the bureaucracy of a few funded centers over the dynamic market that the government was trying to create. MEP centers may now receive up to one-third of their funding from the government and much of the rest comes from state governments. A proposal by the Bush administration to make the centers recompete for their existing funding was widely criticized as being too disruptive.[17] This, of course, means that the government remains a focus of their attention, at the expense of their clients. It reduces the need and incentive for seeking out new ways of helping businesses. And it prevents the government from moving to create centers in underserved areas.

It is not clear how government can make a credible commitment to cut off funding for an organization that it helps create. It is almost inevitable that the organization will fight hard to remain dependent on government funding. In doing so, it can often count on the support of those it serves, who will equate a decline in funding with lack of support for the social problem being addressed. But if the government cannot step away, then its efforts will be limited to propping up old programs, rather than initiating new ones. Agencies will always be more concerned with their relationship to government officials than with serving their clients. The normal process by which the better agencies expand, either by merger or competition, and poor performers either change or die will be stymied. Government agencies will continue to crowd out private investment that might provide better service. And the permanent lack of independent providers will keep clients dependent on subsidized government agencies.

Several tactics might help. One is to create a number of agencies to compete with each other. Part of Fannie and Freddie's power is that they are perceived as being too big to fail. With the MEP, centers are divided into geographical regions that do not really compete against each other. Competition among multiple agencies might encourage each to focus its efforts on clients rather than the government. More importantly, it would reduce the pressure for government to intervene in order to prevent the failure of any one organization. Second, the government should allow for the creation of new organizations by the private sector. Not doing so closes off an important source of possible innovation and investment. All organizations willing to abide by common rules ought to be treated equally. If, for instance, new or existing organizations could compete for MEP funding, this might spur improved services, even if it does not help wean the industry from government.

Third, the government should resist supporting agencies directly and instead channel financial resources directly to intended beneficiaries. The quality of business services might be improved, for example, if businesses, not government, decided which centers received MEP funding by paying the full cost of the services they provide. Government should provide funding to distressed people and neighborhoods, but it should do so by channeling money directly to workers through the income contract discussed above and the tax incentives discussed below, rather than by funding providers. If it does support providers of social services, the assistance should be temporary in order to help them get set up and spread among a number of competing organizations so that none become too important to fail. Government should avoid becoming a source of permanent direct financing.

A NEW ROLE FOR UNIONS

One of the most pressing needs in society is for a set of organizations that can effectively help workers invest in themselves. Unions are ideally suited for this role but only if they are prepared to radically change their view of the economy and their relationship to both workers and employers.

Although workers' unions arose out of a general concern with poor working conditions and depressed wages, they have done remarkably little to advance the cause of the average worker during the last several decades. Union supporters would argue that this is due to the fact that unions represent a rapidly declining percent of the total workforce and that the political climate has been strongly hostile. Neither of these fully explains their lack of effectiveness. Unions have lost power in the private workforce. Unions represented only 13.1 percent of all workers in 2006 compared to 23.3 percent in 1983.[18] Within the private sector, where businesses must compete with each other, unions represent only 8.1 percent of workers. But this decline is the consequence, not the cause, of a lack of effectiveness. Despite union complaints, workers are still free to choose union representation. The fact that the vast majority have not reflects the general feeling in the words of one commentator that "the word 'union' implies enshrined mediocrity, indifference to customers and a closed shop, if not a closed mind. And corruption scandals haven't helped."[19] Traditional unions thus have little to offer most workers in a modern economy.

Although the political climate was definitely not friendly while Republicans controlled both the White House and Congress, the decline in union influence predates that period by several decades. Much of it occurred while Democrats were still firmly in charge of Congress and, often, the White House. And although Democrats are back in power, it remains unlikely that unions will be able to stem their waning relevance without changing their basic business model. Republican politicians were not responsible for the serial decline of industries such as steel, airlines, and automobiles, and Democratic majorities will not be able to shape policy so that traditional unions are relevant to growing industries like software development, health care, or research, except possibly at the lowest income and skill levels.

The truth is that most unions have doggedly pursued policies that offer workers very little future advancement, especially in today's world of global competition within industries that use a great deal of complex, rapidly changing technology. Union philosophy has been built on two pillars. The first involves the relationship between workers and the work that they do. Unions have tended to believe that workers can do little to determine their own fate individually. Workers are homogeneous, allowing managers to pit them against each other in order to keep wages low. There is a fixed amount of labor, so that work done by one worker necessarily reduces work available to others. Workers can only prosper by banding together: workers who resist are traitors or scabs, even if they are merely acting in the best interest of themselves and their family. Because capital replaces labor, its installation should be resisted. Since pay is determined by relative power, not by the productivity of the worker, workers should seek to work as little as possible for as much pay as possible.

Unions tend to represent all workers equally, sometimes expending tremendous energy to keep poor performers on the job. All workers tend to be paid the same: making distinctions based on individual contribution usually faces strong opposition. Therefore, workers have little incentive to improve their individual productivity. In fact, workers who do work harder than their colleagues are often seen as hurting the cause. Unions do discriminate in some cases, however. Pay often rises with seniority, benefiting older veterans at the expense of younger workers, even if the job security of the latter is much more tenuous. In fact, unions often trade increased job security for existing workers in exchange for reduced pay or benefits for younger generations. Building on this, unions usually show no concern for workers outside the union. Unions often support policies that limit competition and therefore reduce jobs for other workers and raise prices for working families.

The second pillar concerns the relationship between workers and management. There is a firm divide between the two. Workers should not seek to advance to management, and if they do, the union no longer represents them. Workers are not responsible for the competitiveness or profitability of the firm within which they work and should resist any attempts to link pay to individual performance or to the performance of the company. Negotiations with management are largely zero sum; whatever one side gains, the other side loses. In negotiations concerning individual plants, a national strategy should be pursued, even if it jeopardizes the jobs of workers at an individual plant. Unions should fight for high retirement benefits but should not worry too much about how companies will find the money to pay these future benefits. Increased productivity should be resisted because it almost always means the loss of jobs.

There are, of course, exceptions to these generalizations, but these tenets still characterize much of the traditional union outlook. It led unions to repeatedly take a hard line in negotiations with companies in the steel, airline, and automobile companies, even when those companies were facing severe competitive pressure from newer companies and losing billions of dollars. Only when companies have been on the verge of bankruptcy have unions made any significant concessions, and even then they have usually resisted linking their future pay to either productivity or profitability. In each industry, unions had succeeded in capturing higher pay and benefits than existed in other parts of the economy, largely by threatening to shut down these capital-intensive industries whenever management resisted their demands. It is possible that these tactics maximized the total amount of pay and benefits workers as a whole received from these companies. But they prevented the companies from raising sufficient amounts of capital or responding to the competitive threats around them and in the end caused the incumbent companies to become much smaller that they otherwise would have been.

The result was an unnecessary decline in the viability of some of America's largest companies. Had the companies been allowed to evolve without union opposition, they no doubt would have reduced the workforce, cut pay and benefits to those prevailing in the rest of the economy, and instilled some of the flexible management rules that their domestic competitors were using. To do so, they would also have had to overcome resistance from several levels of management as well as labor. It is always difficult to turn around a large, existing organization, but it is possible as IBM and other companies have shown. The result would have been stronger, more vibrant companies, employing more workers at higher pay incomes than they otherwise will when the inevitable adjustments take place. Although they would have used fewer workers in traditional jobs, they might have increased total employment, and retirees would not now be worrying about losing their pension and health care benefits.

Some of the union outlook is rooted in a long history of fierce opposition to the improvement of working standards. But regardless of the legitimacy of historical grievances, it is an outlook poorly suited to respond to the challenges facing today's workers. For one thing, businesses compete in a complex environment where capital is fluid and cheap. It is relatively easy for a group of investors to raise the money to launch a takeover attempt or start a rival company. New companies can locate where labor is cheaper, even if they stay in the United States. In doing so they will not have to bear the retirement costs of the established firms, and their workers are unlikely to insist on high pay levels or restrictive work rules when interviewing for a job. Although unions have focused on foreign competition, it is worth remembering that a great deal of competition comes from American production, located in areas of the country that historically were economically distressed. State and local governments in the South and Southwest eagerly sought out companies that would bring jobs to their constituents, often offering significant financial inducements as part of the package.

The traditional union model offers nothing for most of today's workers. If workers are to prosper over the long term, their pay cannot be higher than their productivity, otherwise other workers elsewhere will be able to do the same job for less. And if their incomes are to rise over time, they need to be evaluated on their individual abilities. The best way for workers to increase productivity is through training and by accepting responsibility for using their talents to boost the competitiveness of their employer. Unions have denied that workers in one company need to compete against workers in other companies within the same industry. Their answer has been to unionize all workers within an industry, thereby raising the wages of all. But this only increases the opportunity for new entrants, either here or abroad. By lowering profits and raising prices, this strategy also encourages a decline of the total industry. Unfortunately, unions have been relatively complacent about this because they are more concerned with protecting existing jobs than they are with ensuring an increase in total employment.

Closing off borders is not an option. In order to compete, an industry needs access to the best inputs, wherever they are, and needs to be able to sell into all markets. This means trade has to be open. Unions, trying to defend traditional industries that have long since lost their competitiveness, currently do not feel the need to ensure the growth or competitiveness of high-tech industries. Yet economists are virtually unanimous on the linkage between trade and economic growth. Given that a large portion of the world's future growth is going to occur in Asia, American manufacturers cannot afford to be shut out of these markets. This requires that we remain open to them. Yet this same openness allows industries to source overseas if costs in the United States get too high.

It could be different. Unions could and should be supporting organizations dedicated to advancing the broad economic and social interests of their individual members. Not only do workers have a tremendous need for assistance in job hunting, training, and certification, but also few existing groups seek to provide these services. Unions built on a different model could also provide a great service to employers. Many employers have difficulty finding skilled workers, and job turnover imposes large costs even for employers of unskilled workers. Unions could serve as a source of quality labor for employers, guaranteeing that the employees they refer meet certain qualifications and helping to provide these employees with incentives to stay on the job longer.

One of the first things that would have to change is the nature of union membership. Right now, membership within a business tends to be all or nothing. If 51 percent of the workers want to join a union, then the other 49 percent are forced to join as well, even if they are adamantly opposed. Private groups should never have this type of coercive power. The result has been that, once elected, union leadership often adopts a sense of entitlement that is oblivious to the true interests of any significant minority of their members. Radical members often play a dominant role, intimidating the majority, for whom union politics is merely a distraction. Workers who are dissatisfied with their leaders have no recourse unless they can convince a majority of their peers to ask for a decertification election. In the process of doing so, they can be marked for ostracism and retaliation. Even in Right-to-Work states, unions have often conspired with employers to preserve this all or nothing rule, by agreeing with the employer that nonunion workers will have fees deducted from their paycheck for "negotiating services."

But if it is wrong to force a minority of workers to join a union, it is also wrong to deny union membership to a minority that thinks membership would improve their welfare. If only 10 percent of workers in a plant want to join a union they should still be allowed to. Unions have viewed this right as being worthless because they believe that the minority of union workers will face discrimination from the employer. This is probably true as long as the union follows the traditional tactic of trying to raise wages above free market levels at the expense of either profits or prices. But if the union saw its role as providing a range of services to members that would help increase both individual and collective worker productivity, it could justify higher salaries for its members. As Samuel Leiken observed, "Today's workers need to continually improve their employability through better education and training, and unions are uniquely qualified to help."[20]

If the union sought to work with employers to increase productivity through process changes or other innovations and vouched for a worker's qualifications and suitability, it could become the employer's preferred reference for new workers, even if there was no union shop. The change is not so far fetched. Companies have outsourced many functions that were once considered integral to their operations, and in many firms, employees who are hired and managed by outsiders work side by side with the firm's own employees. A union built on a different type of model could make a compelling case that a firm should outsource all hiring and management for a production line to it. It could also build a more durable relationship with workers, by offering them continued services even if they rose into management, and even if they switched to a different company or industry.

Some unions are already doing this. A decade ago, the Laborers International Union set up a joint foundation with contractors to supply trained workers to employers, even those that were nonunion, while the International Association of Machinists proposed joint efforts with management for high-performance training.[21] More recently, part of the International

Union of Bricklayers and Allied Craftworkers has taken over the training and supply of high-skilled bricklayers for companies that have a hard time finding and keeping them.[22]

In order to make the transformation to this new model, unions would have to welcome the transition to a true membership organization in which each member has the freedom to enter or leave on short notice. Union leaders would have to closely monitor the needs and satisfaction of individual members as well as the needs of employers, so that they could properly advise members about their employment prospects. Different unions might concentrate on different things. Some could focus on working with employers to hire and keep good workers. Others might devote themselves to worker training and certification, keeping a close eye on employment trends to ensure that their clients easily found good jobs. Unions could also help their employees by offering good health care and pension plans, as well as advice on personal health and financial planning. Some unions, such as the National Association of Letter Carriers, already offer nationwide health plans to their members as well as to a wide variety of other federal employees. Other commentators have advocated a return to unions' historic roots as voluntary craft guilds or benefit societies that offered their members a range of services.[23]

A few unions go even further. One of the most innovative is the Freelancers Union, with thirty-seven thousand members. Membership is voluntary and free. Members may purchase a range of services from the union, including health care, disability and life insurance, tax advice, and social networking. In addition to providing benefits, the union engages in social advocacy on issues that matter to its members, such as the ability of freelancers to obtain unemployment benefits.[24]

THE NEW WORK OF NONPROFITS

The challenge is to do rather than to complain. It is easy to argue that there continue to be gaps in how the private sector meets society's demand for goods and services. Many of the groups making this argument also regularly complain that the private sector has too much sway in society. It is much, much harder (often impossible) to step into the breach and do a better job, while competing with other companies on a sustainable basis. Some organizations do this, but even they have difficulty applying their model to a broader audience. One wonders why companies like Starbucks and Crate

& Barrel can so quickly expand a local success into a national company generating millions of dollars in social value, while local homeless shelters and job training programs have difficulty replicating themselves.

Part of the problem undoubtedly lies in the nature of the problems they address. But much of the difficulty also lies in the initial framework of those approaching the problem. Other companies, including Jackson-Hewitt and Wal-Mart have built successful businesses serving people of modest means. Although critics are quick to point out the faults of these companies, they would do better to look at the market opportunity that they demonstrate and try to develop alternatives that provide an even better service to the poor.

Private entrepreneurs think from the beginning of creating value and then investing that value in expansion. Nonprofits are also in the value business, whether they realize it or not. The value associated with helping to increase human productivity and well-being through better education, health care, housing, and financial security is large. Giving low-income workers adequate purchasing power through the income guarantee contract would create a new market, devoted to serving the needs of the neediest. The potential of even less promising markets has already been demonstrated.[25]

Whether originating from government, the nonprofit sector, or private companies, whether in the form of new organizations or existing ones, there is a strong need for reliable brands that people of lower means can go to for trustworthy service. The possible services to which these organizations might provide value are practically endless: financial advice, help negotiating the purchase of a car, health clinics, affordable housing, and personal counseling to name a few. Nonprofit organizations could provide these services directly, or they could affiliate with trusted companies who have business expertise. In the latter role, the nonprofit would serve two purposes. For its target clients it would hopefully provide a guarantee of quality, having worked with the supplier to ensure that the products and services were of high quality, fairly priced, and appropriate for their consumers. For the direct provider, the organization would serve as an entry point and guide into a new market. Local community leaders could also serve this role, taking responsibility for making recommendations to satisfy the needs of their constituents.

There are many precedents. Membership organizations like AARP have for a long time contracted with private companies to offer services to their members. In AARP's case, the partnerships produce a steady stream of income that it can then use for other purposes that further its mission. Any organization that does so runs the risk of losing its sense of mission and placing profit ahead of social progress,[26] but active competition to maintain a brand of quality among those using the service should punish those that stray too far from their mission or accept higher payments from less reliable providers.

The active expansion of this market could also help address one of the emerging challenges that middle- and upper-income workers face. The nature of work is rapidly changing, and employers are finding that younger workers are less content to make the traditional tradeoffs that their parents made. Workers are increasingly demanding a better balance between their personal and work lives.[27] They do not expect to work in any one job for the majority of their careers (crippling the argument for employer-provided pension and health care, as we see in following chapters).[28] They do expect their work to have meaning, and right now for many it does not.

Employers are responding in a variety of ways. Many are providing a broader range of benefits that collectively seek to reduce the impact of work on one's daily routine. Herman Miller, a manufacturer of office furniture, has found that the design of its environmentally friendly office building helps it retain workers;[29] Hilton Hotels offers pet insurance to its employees;[30] KPMG is helping employees who have to care for elderly parents;[31] and Google provides a broad range of attractions, including free meals.[32]

Behind all this is an increased search for meaning in the forty-odd hours per week that one spends at work (often much more for the best and brightest workers), as workers seek their own higher needs for self-actualization. One of the most direct ways to address this desire would be to provide jobs that focus on the most pressing social problems. Enterprises that do this and do it successfully are likely to find that many of the best young workers are willing to forego higher incomes in return for meaningful work.

The nonprofit sector has a long and distinguished history in America. Alexis de Tocqueville spoke at length about the importance of associations to democratic government.[33] Civic and religious organizations have long provided a number of important services to the poor, retreating only when government agencies crowded them out. Yet the promise of this sector remains unfulfilled. A great deal of energy and government support goes to organizations that largely serve the middle and upper classes. The Metropolitan Opera, although a great cultural institution, has far less need for a subsidy than organizations that address the most important needs of our poorest citizens. Those who argue that organizations like the Met and the Kennedy Center for the Performing Arts could not survive without subsidies should at least consider the fact that these subsidies themselves might partly explain the lack of support among the private sector. The heavy subsidies give nonprofits a significant advantage over organizations that seek to raise capital by giving interested parties an equity interest in the enterprise. But shutting this avenue off also guarantees that much of the cultural sector will remain dependent on continued government help. It also creates a permanent lobby arguing for higher marginal income and estate taxes, since these taxes reduce the after-tax cost of charitable contributions. Strictly limiting the charitable deduction to those organizations that directly serve the neediest citizens would raise government revenue that could be better directed elsewhere, would direct more charity to the most vital purposes, and would blur the line between profit and nonprofit organizations, attracting new sources of capital into all cultural sectors.

5

IMPROVING EDUCATION

In virtually every circumstance markets work a lot better than government, provided that the government takes care to see that the market is properly structured. The advantage of markets will tend to widen even further in the coming decades, leading to radical change or collapse in programs that rely on centralized control. This applies to large government programs such as Social Security and Medicare, as well as to less formal government commitments, such as the retiree obligations of state and municipal governments. It also applies to many areas of the private sector, such as industries that follow the traditional union model or commit to long-term employer-provided benefits that must be provided even if the business becomes unprofitable.

It is therefore critical to introduce more flexibility and autonomy into economic and social situations. A minimum income contract linked to personal behavior establishes a much better dynamic than current approaches because it lets individuals adapt to the specific challenges and opportunities facing them as they pursue their own interests and goals. For most markets, government can then safely withdraw, confident that consumers with adequate purchasing power will be able to find a sufficient array of suppliers for the goods and services they want. For instance, government programs to encourage agricultural production make little sense. There is no evidence that food production would significantly decline or that prices would significantly rise in the absence of current programs. In fact, the programs have perverse results because they speed the consolidation of family farms and discourage younger farmers from entering the market. The argument that farm programs are needed in order to raise the income of farmers who would otherwise lack an adequate standard of living has not been true for a long time and in any case would be made obsolete by the presence of an income guarantee contract. Farm programs are also not needed to encourage consumption.

Programs like Food Stamps and Medicaid do not address an agricultural or health care problem. They address an income problem. And once an adequate income is assured, the government usually has far less of a legitimate interest in seeing exactly how it is spent. In these specific cases, the government can rest assured that individuals already have adequate incentives to purchase a sufficient amount of food and health care and, with a properly structured income guarantee contract, that they have the resources to do it.

Similarly, the government need not worry about a wide range of other goods and services. Individuals have a broad array of needs and wants that they will readily demand from producers. With adequate income, they are able to translate these needs and wants into effective purchasing power. The exact prioritization of the various goods and services is usually not a public concern. To take one example, individuals will decide to spend a certain amount of their income on computers. The exact shape of the market will depend on the aggregation of millions of individual decisions, but there is no reason the government should care how many computers are sold, what models are demanded, or at what price sales take place. Even though consumers will not always find exactly what they are looking for at a price they are willing to pay, they will have a vast array of choices, and over time the real price of many of these products should decline even as the quality increases.

This is not true of every market, however. For a few markets government intervention is still needed. In the case of public goods, such as national defense and law enforcement, the rationale for government activity is well established, although even in these cases, private markets may play more of a constructive role than is commonly acknowledged. But there are other cases where the good or service in question is essentially private, but government involvement is still desirable because

1. forces inherent to the market make it difficult for at least some individuals to make purchases at a "fair" price;
2. purchase of the good conveys large social benefits, causing individuals to purchase less than is desirable;
3. services are expensive, so that individuals may not purchase as much as they would like, because they either lack the immediate resources or are reluctant to commit so much money;

4. if individuals do not purchase services for themselves, government may be forced to do so in order to prevent them from becoming destitute; or

5. structural impediments in the market prevent efficiency.

In the last case, where the structural impediments are introduced or supported by government itself, the first priority should be to remove them, rather than to regulate even further.

Education is one of these markets. This chapter will briefly review the structure of the broad educational sector, from preschool to worker training, including K–12 and higher education. Significant reform is needed in each of these areas in order to reorient educational institutions toward meeting the needs of their students in an increasingly changing world. Without such reform, the United States will continue to find that the costs of education rise even as its quality stagnates or deteriorates. This outcome will have its most severe effects on those at the bottom of the socioeconomic ladder, which is why liberals should be leading the charge for structural reform.

Even beyond reform, a continued government presence is desirable because of the social benefits that education brings. There is a widespread belief that better educated individuals make better citizens. The economic argument is even clearer. In 2006, workers with a high school education made ten thousand dollars more than those without a diploma,[1] a gap that is widening because of the growth in skilled jobs and increased domestic and international competition. Those with a college education earn an even higher premium. In light of this wage differential, one might assume that individuals already have a sufficient incentive to purchase education on their own. To a large extent this is true. However, three impediments exist. First, not all parents will make responsible decisions regarding the education of their children. States have therefore made education compulsory up to a certain age. But in the cases where this requirement might matter, it is not clear that it has worked, due to poor-quality schools and high dropout rates. Second, the supply of K–12 education is heavily dominated by local governments. In almost all cases, rhetoric aside, the interest of teachers and administrators dominates that of students and their parents. This tends not to matter too much in upper- or middle-class neighborhoods where parents have other options and are politically active. However, it has left large pockets of destitution in many poorer areas, depriving the neediest students of an education or even physical safety. Without the introduction of significant choice and flexibility, improvement is impossible and even middle-class schools will increasingly fall behind what the market is demanding. Finally, the cost of higher education, where a student can be expected to learn those specific skills attractive to an employer, is rising at an unnecessarily fast rate. Government reform is needed to slow the growth of these costs, and a subsidy is needed in order to ensure that students can afford to invest in their careers.

The selection of a sensible policy depends upon the goal one is trying to achieve. For education, the primary goal should be to ensure that all individuals have an affordable and easy way to acquire whatever skills will allow them to increase their earnings, at least up to the point where they have a middle class income. There are a number of other benefits to education, including the development of the critical thinking skills and intellectual maturity needed to approach life as a well-rounded individual and the pursuit of knowledge for its own sake. But the pursuit of these goals is secondary to government's main function of providing each individual with the means to become self-sufficient. Beyond that, the strong presumption should be that individuals are capable of making their own decisions. If they choose a path different than the one we might have preferred, the most likely explanations are that we failed to make a persuasive case for the available alternatives or that our preferred path is not suitable to their individual goals. Either way, the case for government involvement is weak.

PRESCHOOL

One of the key challenges that low-income parents face is the heavy implicit tax imposed by child care. When going to work necessitates placing a child in day care, the parent only receives the difference between his or her salary and day care expenses in return for working. Due to their lower salaries, this burden falls relatively hardest on the working poor. This significantly reduces the net rewards from working. The impact is only partially offset by the fact that current law gives parents a tax credit for up to three thousand dollars of work-related child care.

Federal tax law also provides a $3,300 exemption for each child. In many ways this assistance is mismatched to the cost of care. Parents are likely to face the greatest effective costs in the early years before the child can attend first grade. Prior to this, parents must either forego income in order to stay at home or pay for day care. Changing the exemption to nine thousand dollars but limiting it to the first five years of a child's life would provide assistance when it is most important. Changing the exemption to a fully refundable credit would broaden the aid to those who need it most.

There is some evidence that preschool education makes a difference in how children perform later in life. An ongoing federal study recently found that children who receive care by an engaged, responsive adult in a rich, nurturing environment have better vocabulary skills through the fifth grade.[2] But this does not mean that children will do better if government simply makes day care more affordable. Higher scores in math and reading disappeared by the first grade. The same study also found that children who attend day care are slightly more disruptive later in school, an effect that apparently lasts at least through the sixth grade.[3] More importantly, the effect of child care was small compared to the effect of parenting.

There has been a long-running battle over whether children suffer when their mothers place them in day care in order to work. They apparently do, but this effect may be largely overcome by quality day care. In any case, staying at home may not confer great benefits if the quality of parenting is poor or if the family needs the parent's income.

It would be a mistake to confuse the importance of early care with enrollment in day care as the Center for the Child Care Workforce apparently does. Good parents can do a better job than poor day care centers. It is possible that day care centers would improve if federal support was increased, but any increased assistance is better channeled through the parent rather than the institution. The preferred alternative is not day care: it is for parents to spend more time with their children delivering the kind of education and guidance that make a difference. Even if federal policy does not explicitly encourage this policy, it should not actively discourage it by further increasing the effective cost of staying at home during the most formative years. Expanding public education to day care without also subsidizing stay-at-home care would have precisely that effect.

The government should therefore not encourage broader use of day care by creating a federal program that benefits only those who chose to enroll their child. This may be convenient for many parents who are reluctant to believe that there is a tradeoff between pursuing their own careers and the development of their children, but it may not be in the best interests of the children. It mainly supports the interests of the day care industry, including its workers. This tension between these interests appears in the response of the Center for the Child Care Workforce, whose deputy director is quoted as criticizing the study cited above for not taking into account some of the faults of day care centers, which presumably would show that the fault was insufficient federal funding, not day care itself.[4]

However, there is a case to be made for greater public support for parents of young children. Greater financial support would help parents strike a better balance between spending time with young children and enrolling them in early development programs. Although different parents will make different choices given their individual situations, many might decide to spend a greater portion of their time at home, especially if the government was willing to channel the resources it would otherwise spend on the child's development through them. Others might still send their child to development programs, but only part time, perhaps participating with them. The result would be greater bonding and greater social support for both parents and their children.

The difference is likely to be especially great in lower-income families, where the prevalence of single-parent families, lack of education, and poverty may make adequate parenting rarer. Society has a strong interest in ensuring that disadvantaged children receive a strong start within a supportive environment that extends well into grade school. For this reason, it would be wise to allow one parent to meet the work requirement of the income guarantee program by staying at home with a child under the age of five, provided he or she participates in a structured program that ensures that (1) the parent develops sound parenting skills, (2) the child develops the social and cognitive skills needed for school, and (3) the parent possesses the skills needed to reenter the job market when the child enters school.

K–12 EDUCATION

In 1983, a federal commission recommended significant changes to the nation's system of primary and secondary education. The authors concluded that the status quo was failing to prepare America's children for the world that awaited them upon graduation. The report's language was harsh:

> If an unfriendly power had attempted to impose on America the mediocre education performance that exists today, we might well have viewed it as an act of war. As it stands, we have allowed this to happen to ourselves. We have even squandered the gains in achievement made in the wake of the Sputnik challenge. Moreover, we have dismantled essential support systems which helped make those gains possible. We have, in effect, been committing an act of unthinking, unilateral educational disarmament.[5]

Almost twenty-five years later, little has changed. In 2005, a different panel warned that without decisive action America could lose its privileged position as the world's leader in science and technology.[6] In the intervening years the challenges have only gotten greater. The pace of technological change has increased, widening the income gap between those without an education and those with one. International competition has intensified; countries like China, India, Mexico, and Brazil are increasingly interested in and capable of performing competitive low-skill production.

Although some observers emphasize the positive,[7] even if on average schools have not gotten worse, the world around them has gotten much more demanding and competitive. The fact that most Americans are satisfied with their schools does not mean that their children are receiving the skills needed to succeed in the private sector. In any case, few would question that the current system consigns large numbers of children, typically those who are already facing the greatest disadvantages, to failing schools where neither their education nor their physical safety is assured. Recent results from the National Assessment of Educational Progress showed only slight progress in the reading performance of fourth and eighth graders over the past decade.[8] Significantly, less than a third of the students in both grades were judged proficient at reading. Less than 40 percent were proficient in math. In recent SAT scores, only about half of high school graduates had the reading skills they needed to succeed in college, and even fewer had the necessary math and science courses.[9] At the same time, the system holds back the smaller minority of students who are capable of advancing at a much faster pace and who promise to make the greatest contributions to society's future.

The current system gives the well-to-do a built-in advantage. Primary and secondary education is financed largely through local property taxes, allowing wealthier jurisdictions to spend much more on their schools than poorer ones. Federal tax law further subsidizes this advantage by allowing taxpayers to deduct these taxes from their federal income, but only if they already itemize their deductions, a policy that further tilts the benefits toward those who have money.

In general, tax deductions further skew the disparity between the rich and poor. First, deductions are only valuable to those individuals who would otherwise owe tax on their income prior to the deductions. This excludes most couples earning about forty thousand dollars per year.[10] Families making less than that receive no benefit from a deduction. Second, most families with little tax liability do not itemize deductions unless they happen to own a home and can take advantage of the deduction for mortgage interest. Thus, they also do not benefit from the deduction. Third, even when comparing families who benefit from it, a deduction gives a greater subsidy to those in higher tax brackets. A $5,000 deduction is worth $1,400 to an individual with a marginal tax rate of 28 percent. The same deduction is worth only $750 to workers whose marginal tax rate is 15 percent. The government therefore provides the greatest subsidy to those with the greatest ability to bear the cost themselves. For these reasons refundable tax credits are a much better means of funding social benefits. They provide the same benefit to every person, and they provide it regardless of one's tax liability.

The Democratic Party, which prides itself on its attention to education and concern for the poor, should be arguing for radical changes in how primary and secondary education is funded. But their main lament is a lack of money. Whether phrased as a demand for smaller classes, higher salaries, or longer school days and years, the solution is always to spend more on what we have rather than to make what we have better.

But the problem is not money: it is institutional structure. Nothing can absorb money faster with no visible effect than a poor institutional structure. Even one of Senator John Kerry's (D-MA) education advisors during his 2004 presidential run acknowledges that the United States has tripled education funding per student since the 1960s with only modest achievements.[11] School districts like Washington, D.C., and Detroit spend over eleven thousand dollars per student yet still totally fail to serve the needs of the poor. In Kansas City, a massive increase in expenditures was accompanied by a significant upgrade in physical facilities but not reform of the fundamental system. The result was failure.[12]

In spite of this, and despite all the evidence that, whenever politics intrudes on education, wealthier, more powerful parents usually come out ahead, why have liberals refused to consider fundamental reform? Two reasons are prominent. The first is the dominance of unions, and teachers' unions specifically, in the Democratic Party. With only a few recent exceptions, the unions have steadfastly refused to consider any reforms that would increase parents' choice, link teacher pay to performance, or make schools more accountable for the actual performance of their students. Second, the Democratic Party itself is heavily responsible for a large part of the failure. Many of the most troubled schools are in cities where government, teachers' unions, and school administration have been firmly entrenched in Democratic hands for a long time. In cities like Detroit, Washington, D.C., Chicago, and New York, Democrats have set the taxes, negotiated the contracts, established the curriculum, and run the schools. Advocating reform would mean giving up control and accepting wrenching change to the power relationships that they have created.

Yet several reforms are needed. The first is a clear definition of what students ought to know when they graduate from high school. Both students and colleges have the right to expect that a high school diploma implies an ability to succeed in entry-level college classes. The standards do not have to be mandatory, but they should be widely seen as being legitimate. This in turn will help exert pressure on school districts that fail to meet them. This can only be accomplished if we have a clear set of benchmarks for all twelve grades so that parents, teachers, and students know what a student is supposed to know after completing each grade and can tell whether a student is falling behind in time to correct it. E. D. Hirsch has written a good set of books that give parents one set of guidelines for what their child should know by each grade, but he stops with grade six.[13]

The standards need not be unanimously agreed to or even unique in order to be useful. A vigorous debate about exactly how well graduates ought to read and write and what proficiency in math and science should be expected would be a healthy development and would focus attention on the need to convey useful knowledge and hard skills. Structured properly, it might even result in jurisdictions competing upward in deciding what they will commit to teaching their students.

A second reform is regular testing that is clearly linked to commonly accepted standards. Those who argue against testing for testing's sake miss the point. It is impossible to improve performance, or even adhere to an existing standard, without the ability to measure outcomes. How else can we identify which students are falling behind in a certain subject and therefore need special attention? Tests could be administered at school and become a formal part of the educational process. Alternatively, the government could issue a suggestive set of tests that reflect the expected proficiency in a certain grade and suggest that parents administer these to their children on their own. The latter approach should encounter fewer hurdles, since it is voluntary, but still promises to create pressure for improvement when children demonstrate a deficiency.

Opponents of testing raise two objections. The first is that teachers will only teach to the test. But if the test adequately reflects the general knowledge a child is expected to have in a certain class, it is hard to see the objection. The alternative surely cannot be to give the teacher total freedom without any check on whether knowledge is being conveyed. The object of the classroom is neither to have fun nor to fulfill the teacher's desire for professional fulfillment. The object is for students to learn, and that object cannot be made subject to any others. It is a fallacy to think that, just because giving teachers freedom to make their classrooms fun might enhance learning, stressing fun and professional fulfillment will automatically benefit students. A fun classroom in which both teachers and students are engaged, but where students are not acquiring the skills needed to succeed, is a failure. The second objection to testing is that testing in itself does not solve any problems. True, but it helps identify them, and it helps measure whether structural reforms are making a difference.

Assuming that tests adequately reflect what students at each grade level should master, the debates over methodology will become less important. Educators have spent a great deal of time arguing over the respective merits of traditional versus new math, whole language versus phonics, and Spanish instruction versus immersion. If the objective is to improve test scores, then an answer to which method works best will gradually emerge. Most likely, different students will respond differently to different approaches, and teachers equipped with a mix of approaches will demonstrate a greater ability to improve the performance of each child under their care. Only when there is no testing or emphasis on results can teaching methods be pushed for their own sake, regardless of effectiveness.

There is a mistaken desire to make education "fun" for its own sake. Certainly anything that inspires actual learning should be strongly encouraged, but the evaluation of programs should focus on what knowledge was conveyed, not whether children enjoyed or felt good about the process. The job market has fairly strict standards for performance. Children who enter it unprepared but satisfied with themselves are unlikely to do well.

This raises another basic point about education. Manufacturing executives are familiar with the concept of a bottleneck: that key resource that single-handedly constrains efforts to increase production. In the presence of a bottleneck, adding other resources such as money or manpower leads to no improvement in performance.[14] In education, the bottleneck toward faster learning is usually the student's time and willingness to absorb the material. Any diligent student knows that learning occupies a certain minimum amount of time and concentration. Any parent knows that, without the student's cooperation, other factors such as greater teacher involvement, punishments, rewards, and study aids have little, if any, effect. For this reason, we should be especially dubious of claims that more money or technology will have a significant effect on learning as opposed to cost. Better technology will likely make a difference only to the extent that students are already exerting themselves. Computer instruction and software may play an enabling role, but absent a desire to learn, it may only increase costs without raising performance.[15] On the other hand, innovations in distance learning may reduce the cost of education, an improvement even if the instruction is no more effective than traditional methods.

The third reform is to give parents more choice in which school their child attends. Only in this way can those with the greatest interest in a child's education exert the maximum direct pressure to improve the quality of education. There is not much difference in the long-run between vouchers and charter schools, both potentially introduce a variety of choices, but both can also be artificially restricted by rules designed to protect the employees of existing schools. The only significant difference seems to be who owns the capital invested in the school. Although still fiercely opposed by the education establishment, vouchers will continue to gain support, especially among poor voters who suffer the most from existing schools. This is because these schools will continue to fall further behind the increased standards of a competitive world, even if significant additional resources are devoted to them in their current form.

In an ideal world, all parents would be able to pay for their own child's education. Absent that, society has made a commitment to universal publicly paid education through high school. Universality gives the upper and middle classes an interest in the quality of public schools, although this interest tends in practice to be limited to their own school districts, which usually exclude outsiders from attending. It also helps to promote a uniformity of education, at least within a school district, which may reduce racial and sectarian differences and promote assimilation.

But the willingness to pay for every child's education does not imply the need to actually own the school, employ the teachers, or direct the curriculum. Medicare subsidizes the health care of seniors but does not run the hospitals to which they go or directly employ the doctors that see them. In housing, the government has already moved toward a much greater reliance on housing vouchers instead of direct landlord subsidies. Seldom has it thought of owning and leasing apartment buildings itself. The Food Stamp Program operates exclusively through vouchers. Within education, other attempts to introduce innovation, such as magnet and charter schools and open enrollment, have also faced initial opposition before gaining general acceptance. Where vouchers are tried, such as Milwaukee and Cleveland, they quickly create broad parental support, making it hard for later politicians to remove them.[16] The sole reason a similar movement has been delayed elsewhere is because organizations representing teachers and administrators put their own interests above that of parents and students.

The arguments for vouchers are simple. Although the evidence is not as clear-cut as voucher proponents would like, it does appear that greater school choice leads to improvements in school quality and student performance.[17] Not all of this improvement comes from the voucher or charter schools themselves. Much of it comes from public schools as the threat of losing students and budgets forces an openness to reforms that would otherwise not exist. Two studies of the voucher program in Milwaukee found that, as the program expanded, performance at those public schools most threatened by the program improved.[18] The tendency of competition to improve the performance of all schools often makes it difficult to measure the effects of choice. For example, a recent study by the U.S. Department of Education found that, when test scores are adjusted for race, socioeconomic, and other factors, students in public schools performed just as well as those in private schools.[19]

This leads us to the second justification for choice. To a large extent, the question of performance should be largely irrelevant. Democratic government should strive to give individuals the maximum amount of choice consistent with maintaining a functioning society. Proponents of centralization would be wrong to use the Department of Education study just cited to deny parents the right to send their child to a private school that they felt was better for their child. The lack of clear-cut evidence regarding the superiority of charter schools or voucher recipients should not be used to defeat parental choice. Such an outcome is equivalent to deciding that, because there is little difference between Land's End and L.L. Bean in the type of clothing they sell or the prices, competition between the two is socially destructive and consolidation would lead to efficiency—or that the existence of L.L. Bean is inefficient because it forces Americans to pay for two outdoors stores. Competition introduces a strong dynamic for continuous improvement. Moreover, even if voucher programs produced no improvements in the quality of education, they would still be a success if they either reduced the cost of education or led to greater student or parental satisfaction. Most voucher opponents tend to totally discount the latter goals, however. Despite the fact that private and charter schools occasionally fail, wherever choice is tried growing popular support will make it difficult for politicians to reverse reforms.

Who should determine where a child goes to school, an administrator or teacher, or the parent? The rich already have choice, although they have to pay for it through higher home prices and local taxes. It is time the poor had it as well. We have been through this battle before. The education establishment used its power to try to stop home schooling, charter schools, and reforms to make it easier for individuals with experience in math and science to teach in high schools. Each of these innovations is now accepted as part of the overall educational mix, although each continues to face opposition from established interests.

If the federal, state, and local governments provided every person with a $10,000 refundable tax credit every year between the ages of five and twenty-one that could be banked if not spent, parents would, for the first time, be able to truly shop for the best education for their children. If the credit then dropped to $500 from ages twenty-two to sixty, workers could invest in continued training throughout their careers.

Despite setbacks, support for vouchers will continue to grow within both parties. Already Wisconsin, Ohio, Utah, Colorado, and Florida have experimented with voucher programs, although state courts have ruled that the latter two efforts violated their state's constitutions. The inertia of public systems will cause them to fall further behind the needs of the economy, while districts that do adopt greater choice, whether in the form of vouchers, charter schools, or even open enrollment, will improve their performance relative to others.

But if choice is to be tried, it should be done correctly. A first reform is to address the disparity between school districts. Although there is strong reluctance to dramatically increase the federal role in education, a program of matching grants should be put in place to ensure that every district spends a minimum amount of money per student. Ideally, state and local governments would allocate a uniform amount for each child's education, and the money would flow directly from the government to whatever school a parent selects. Unfortunately, there is no good study of what it should cost in order to teach an average child in an efficient system. Without such a study it is difficult to know what the minimum expenditure should be. The amount probably varies by locality and grade. Rather than trying to set a specific level for each area, the federal government should concentrate on setting a reasonable uniform national floor. Tax reform that eliminated the deduction for state and local income taxes would also level the funding disparity by making wealthier districts pay the full cost of the education they provide.

Opponents of vouchers do have a good argument that vouchers of a token amount do little to give poor parents effective choice. The voucher size should therefore be substantial, sufficient to ensure that parents can find alternative schools willing to enroll their child. This will win over very few voucher opponents, however. Matthew Miller once suggested experimenting with a voucher program set at 120 percent of what the school system is currently funding per student.[20] Although people on both sides of the political spectrum supported the proposal, the teachers' unions remained steadfast in their opposition. When presented with the proposal, Bob Chase, then head of the National Education Association, said, "It's purely and simply not going to happen. I'm not even going to use the intellectual processes to see if in fact that could work or not work, because it's not going to happen. That is a fact."[21]

A second legitimate complaint is that vouchers might allow private schools to pick only the best students, leaving others to an inferior school system. But sensible rules can deal with this and other potential problems. A school that wishes to accept vouchers for tuition payments should have to commit to accepting any child that applies. It should also be required to accept the voucher in full payment of tuition, ensuring that poor students are not priced out of the best public schools. If a school finds itself over-subscribed, it should conduct a lottery to determine who is admitted. In some cases, such as students who live nearby or whose siblings already attend the school, the district may decide to allow guaranteed enrollment, but these exceptions should be relatively few. Rules of this type are already used by many districts to determine admission into some public schools. In cases where tuition is less than the amount of the voucher, parents should be allowed to bank the difference for college. Religious and private schools ought to be allowed to participate, provided they make the same commitment to take everyone on the same terms. The role that parochial schools could play can be seen by the fact that they produce a quality education at a fraction of the cost of public schools and the fact that a large portion of the students in Catholic schools are not Catholic. Parents presumably value the quality of the education and the learning environment enough to overcome both the cost of tuition and any religious differences. Since the federal government currently allows college students to spend federal subsidies at Catholic universities such as Georgetown and Notre Dame, constitutional objections to similar policies on the primary and secondary level seem to be motivated more by the desire to protect the status quo than by true legal concerns.

What would a fully implemented voucher system look like? Probably a lot like the current one, only more effective and with higher parent satisfaction. Existing public schools would continue to have a strong advantage due to the fact that they are already operating and most parents are satisfied with them. Testing would be more frequent in order to measure progress and evaluate reforms, and schools would advertise both test scores and college admissions. Good teachers would have more freedom and probably better salaries. Schools might introduce more options to help parents, especially those with young children, home school at least part time, a reform that would lower costs and have strong benefits for both parents and children. Most jurisdictions still adopt an all or nothing approach to home schooling. Despite a greater degree of choice, most parents would probably prefer the convenience of sending their children to a neighborhood school, even if others were slightly better. It is not clear whether the size of the average school or class size would increase or decrease, although a decrease in both seems more probable if the size of the voucher admits it. Schools trying variations such as same sex, military training, uniforms, a stress on math and science, or unstructured learning would find a niche.

Few proponents claim that vouchers are a magic bullet promising instant improvements. Rather, they believe that competition at the edge promotes a process of continuous change that allows the best schools to expand, eliminates the worst, and forces the rest to constantly worry about their relative performance. In contrast, systems that are as long standing and centralized as the current public school model seldom are able to introduce necessary changes in time to adapt to external events.

HIGHER EDUCATION

Significant structural reform is also needed in higher education. The United States currently has the world's best system for higher education. Every year, large numbers of foreign students come here to study for undergraduate and graduate degrees. Yet the system is also extremely expensive, lacks competition, and to the extent that it forms an unnecessary barrier to entry into better paying jobs, tilts the playing field further against those with limited means.

College education, as most middle-class families know it, actually has two aspects, and it is important not to confuse the two. The first is to acquire the knowledge and skills needed to enter either higher-paying jobs or graduate school. Attainment of this standard is typically inferred from a college diploma, although in many fields very little of college is specifically devoted to preparing one for the next step. Instead, the focus is on acquiring a general education that presumably prepares a student for a variety of possible careers. Colleges do not typically consult potential employers about the skills they should be imparting to students. One significant exception is engineering schools, which often work closely with local businesses to ensure that graduates depart with skills and experience that companies value. Colleges instead stress more general skills such as writing, critical reasoning, and breadth of knowledge that are commonly thought to be needed to enter high-paying jobs. While these skills are important, they might be better taught in settings that bear a closer relationship to those in which they will actually be used. In any case, it is difficult to tell just how well colleges are performing this function since they do not test according to a uniform and objective measure.

This leads to the second aspect of college. For most students much of the attraction of the college experience centers around the opportunity to finish one's maturation process separated from parents, among peers, pursuing general courses of interest, with only minimal concern about their practical relevance. There is certainly a great deal to be said for this college experience, but it might more accurately be classified as luxury consumption rather than an investment in human capital. The problem has been compounded by the tendency to increase the quantity and quality of attractions available to students on campus. While these attractions may make college more enjoyable, they do not contribute

to learning. And by adding to the cost of college, they make higher education increasingly unaffordable to more Americans. Whether these practices
should receive public subsidies is an open question.

Of course, separating the two aspects is difficult, especially in a setting
that artificially constrains the ability of competitors to offer the same education at a lower price. But the distinction is important if institutions of
higher learning are requiring courses that are irrelevant to the immediate
needs of students that just want the ability to get a better job at an affordable price or are requiring them to stay in school longer than is needed to
acquire the necessary skills. The direct costs of college are significant as are
the indirect cost of earnings foregone while attending classes.

The basic problem of higher education is that cost has become largely
divorced from benefit. This separation can be illustrated in three ways. The
first is that too often both students and employers concentrate on the college diploma rather than the specific courses taken and knowledge gained.
This is understandable but creates an opportunity for the implicit value of
a diploma as an entry ticket to a better future to far exceed the explicit value
of the education in terms of the value that a graduate can actually generate
because of the education. The diploma becomes the goal in itself, and because it becomes the goal, its price can become inflated.

Second, too many parents equate cost with quality. In 2000, Ursinus
College in eastern Pennsylvania raised its tuition and fees over 17 percent,
to $23,460. It received nearly two hundred more applications the next year,
and within four years the size of the freshman class had risen 35 percent.[22]
Average tuition at private, nonprofit colleges rose 81 percent from 1993 to
2004. At the same time campus-based financial aid rose 135 percent.[23]
There is no one price tag associated with college, and to the extent one does
exist, few people actually pay it. As a result, price bears little relationship to
the quality of the particular education purchased. In such a setting, we
should not expect prices to remain at reasonable levels. A recent study spon-
sored by the U.S. Department of Education concluded that "affordability is
directly affected by a financing system that provides limited incentives for
colleges and universities to take aggressive steps to improve institutional efficiency and productivity."[24] Recent research has cast doubt on whether
elite universities are worth the high tuitions that they charge.[25]

In private markets prices serve as an important signal in allocating resources and signaling quality. They do not perform these functions in
higher education. Each parent often pays a different amount of tuition, and
the amount paid is not always related to either the ability to pay or academic
prowess. In fact, to the extent that financial assistance is linked to income,

it often has perverse results. Parents who save up for college and therefore demonstrate an ability to pay are given less assistance than those with the same income who neglect saving. The disincentive to save is even more striking for students themselves. One article reported that, in determining eligibility for financial assistance, colleges consider 20 percent of a child's assets as being available to pay for college.[26] More disturbing is the assistance given to families with a preexisting tie to the university. It is hard to begrudge giving automatic entry to the child of someone who has donated a million dollars and therefore paid the tuition of several other students as well as that of their own child. But pure favoritism without such largesse is yet another way that the existing system, often with the support of both liberals and conservatives, subtly discriminates against those with few means.[27]

A third fault is the lack of competition in higher education. It is true that competition exists to a much greater extent than it does in secondary schools or in other parts of the world. High school graduates have thousands of colleges to chose from, each offering a slightly different approach to learning. Schools differ from each other across a wide range of criteria including size, location, prestige, cost, and academic concentration. And schools often do compete outright for the best students. But in many ways, the game is rigged to limit this competition.

Several years ago the Department of Justice alleged that Ivy League colleges were conferring with each other about which students to admit and how much assistance to offer them. The goal of this collusion was to reduce the total amount of assistance that an attractive candidate could receive by limiting the degree to which colleges bid against each other.[28] Although colleges agreed to stop this practice, there is little evidence that they engage in the type of active competition that in other markets keeps prices down and ensures that a more expensive school delivers better quality. Colleges tend to set their tuition close to what other colleges choose. The outputs that colleges produce are also not well measured. The Department of Education report quoted above noted that colleges face inadequate transparency and accountability for measuring performance.[29]

Of course, private businesses also keep a close eye on the prices that their competitors charge. But they face a broader range of near substitutes and consumers who have a strong incentive to ensure that they get value for their money. Current federal programs largely protect colleges from this pressure. The discussion of how government policy makes college education more of a necessity than it might otherwise be occurs later in this chapter. If parents receive an increase in income, they have a choice of a wide variety of things to spend it on, of which higher education is only one. As a result, they are likely to insist that the college deliver value that is close to or greater than any other good or service they could buy. But federal loans and grants can only be used for college, not for job training or other investments. As a result, an increase in federal assistance has the direct effect of increasing what parents are willing to spend on tuition, precisely the measure that colleges look to in determining needs-based assistance. An increase in federal assistance therefore feeds directly into an increase in the actual tuition that a parent must pay. If all federal assistance was terminated tomorrow and equivalent sums were given to parents as general income, tuitions would fall significantly because parents would have more alternatives for the money.

The problems of federal assistance are exacerbated by the structure of student loan programs and unnecessary regulation of colleges. A recent report noted that the existing financial aid system is "confusing, complex, inefficient, duplicative, and frequently does not direct aid to students who truly need it"; moreover, this reliance on third-party funding insulates colleges from the need to control costs.[30] Adding to the problem is the fact that institutions of higher learning must comply with more than two hundred federal laws, many of them unnecessary.[31]

Ideally, the government would make private companies bid for the right to make and service student loans. Since the government is guaranteeing repayment, the creditworthiness of the student is not an issue and the only question should be what interest rate lenders will charge to make the loans. The best way to find this out is through competition. In theory these loans should be highly attractive to investors. Since the government guarantee exposes lenders to less risk than most other loans, they should command higher prices as investments, allowing lenders to lower the interest rate. Unfortunately, the government has become convinced that lenders are unwilling to make these loans without a guaranteed rate of return. As a result, the government has been paying above-market rates, which raises the cost of a college education to both the government and the student. Lenders have paid colleges to steer students to them, in some cases sharing the profits with individual college officials.[32] This protects the companies from having to compete on the basis of loan rates. Some legislators have pointed out that it would be cheaper for the government to issue the loans directly to students. A better option would be to properly structure the market so that private lenders truly compete with each other the way home lenders do. The result would be lower interest rates and more affordable education.

Colleges also benefit from enormous tax breaks as a result of their nonprofit status. They do not have to pay property tax on the often substantial value of the real estate their campuses occupy, nor are the gains on their endowments taxed as income. In return, they face few requirements on how they must use their endowment to benefit students. Endowments do have a large effect; for example, Swarthmore estimates that its average cost of educating a student is $73,690, even though full tuition is only $41,000. The difference is made up by tapping into its endowment.[33] If true, this would mean that even those students who are paying full tuition receive a subsidy of over eighty thousand dollars over four years. But it is difficult to document such facts in an industry that is largely divorced from economic forces. What is known is that college endowments are growing rapidly partly because colleges are spending only a fraction of the principal built up.[34]

Too often proponents of government involvement support policies that are more effective at propping up existing institutions than they are at helping disadvantaged people. This is partly because the institutions, not the people in whose name the help is justified, are organized into an effective lobby. But it is also possible that many policy makers do not quite believe that lower- or middle-income individuals can make the right decisions by themselves. According to this belief, it is not enough to help a family get enough income so that they can afford a decent college education if they want one; the assistance must be linked directly to the education so that it can only be used for that purpose and no other. Such policies disadvantage the poor who are least able to afford the traditional path to college, and it is not clear that efforts to specifically target the poor in other ways counteract this discrimination. Progressives also commonly neglect the role of competition in keeping goods and services affordable. Too often strong competition is discouraged as threatening jobs rather than encouraged for its progressive effects.

Higher education also is protected from competition by accreditation policies. Generally, an advanced degree has little worth unless it comes from an accredited institution. Accreditation standards are set and enforced by private bodies that ultimately respond to the very institutions they oversee. Moreover, many of the accreditation standards seem geared more toward ensuring that an institution matches the existing model of education than Toward whether it actually conveys knowledge to its students. This is especially relevant as modern technology makes distance learning increasingly possible.

Distance learning opens the way for students to study from home on weekends and evenings, the times when older students or those who must work are available. It also makes it easier to study at one's own pace, another advantage that is likely to have the greatest benefit for the least well off. Finally, by making physical location less important and increasing the number of students that can potentially access the best teachers, distance learning may dramatically lower the minimum cost of higher education.

Some schools are already experimenting with this trend. The University of Phoenix has established a large presence in Internet learning, although it has lately suffered from criticism about the quality of its programs.[35] Some universities, such as MIT, post course materials, including syllabi, lecture notes, and tests online. Still others are experimenting with virtual classes in virtual reality programs like Second Life.[36]

But distance learning will have difficulty taking off if accreditation bodies discriminate against it. Standards that require permanent faculty, a large physical library, and tenure are irrelevant to a new business model that could potentially open up high-quality education to those who cannot afford it. The problem is compounded by the large number of diploma mills that pretend to teach classes but provide little education. There is a tendency to confuse the two groups. But government loan programs themselves enable diploma mills to exist because students often do not think that they are spending their own money, even though they must eventually repay their loans. Some type of accreditation is useful, but it should be closely tied to the quality of the students emerging from the institution as measured by test results and employer interviews. And the results should be widely available to all prospective students.

JOB TRAINING AND PROFESSIONAL CERTIFICATION

The purpose of education is much broader than simply finding a job or earning a better salary. The development of reasoning and communication skills is a prerequisite both to making a greater social contribution and to self-actualization. The pursuit of knowledge should never be evaluated solely on whether it creates immediate economic value.

But it is both unfair and unrealistic to impose broader criteria on those who are struggling to climb the economic ladder. For this reason, the central focus of public policy should be on ensuring that the cost of entry into higher-paying jobs is kept as low as possible so that they are truly accessible to all. In this regard three reforms are important.

The first is continued focus on involving employers in job training. The purpose of training is presumably to find a job, and employers, not teachers or administrators, have the best knowledge about the specific skills and experience needed by the private sector. In fact, employers are in a position to commit to hiring workers who complete certain training. To the maximum extent possible, training should be evaluated according to whether it increases net income. Unfortunately, current labor rules often prohibit some of the most effective means of training. For example, no one thinks anything of charging a worker several thousand dollars for a six-week training course and then sending him or her out to find a job. However, if an employer asked a worker to work for free for six weeks, in exchange for giving the worker the same training, the employer would violate wage laws. Yet the second path is clearly in the worker's interest: not only does the worker save the cost of tuition, but he or she also gets exposure to an employer, who then might give the worker a permanent job. Since current training programs show mixed success at raising worker incomes,[37] the federal government should encourage employers to engage in more entry-level training themselves and allow them to offer lower or even no wages. This, combined with an annual refundable tax credit of five hundred dollars that workers could bank for times of transition, would increase the number of options available to them. With more options and with the resources to pay for training coming directly from the worker, not the government, the probability that workers would be taken advantage of by either employers or training centers decreases. This is especially true if unions restructure themselves to provide guidance and services to workers at all stages in their careers.

A second reform is to restructure the process for admitting individuals into a profession. Too often state licensing requirements are more effective at protecting incumbents from competition by raising the cost of entry than they are at ensuring the quality of those practicing. People wishing to enter the practice of medicine or law typically have to take a test at the beginning of their career but are never tested again to ensure that their skills remain up do date. Even if continuing education is required, the substantive demands are not very difficult. If quality is the goal, then testing should occur throughout one's career. When testing is only done at the beginning, on suspects that the main purpose is to limit the number of new entrants that can compete with existing professionals.

A more important reform would be to ensure that professional standards are not applied inappropriately and to permit individuals to obtain the necessary qualifications through job training rather than through formal education. Law serves as a good example. Some states have inappropriately tried to shield lawyers from competition by charging individuals for practicing law without a license for the following activities: writing do-it-yourself legal guides,[38] representing their child in a suit against the local school board,[39] helping clients understand and fill out legal forms,[40] and helping with real estate closings.[41] Bar associations have been especially aggressive in seeking to limit competition.[42] Similar battles over licensing have been fought in the medical profession.[43] There have even been attempts to require a license to braid hair.[44] Yet, no formal certification is needed to practice as an economist or business manager. Why should one be needed to practice as an attorney or school teacher?

To the extent that licensing requirements are successful, they raise the cost of professional services, often pricing them beyond the reach of low-income workers. They also raise artificial barriers to new workers seeking to enter the field. These barriers can be lowered by allowing individuals to sidestep professional school and obtain their training on the job. If the government strongly feels that licensing should be required, it should establish a test of abilities that is open to all but not restrict the means by which individuals obtain the necessary experience. Many future lawyers would be better off if they were allowed to work at a low wage for a few years in a law firm in return for the opportunity to learn the profession. This type of training might actually be better in terms of practical experience and professional contacts than law school, which tends to focus on theory rather than practice. In the legal profession, four states currently allow students to do exactly that, admitting them to the practice of law once they pass the state bar exam, even if they have not gone to law school. Three other states allow a combination of law school and experience.[45] While few students currently pursue this option, determined efforts to expand and encourage alternatives to formal education and reduce unnecessary licensing requirements would lower the cost of professional services and remove barriers toward upward mobility.

6

MAKING AFFORDABLE
HOUSING AFFORDABLE

Because individuals normally have adequate incentives to purchase decent housing, it may seem that the role of public policy should be limited. This is largely true. Given adequate income most people will make intelligent decisions about how much of their income to spend on shelter. Some will decide to buy large living spaces to store possessions, entertain friends, and enjoy living. Others may prefer small efficiencies or one-bedroom apartments that meet their immediate needs and devote the rest of their income to other goods and services such as a newer car, a longer vacation, or increased savings. Individuals will also normally make intelligent decisions about whether to purchase or rent housing. Some will prefer the freedom of renting, either because they anticipate moving soon or because they do not want the responsibility of mortgage payments, while others will choose to buy a house, either for the security of owning their own home or as an investment. Although some individuals may make choices that they later regret, there is no reason to believe government could make better decisions for them, nor is it clear why the government should prefer that they make one choice over another.

Given this, what is government's interest in the housing sector? To begin with, every market requires rules and norms in order to help individuals arrive at voluntary agreements that increase total welfare. This point is usually discounted by those who distrust market forces. Decisions regarding government involvement are almost never between regulation and the free market. Few markets would work under total freedom. There is always a need for common understandings imposed by government. Markets need to be properly structured in order to work well. But this structure may take many forms. Regulation relies on political bodies to write and enforce rules and may incorporate market forces to a greater or lesser degree. Alternatively, markets can rely on common law principles crafted by a series of judicial decisions. Both systems have their strengths and weaknesses.[1] Under either, conscious attempts to align market rules with economic incentives usually result in a greater achievement of public goals at a lower price.

Some level of government involvement is needed for every market, if only to enforce contracts and prevent coercion. This book concentrates on those few sectors where greater government involvement is needed, presumably because of inherent flaws in the normal market. Neither housing nor education are more important than ensuring adequate nutrition, yet there is no chapter on food policy because there is no reason to think that, once given adequate income, individuals will decide to purchase too little of it. There is also no reason to think that private producers will not supply sufficient quantities at affordable prices. In fact, the central flaw of government agricultural policy is that it is too involved, sending huge subsidies to large capital-intensive operations and putting younger and smaller farmers at a competitive disadvantage.

Housing presents a similar story. Federal policy should be significantly reduced and reformed in a number of ways. Doing so would produce a more flexible sector that provides better housing at more affordable rates. The historic case for housing policy was built on its unique nature as the largest capital item that most families buy. As more areas of the United States became developed, the cost of housing rapidly became a significant portion of a person's income. Housing is the single largest expenditure for most individuals. The average household spends approximately one-fourth of its income on housing. The portion is one-half for many poor families. One study estimated that poor households devoted 64 percent of their income to rent.[2] For families that want to own their own house, the purchase price can often be several times their annual salary.

Until the last few decades, the market for housing purchases was significantly constrained by a lack of credit. In order to make housing affordable, workers had to be able to borrow several times their annual salary and pay it back over several decades. Few banks were either willing or able to make these loans. It therefore made some sense for the federal government to encourage this type of long-term credit by providing loan guarantees and, more importantly, by purchasing long-term mortgages at a fair price so that lenders could use the proceeds to make additional loans.

Over the last several decades financial innovations have revolutionized the housing market. The vast majority of mortgages are now sold to private institutions that package them into pools and then sell collateralized securities specifically tailored to the desires of a large variety of financial investors. The ultimate product has gone from unique thirty-year mortgages whose value can fluctuate wildly with interest rates and credit quality and which therefore appeal only to those with an intimate knowledge of local real estate and the individual borrower, to an increasingly standardized financial interest in a large pool of mortgages with statistically predictable characteristics that increasingly form just another part of a well-diversified financial portfolio.

A specific part of the market has been born specifically to extend loans to individuals with poor credit histories. These loans have enabled a large portion of the population to finally afford their own home, by tapping into the same credit markets that once were available only to the rich. Recently subprime loans have been the source of much higher delinquency rates and increased fraud by both lenders and borrowers. This should not be seen as an indictment of the new financial system as much as a reminder that good underwriting standards and financial due diligence continue to be important to any financial market. It also shows that poorer and less educated borrowers could use greater access to trusted sources of advice that can link them to reputable lenders. The markets are already adjusting to the need for greater financial scrutiny. Despite the current credit crunch, it is important to remember that, whatever problems the mortgage market has, a lack of capital is not likely to be one of them.

The maturation of modern financial markets significantly diminished the rationale for government involvement in the housing markets. Unfortunately, housing is still heavily influenced by government programs that take a variety of forms. This involvement stems in part from the concern that housing is becoming unaffordable. For that reason, a recent bipartisan commission recommended a series of new initiatives to subsidize both the demand and supply of additional housing.[3] But programs like this seek to address a problem that largely does not exist, and in doing so, they create the very problem they seek to solve. A recent study found that for two-thirds of U.S. households there is little evidence that housing became less affordable over the past four decades.[4] For the one-third of households who rent, the proportion of income that the median household spent on housing rose only modestly. This study did not include the steady increase in home prices that has occurred since 2000. But since many of those gains are currently being given back as housing prices stagnate or fall while inflation and wage increases continue, once supply adjusts the results should not differ much from those of the last four decades.

The authors did, however, find that the price of rental units had increased significantly for poor households. Whereas these households used to spend 44 percent of their income on rent in 1960, by 2000 that figure had risen to 64 percent. Only 4 percent of the rental stock was affordable to the median poor renter.[5] Much of the rise was due, not to the failure of the private housing market, but rather to specific government policies.

John Quigley and Steven Raphael found that much of the increase in rents reflected increases in the quality of the rental units. Yet the dramatic rise in the proportion of income that the poor devote to housing suggests that much of this increase in quality was imposed on them by government policies. Three of these are particularly important.

The first is the massive subsidization of middle- and upper-class housing. Interest payments on mortgages of up to a million dollars are currently exempt from income tax. At the federal level alone, this subsidy cost sixty-eight billion dollars in 2006.[6] The exclusion of capital gains tax on home sales subsidizes housing by another thirty-five billion dollars. The ability to deduct state and local property taxes adds another twenty-one billion dollars. The vast majority of this benefit goes to the wealthiest Americans. According to one estimate, nearly 80 percent of the benefit from the mortgage interest and property tax deductions goes to the top 20 percent of taxpayers.[7] In fact, the structure of the interest deduction means that the after-tax price of a home is lower for people in higher tax brackets. The rich therefore have a built-in advantage in bidding for homes against the middle class and poor.[8] The very structure of the subsidy ensures that this is the case. To begin with most poor and younger workers rent rather than own their housing. Since rental payments cannot be deducted, only homeowners benefit. Second, the deduction is available only to those who itemize their deductions. Once again this tends to be wealthier Americans since a combination of mortgage payments and state and local taxes often makes itemizing worthwhile. Last, the value of the deduction is directly proportional to one's tax bracket, which rises with income.

Another subsidy is the ability to protect one's home from seizure in bankruptcy. Although some states cap this ability, others, such as Florida, do not. Wealthy Americans are therefore able to protect large sums from creditors by purchasing multimillion-dollar homes prior to declaring bankruptcy. After the process is completed, they are of course free to sell the property and spend the money as they see fit. In these cases it is not so much the exemption of housing that is the issue, as much as the unlimited aspect of it, which can only benefit those who are already best off.[9]

These subsidies have three effects. The first is to significantly increase the amount of housing that Americans purchase. It is not clear why government should care how Americans allocate their income between sectors such as housing, transportation, health care, education, and food as long as they have enough of each. But because subsidies keep the after-tax cost of housing artificially low, Americans overinvest in it. Middle- and upper-income workers purchase bigger, more expensive houses than they otherwise would because the relative cost of housing is artificially cheaper than the price of other goods and services such as education and health care. Partly as a result, the value of one's home becomes one of the major assets of a typical family. Yet it is not clear that this is the best investment for families to make because the government-induced overinvestment also causes the risk-adjusted social rate of return from housing to be substantially below that of other investments such as a college education or nonhousing fixed capital.[10]

The strong rise in demand caused by tax subsidies inflates the price of housing. Although builders respond by increasing the supply, the net effect is almost certainly larger homes at higher prices than would exist if government policy was strictly neutral.

Second, the subsidies significantly skew the decision of whether to rent or own property. Advocates of housing subsidies argue that home ownership brings social benefits such as neighborhood stability, higher property values (since people generally take better care of property that is theirs), greater support for property taxes (since the people directly paying the tax also enjoy its benefits), and a source of wealth generation as the value of residential property rises. There is some evidence that these benefits do exist, although their exact size is difficult to measure.[11] But even assuming that they exist, they do not justify the current subsidies. Moreover, despite their large cost to taxpayers, it is not clear that these subsidies have much of an effect on homeownership rates because the elasticity of ownership with respect to price is relatively small.[12]

One problem is that, since they are difficult to measure, it is hard to say that the social benefits outweigh the cost of the subsidies, which clearly distort private markets and use scarce resources that could be devoted to other, more valuable purposes. Another problem is that home ownership is clearly not desirable for every person.[13] Younger workers who are just starting their careers and paying off loans and transient workers who anticipate moving soon, either into a bigger residence or to another city, usually are better off renting than owning. Even over the long term, housing is not all that good an investment. Although housing prices have risen over the long term in many areas, other parts of the country have lagged well behind and even seen dramatic decreases in property values. Measured against a well-diversified portfolio of financial products, it is not clear that the hope of a higher return justifies concentrating most of one's savings in a single asset. Individuals are generally in the best position to make their own decisions, and the government tilts the playing field unfairly when it gives massive subsidies to homeowners but not to renters.

A third problem with the deductibility of mortgage interest is that it encourages households to borrow. A homeowner who owns his house free and clear receives no benefit from the interest deduction, except to the extent that it inflates the market price of his or her home. The higher the loan-to-value ratio that a homeowner borrows up to, the greater the tax benefit. Once again, the value of the subsidy is greatest at the higher marginal tax brackets.

Housing markets would work better and society would be better off if the government reduced its role. Specifically, reducing the heavy tax bias toward homeownership would benefit lower-income individuals by reducing existing home prices and encouraging the construction of smaller, more affordable houses. A recent presidential commission suggested limiting the mortgage interest deduction.[14] While politically difficult, such a policy change is feasible. Britain eliminated a similar subsidy over a period of twelve years. If the government wished to subsidize housing in general, a flat refundable tax credit available to everyone to use for either rent or mortgage payments would be preferable. Implementing such a credit could cushion the impact on families who currently benefit from the deduction and also substitute for current government programs that assist low-income individuals.

HOW ZONING LAWS WORSEN
THE HOUSING SHORTAGE

Most local governments also interfere in the housing market through zoning laws. The stated purpose of these laws is to protect property owners from the "unfair" use of neighboring properties. Proponents claim that these laws increase property values by preserving the character of neighborhoods. Politically, they are backed by the fact that most homeowners are uncomfortable with the possibility that a company might build a factory on the block next to their house or a ten-story apartment building on the lot across the street. But it is not at all clear that zoning laws increase social value.

The first questionable assumption is that local governments will make wise decisions in drafting and applying zoning law. In many cases the decisions will be influenced by political pressures that are more likely to hurt the least powerful than help them, nor are local officials more likely to know which uses would maximize social value than are developers who get a return on their investment only if they are right about the marketability of a project. There are many reasons industrial uses are most likely to occur in poorer neighborhoods where land is cheap, but the political calculus that lies behind local zoning ordinances is likely to increase these factors, not ameliorate them. As actually applied, housing standards often prohibit the type of units that the poor are most able to afford, such as apartments without private baths and private kitchens.

Zoning regulations often reduce building density or require minimum dwelling and lot size requirements and make single-room occupancy units and dormitory-type rooms almost impossible to build.[15] They also significantly increase the cost of housing. One study showed that, by 2000, in twenty-seven cities over 40 percent of the price of property reflected the value of obtaining permission to build it.[16] In Manhattan, a similar study estimated that the regulatory "tax" of planning laws accounted for over half of the average rent.[17]

There is an alternative. The owner of a home can purchase an easement in nearby property that prevents it from being developed for certain uses without her or his consent. Having each owner negotiate deals with every other owner is difficult but not impossible. Alternatively, the initial developer of an area can impose restrictions on units as he or she sells them. Since the buyers are aware of the covenants, they presumably will purchase the homes only if the value of having an easement on everyone else's property outweighs the burden of accepting one on theirs. Both alternatives require the owner to give up something in exchange for the building restriction.

Instead, what too often happens is that wealthier neighborhoods use zoning laws to prevent other families from building lower-cost housing in the neighborhood. For instance, a subdivision might seek laws requiring that new houses be a certain size in order to get approval. The effect is to increase the price of building new houses. Zoning laws are also used to prevent the construction of apartment buildings. Because of the existing pattern of residential and business construction this often makes it very difficult to create low-cost housing near where jobs are being created. For many of the nation's poorest workers, the construction of low-cost efficiency or one-bedroom apartments might be the best means of assuring convenient, affordable housing at least for a short period of their lives. But there are few areas where such construction would be allowed. It is not enough to buy the land and find a willing developer. In virtually every city, such a project would need the approval of the local government, and neighborhood opposition could be expected in almost any area worth building in.

The assumption that wealthier property owners should have a say in whether a plot of land in which they have no ownership interest should be used to benefit the poor usually goes unchallenged. In Arlington, Virginia, a local church recently decided to further its mission by building a ten-story building on its current site. Most of the capacity would be devoted to apartments, and the church planned to use the profits from those apartments to subsidize several low-income units in the same building. The plan was significantly delayed by the need to obtain approval from the county board, where it faced strong opposition from surrounding neighbors.[18]

The negative impact of zoning restrictions falls mainly on the poor. In their study mentioned above, Quigley and Raphael find that housing rents have risen higher than quality increases would justify.[19] They attribute this increase to government policies that impact both the supply and demand for housing. As they put it, "Local land use regulations drive up rents and force poorer households to spend large fractions of their incomes on shelter."[20] Reducing zoning laws, whether they deal with restrictions on building size and use or with occupancy, would make it easier to build housing close to where jobs are. It would also make it easier for nonprofits and other organizations to build low-cost housing wherever they thought it was most valuable to the poor without battling special interests who either do not want high-occupancy dwellings in their neighborhood or want to force the developer to convert them into more expensive condominiums that will attract "better" people.

Thus, the result of zoning laws, like many other government restrictions whose stated intention is to protect the population, is to raise further barriers on the ability of markets to meet the needs of those with the fewest means. Left unregulated, the housing market is far from static. Housing buildings evolve through a process of "filtering" by which they move up and down the quality range. Certain units can move from middle to low income by depreciation that exceeds new investment in maintenance. But as quality deteriorates, owners must accept lower rents in order to entice people to stay. Alternatively, renovations can move a low-income building into the high-income rental market. The process of filtering is especially important to low-income renters because developers tend to find it more profitable to devote new construction to high-quality apartments.[21] As a result, the supply of low-cost housing depends on new housing construction at all levels, not just new affordable housing. Studies have shown that, by making it easy for any type of housing to be built, cities can increase the available stock of low-cost housing.[22] Economic studies also demonstrate that zoning ordinances and growth controls tend to increase housing prices and reduce construction in the municipalities that impose them. They also have spillover effects on housing costs in neighboring areas that do not have them.[23]

Quigley and Raphael cite several reasons wealthier neighborhoods might want to prevent the free markets from working: the users of low-cost rental units are likely to pay less in local taxes but consume more public services; low-cost housing may negatively affect other home values; and low-cost rental units may include people who differ by race, ethnicity, and language.[24] Aside from possible moral objections, it is not necessarily wrong to have these concerns. But rather than pursue them by purchasing the necessary property rights in surrounding lots, those who are better off seek to use their political power to impose extra costs on the poor.

The ability to evaluate changes in zoning and other existing laws is significantly handicapped by the Normative Power of the Present, which attaches a normative preference to the existing laws, even if other untried laws are demonstrably better. There are some good reasons for this preference. All things being equal, one might prefer to stick with laws that are integrated into the system rather than switch to others that entail transition costs and that might not work as planned. But this normative power is usually stronger than that. It can often lead otherwise rational people to reject out of hand systems that are different from those they are comfortable with, even if there is clear evidence that change would be better. Even when self-interest is not clearly involved, people often have a difficult time imagining that radically different systems could actually work in practice.

Houston, for example, has no zoning laws. No doubt one could criticize a number of aspects of the way the city has developed. But are its flaws noticeably different than those of other cities, where development has had to pass through complex and laboriously planned committee hearings designed to prevent those very mistakes? Do the type of horror stories people imagine must happen without zoning laws actually occur? Evidence suggests that, even after several decades, the answer is at least debatable.[25] In reality, developers have very good reasons for trying to make the best use of their land, and that use is usually one that is complementary to surrounding land. Moreover, nearby landowners always have the right to try to buy the property themselves to use as they wish. In fact, they seldom do, presumably because the zoning "right" that they seek is not worth the cost if they actually have to pay for it.

THE FAILURE OF HOUSING PROGRAMS

Having helped create a shortage of affordable housing, the government now seeks to address it, not by reversing the policies that restrict private developers from offering new housing, but rather by implementing new programs that create new problems. Thus, a final area in which government programs have failed is the subsidization of housing for the poor. In this area more than most, government officials during the 1960s and 1970s engaged in grandiose exercises in central planning. Rather than let private developers decide what housing to build and where based on what the developers thought they could rent to the public, they pursued their own visions of a better society by arranging the construction and operation of large housing projects.[26] These projects often had a secondary motive of separating poor blacks from middle class whites by dictating where the former could live if they wanted any type of government support. But to the average planner, the vision of a more planned, and therefore better, system had its own strong appeal.

Housing projects and other exercises in urban planning often removed large numbers of poor-quality apartments in the name of urban progress. Although these units were often dilapidated, they served the purpose of giving the poor a place to stay that was within their means. Private landlords had some incentive to make sure that the quality was at least equal to the rent and to ensure at least some safety by providing security and screening tenants. The government replaced very few of these units with anything better. Arthur O'Sullivan notes these redevelopment efforts removed 600,000 low-income units from the housing stock but only added 250,000 new ones. Many of the latter were targeted to middle and upper income families rather than the low income workers who had been living in the original buildings.[27]

Like many other grandiose plans, the projects by and large were massive failures. Devoted only to those who needed housing assistance, they became concentrations of poverty and crime. Landlords had little incentive to maintain the property beyond what the government required. Tenants who succeeded in improving their incomes were forced to move out because they no longer met the income tests. Few other developers wanted to build any moderate or higher quality apartments nearby because of the fear of crime. An article on the Hole in Chicago described it this way:

> From the beginning, city officials used them, along with the expressways being built at the same time, to contain the city's growing population of

poor blacks. . . . Working families moved out as their rent rose while neighbors on welfare paid almost nothing. Housing officials, wary of discrimination suits, stopped screening tenants. Single mothers as young as sixteen were given apartments.

As the project filled with impoverished people, rent income fell and maintenance had to be cut. Tenants threw things off exterior gangways that linked apartments, so they were covered with steel grating, like a prison. Leaks and broken windows went unfixed. Elevators and hallways reeked of urine.[28]

Some have argued that the removal of low-quality rental units through urban redevelopment and housing ordinances has been directly responsible for the rise in homelessness.[29] Over the past few decades, the U.S. government has begun tearing down many of the worst projects.[30]

Another massive failure has been rent control. In an effort to keep housing affordable, many cities, including New York, Washington, D.C., and San Francisco, enacted laws that limit the rate at which landlords can raise rents. In every city in which rent control has been tried, the long-run result has been a reduction in the amount of affordable housing, without any clear evidence that new tenants who move into rent-controlled units benefit.

As the beginning of this book argued, economic forces are powerful and persistent. Laws that seek to thwart them, especially in such a broad sector, are almost always doomed to failure. Normally, evaluating social policy is complicated by the fact that policy makers cannot run pure experiments. In a lab, scientists can randomly give a hormone to half of their laboratory animals and then see if there is any difference in how the two groups grow over time. In evaluating social policy, this type of controlled experiment is difficult but not impossible. What is impossible is running a counterfactual scenario. In those cities that resisted imposing rent controls, we can never know exactly how much slower rents would have risen if controls existed— nor can we know what the effect on apartment construction would have been. In the cities like New York, which did impose controls, we can never definitively show how many fewer apartments exist because potential landlords saw no point in building them.

But we can do some things. We can look at the pattern of investment in a city both before and after rent controls are imposed and compare it with cities that do not have controls. We can study how the limited number of apartments are maintained and how they are allocated to the people who want them. We can also conduct surveys to see who actually benefits from the controls. Each of these efforts shows quite clearly that rent controls transfer a large sum of wealth from existing landlords to existing tenants, but they do this at the cost of a long-run decline in housing markets. This decline imposes severe costs on both future tenants and future landlords that outweigh any initial gains to the original tenants. They also show that much of the gain goes, not to the poor, but rather to middle- and upper-class people.[31]

As hinted above, housing markets are well established and extremely sophisticated. Developers can quickly raise large sums and arrange the necessary contracts to construct housing of the type they think workers will pay for. The market for existing apartment buildings is also vibrant. The birth of real estate investment trusts allows ownership to be widely diversified. Now that investors can add real estate to a diversified portfolio without having to manage buildings, an influx of capital has gone into the sector. Zoning delays and corruption in the building trades often add significantly to cost, but these costs are simply passed on to renters or buyers.

As a result, the housing market reacts quickly once rent controls are imposed, although the effects can take years and even decades to surface. To begin with, few new apartment buildings go up because investors no longer have any assurance that they will be able to get a fair rate of return. A natural response is to shift to condominiums. Since these units are sold rather than rented, developers can take their profit and move on without worrying that the government will change the rules of the game on them. The problem is that it is not at all clear that strongly preferring the construction of condominiums over apartments is wise public policy. It forces workers to own their housing rather than rent it, regardless of what they think best fits their income, age, or future plans.

Workers are normally split between those who want to own and those who want to rent. In a free market developers and building owners would quickly respond to this mix. Under rent control, few investors will agree to support apartment construction even if workers clearly want it because of the risk that controls will reduce their income. The shift to condominiums probably hurts low-income workers the most. Despite the growth in subprime lending, low-income workers remain less able to obtain the credit necessary to purchase their home. They also have the fewest assets with which to diversify their exposure to the risk in housing markets. And they receive the fewest subsidies for owning their own home.

Rent control also affects the future of existing apartment units. In a free market, workers of all incomes would create a demand for a variety of rental units in different price ranges. Landlords who wanted to respond to the demand for luxury housing would furnish a great deal of service in exchange for high rents; if demand outstripped supply they might purchase an older building and completely refurbish it. At the same time, some landlords might use older buildings to respond to the demand for low-cost units. Although the physical state of these buildings might be poor, their quality would be reflected in lower rent. As long as the market is free, landlords face pressure to keep quality from slipping too low or rents from creeping too high—otherwise tenants will leave. Under rent control, landlords have less incentive to invest in maintenance because alternative apartments are hard to find, and they are prohibited from raising their rents even if better quality justifies it.

The tendency will be for the quality of the building to deteriorate down to the level that would justify the controlled rent in a free market. In many cases, the government itself causes this deterioration by making it all but impossible for landlords to make a profit. An article on New York City noted, "As expenses for landlords are rising and tenants' incomes are falling, the dynamic is particularly unhealthy. When rents cannot be met consistently, even the best intentioned landlords cannot afford to maintain their properties. So they let them deteriorate, or simply walk away, leaving the tenants' fate in the hands of government."[32]

Of course, supporters of government intervention may hope to combat this trend through building codes, inspections, and fines, but since the government's resources are limited compared to the amount of housing that needs to be inspected and supervision of housing is likely to be a low priority, it would be naive to think that such efforts will have much success. An article on New York's housing agency found that there was no routine inspection of residential buildings, that most violations are simply logged into the computer without action, that the agency lacks correct addresses for up to a third of landlords, and that it allows landlords to self-certify that they have made repairs mandated by the city.[33] Companion pieces showed that regulation had merely driven some of the poorest housing underground, as individuals illegally subdivided both apartments and houses to crowd low-income workers in.[34]

Assuming that rent control succeeds in keeping real rents below what they would be in a normal market, there will be a surplus of individuals who want to live in them. By lowering the price of rental units compared to condominiums, controls will induce some individuals who otherwise would have preferred to own to rent instead. And, as we have already seen, by discouraging the construction or renovation of new rental units, rent controls also reduce the supply. In order to combat these foreseeable market effects, many governments weaken the laws' application to new buildings. But even in these cases, the housing market is likely to pay a price because developers will not fully trust the government's intentions about the future. The rental rates they set will surely contain some premium to cover the risk that at some future time the government will not allow them to increase rents to the point where supply clears demand.

Much more interesting is the manner in which scarce rent-controlled units will be transferred. A variety of effects are likely, all of them perverse. To begin with, many renters will become trapped in their units, no longer in the best housing for them but unable to relocate due to the huge opportunity cost. Whether this means passing up work transfers to another city, forgoing the purchase of a home, or accepting a much longer commute than necessary, renters who are paying rents that are significantly below market rates will lose much of their flexibility in life. Second, a large variety of extra expenses will likely appear that raise the real cost of the rental unit toward its implicit market price. These may take the form of long waiting lines, which have a cost in themselves, move-in fees, finder's fees, payments to existing renters, and bribes. In each case, the new tenant loses some of the benefit that the rent restrictions were originally meant to deliver.

Finally, rent control also hurts city coffers. There is no question that an apartment building subject to rent controls is worth less than one that is not. The difference shows up in property values and purchase prices, both of which affect tax revenues. By one estimate, New York City lost one hundred million dollars in tax revenues in 1990 as a result of the lower value of rental properties.[35]

The perverse effects of rent controls accumulate over time unless the law is largely rolled back. In each case the result is less rental housing and an environment in which more people have a difficult time finding affordable housing. The negative effects fall most heavily on the poor, while wealthy individuals often receive significant subsidies. The magnitude of the effects can be seen in the sharp cry of protest in San Francisco when one city official merely suggested studying the effect that rent controls were having on the city's housing.[36]

An article about the effects of rent control stated the results well:

> While immigrants are crowded into bunks in illegal boarding houses in the slums, upper-middle-class locals pay low rents to live in good neighborhoods, often in large apartments they no longer need after their children move out. Half a century of rent regulation has created a permanent shortage of decent homes by keeping apartments off the market and encouraging landlords to neglect their buildings. The shortage isn't being eased by new apartments, because developers have been frightened away by the rent regulations and stifled by a host of other restrictions.[37]

As the quote hints, these effects fall hardest on the poor. Another article detailed the enormous power landlords have in choosing which renters will receive these coveted apartments: "Rental agents are suggesting that prospective tenants come armed with renters' resumes detailing their credit and job history, credit reports and references. They also suggest that renters wear professional attire and show enthusiasm for the apartment."[38] The president of an apartment listing service was quoted as saying, "You have to kiss up to the landlords. The landlords can pick the *crème de la crème* of tenants, the absolute perfect person for their space." Landlords reported that it is not uncommon for prospective tenants to offer to redo floors or remodel the bathroom.[39] What hope do less affluent, less sophisticated workers have in this sort of competition?

The effects of rent control are so clear that cities in only a few states such as California and New York still impose it. A majority of states have passed laws prohibiting their jurisdictions from controlling rents.[40] When Massachusetts eliminated rent controls, the city of Cambridge experienced a boom in housing construction and an influx of new tenants.[41] Of course, average rents also increased, doubling over four years. Yet these rent controls had not been helping primarily the poor. When the state legislature passed a measure protecting low-income tenants from eviction for up to two years, only 9.4 percent of all tenants qualified.[42]

ASSISTING THE POOR

Yet if government controls usually make housing markets worse, their removal does not automatically ensure a healthy supply of low-cost housing. The economics of multifamily construction may be such that a developer can usually obtain a higher rate of return by spending marginally more money on upgrades in order to get significantly higher rents. To the extent that this is true, the private sector may lack an incentive to build new low-cost housing. In this case low-income units are likely to appear only as neighborhoods and buildings deteriorate. This poses several problems. For one thing, it takes several years for this process to turn new construction into low-rental units that poorer workers can afford. More importantly, it does not do enough to separate low-cost housing from poor neighborhoods. Research shows that moving families out of distressed communities improved measures of well-being such as safety, health, and behavior problems among boys,[43] although there was no evidence that the move had a significant impact on employment, earnings, or the need for government assistance.

Yet the answer is not to have government build the housing. A recent study estimated that, for every three units of housing that the government built, it drove out two units that would otherwise have been supplied by the private sector.[44] In other words, the government had to devote enough resources to build three units just to increase final supply by one. Government simply does not have the resources to rebuild private sector housing on its own and then also add enough houses to existing supply to provide low-cost housing to everyone.

One popular alternative is vouchers. Under Section 8 of the U.S. Housing Act, the federal government provides vouchers to some eligible families to help them with housing. Families must find their own unit, but they may use the voucher in any complex that accepts them. The tenant pays a portion of his or her income as rent (usually around 30 percent), and the voucher covers the rest up to what the government determines is a "Fair Market Rent." Unfortunately, in many cities it can be extremely difficult to find an eligible apartment, and waiting lists to obtain a voucher can be so long as to be useless.[45] Although rental payment is guaranteed by the government, many landlords will not accept vouchers, either because they fear that low-income tenants will not maintain the units or because they prefer not to deal with government regulations. As one landlord explained it, he "can get better rents and not have to deal with the bureaucracy of the federal government."[46]

Of course, these motives are most likely to dominate when housing is tight, precisely the time when the poor most need assistance in finding and affording it. According to a 2001 study, more than 40 percent of voucher holders failed to find a private rental unit before the voucher expired.[47] Quigley and Raphael conclude that only a fraction of households deserving assistance on income grounds receive it, and in tight markets, many participants find it difficult to locate and acquire acceptable units in the private market.[48]

The wide acceptance of housing vouchers among liberals is somewhat surprising, given their strong opposition to them in the case of primary and secondary education. One is tempted to inquire whether this acceptance would extend to using a Section 8 voucher in a housing complex operated by a religious institution, such as the one in Virginia discussed above. The opposition to school vouchers also reflects the strong influence of teachers unions in the Democratic Party and the consequent inability to base political positions on the merits of an issue. In fact, liberal support for housing vouchers is largely a response to the demonstrated utter failure of most government-run housing projects. This point of indefensible and unyielding quality failure has been widely acknowledged with regard to housing projects but not with regard to education.

Yet, as Howard Husock writes, "why, after all, should a small minority of families gain amenities and low rent, not because they've worked hard and improved their station but because of a combination of need and luck?"[49] By setting maximum rents, vouchers interfere with the normal residential market and prevent families from accepting units that they otherwise might find acceptable. By paying only the difference in rent above 30 percent of the recipient's income, the program subjects workers to the equivalent of an extremely high marginal rate of taxation and discourages efforts to earn more income. Husock describes the traditional housing sector as a ladder offering different quality housing to different individuals depending on age, taste, and income. The desire by most to move up the ladder served as a powerful incentive for personal initiative.[50] Yet government has removed most of the bottom rungs and widened the spaces between them.

The solution is to create a freer, more diverse housing sector that encourages people to seek out the best mix of business and residential construction, single-family homes and multifamily units, and rentals and homeownership. A newspaper article stated the logic that for too long has justified government involvement: "The private market cannot do it alone, many people say, because the cost of building and operating housing . . . simply exceeds the ability of many poor people to pay."[51] The statement fails to acknowledge that much of the cost of housing has been imposed by government itself. Experience shows that without these costs and controls the private sector would respond by offering a much larger supply and variety of housing.

Americans need more choices, not less.[52] Current laws encourage urban sprawl, separate jobs from homes, and segregate the poor from the rich. Private builders are savvy enough to figure out on their own what type of development families and businesses want. If they build developments that turn out not to be wanted, the private sector is big enough to absorb the loss without help from government, and the market is flexible enough to recycle the scarce resources back into productive use.

One area in which government could help is to encourage the development of low-cost housing through the use of more appropriate standards and better housing models. Experiments have shown that it is possible to design houses that cost much less than standard ones do, without a diminution of quality.[53] In Oakland, California, officials used a private developer to replace traditional housing project buildings with modern townhouses. A reporter noted that "features more commonly associated with middle-class suburbia—brick detailing, copper trim, warm oak kitchen cabinets, private entrances, and lush landscaping—are fast becoming *de rigueur* in affordable-housing circles."[54]

The focus of most developers is on finding the highest risk-based rate of return, not necessarily on discovering the cheapest way in which to supply shelter of a given minimum quality. But determined efforts aimed at the latter can produce significant improvements in the price of quality low-cost housing. Auburn University's Rural Studio has designed a series of homes that can be built cheaply.[55] Although the design costs for each model were high because they took up a great deal of designer time, these costs would be amortized over a large number of buildings if the models were easily duplicated.

Another productive avenue would be the entry of nonprofits into the housing market. If private developers lack an incentive to build new affordable housing, this need not be true of organizations specifically created for this purpose. Habitat for Humanity operates an international program that enlists volunteer efforts and donations to help low-income workers own their own house, partially through sweat equity. Many of the single-room occupancy units being created in New York City are run by nonprofit organizations, which often offer a variety of supportive services to help residents.[56] Nonprofits have also built more traditional units of housing.[57]

However, the promise of nonprofits is uncertain. While they are likely to play an important role in supplementing private developers, there is no guarantee that they will be able to offer the least cost or best quality housing. A typical misconception is that nonprofits have a built-in cost advantage over private developers. As one economist said, "There's an inherent conflict between low-income housing and the profit motive. . . . There's just not enough of a margin to make it economically viable. That's why the nonprofits are so important: they don't need the rate of return."[58] This is only superficially true. All developers, whether private, nonprofit, or public, have to pay a rate of return on the capital they use. If nonprofits decide to borrow this capital, they will pay an interest rate that reflects both the risk of nonpayment and expected inflation. It is true that nonprofits do not face market pressure to earn a rate of return on their equity investments, but to the extent that they forego profitable investments they have fewer resources to expand their services. Finally, nonprofits can use donations to offset the costs they pass on to tenants, but government policy is the only reason preventing private developers from doing the same. By changing tax law, the government could make it possible for private developers to solicit donations with the promise that they would be passed through to keep rents low for tenants who met certain eligibility criteria. Another cost that is often not considered is the lost sales and tax revenue that a municipality loses for giving property to a nonprofit and then not collecting property taxes because of its exempt status.

If there is no reason to think that nonprofits are inherently low-cost producers, there are some reasons to think that they are not. First, they often do not have the expertise or management resources of a private developer. In addition, they often lack the size to achieve efficiencies of scale. Smaller size also affects their ability to take risk and manage large properties. As a result, nonprofits are likely to be most useful working in partnership with for-profit developers, helping the latter design and possibly subsidize through contributions affordable housing.

In short, those truly concerned with the quality of housing for the poor should treat it mainly as an income problem. Provide sufficient income, either by a new refundable tax credit that replaces the mortgage interest deduction, the deduction for property taxes, and the exclusion from capital gains, or by building the cost of affordable housing into the income guarantee contract. The former would provide middle- and upper-class families with some substitute to replace the lost tax subsidies.

The second action should be to fully embrace private development. The public sector will never have enough resources to address even a fraction of the housing shortage created by its own policies. Shortening the time and reducing the cost of obtaining building permits and eliminating the corruption and artificially high wages associated with union contracts will encourage more construction and lower costs. Encouraging ordinary homeowners to rent out rooms and making it much easier to evict tenants that do not pay is likely to create a new source of supply and, by allowing new homeowners to derive income from their asset by taking in tenants, increase the ability of poor families to own their first home. Finally, greater support for financial innovation in the housing markets would also help. It was not that long ago that reverse mortgages, which give elderly homeowners a loan for living expenses and do not demand repayment until their house is sold, were considered unethical because of the possibility of huge windfalls if the homeowner died early. Now they are an accepted, albeit small, part of the market. Experiments with joint ownership, in which those who reside in a building give up part of the equity in exchange for making only a portion of the monthly payment, with investors assuming the rest, might be equally valuable in making the purchase of a home more affordable to the poor.[59]

7

AFFORDABLE HEALTH CARE

Of all major sectors of the economy, health care might be the most complicated from a policy perspective. Already roughly 15 percent of the economy, the health care sector's role in the economy and its cost to most Americans is rapidly increasing.

The government already plays a large role in health care. In 2006 the federal government directly spent an estimated $538 billion on its two largest health care programs, Medicare and Medicaid, about 35 percent of the nation's entire health care budget.[1] Federal and state expenditures make up 45 percent of all direct spending on health care.[2] In addition, federal and state tax preferences for employer-paid health insurance amounted to $225 billion in foregone income and payroll taxes.[3]

One central point of this book is that private markets, if properly structured, can satisfy private needs with a surprising diversity and ingenuity. A secondary theme is that many of the structural problems in markets are introduced by government itself, often in an attempt to make markets "fairer" or more affordable. These interventions often exacerbate the very problems they seek to address because the discretion they give government is often used to further the interests of those with power and wealth. A more direct solution would be to transfer income directly to the poor and leave markets alone.

In the case of health care, this would not quite solve the problem for a couple of reasons. First, normal health care is different than most types of goods. A great deal of health care consists of normal consumption such as regular eye checkups, visits to the dentist, and annual exams. These expenses are as predictable and routine as regular car maintenance. In an unregulated market there is no inherent reason they should not be paid out of pocket by the patient when they are incurred, the same way that clothing, food, and housing are. The fact that some individuals may not be able to afford these basic services is not a failure of the health care markets any more than hunger represents a failure of the private food markets. What it does represent is a lack of sufficient income, which government can best address through the income contract set out in previous chapters.

Medical care does have another aspect, however. Occasionally individuals suffer from accidents or illnesses that present them with large unplanned costs they cannot pay. Like other catastrophic events such as house fires and auto accidents, individuals need insurance so that they can spread the risk of occurrence among the general population. Individuals therefore need adequate health insurance to ensure they are able to purchase treatment even when they are seriously ill.

It is important to note, however, that insurance does not reduce the overall risk; it merely spreads it, hopefully, to others that can bear it better. If one in ten individuals get cancer, then each individual will have to pay roughly one-tenth the cost of obtaining treatment for cancer over his or her life in the form of insurance premiums. Alternatively, if everyone can expect to need one major operation sometime during their life, then each individual will eventually end up paying for the cost themselves, even if they are insured, since the premium will reflect this expectation. In this case insurance merely becomes a way of spreading the cost out over one's lifetime.

Although these two separate aspects of health care are clear in theory, they are often confused in fact. Many individuals purchase insurance even for predictable, routine visits, such as an annual checkup. The reason does not stem from any inherent market inefficiency or popular preference. As with many other aspects of health care in America, the conflation of routine consumption and insurance is driven by government policies.

The strong tilt in the market toward employer-paid health care results from decisions that were made over half a century ago with no real thought of how they would impact health care. World War II imposed severe manpower shortages on the U.S. economy. In order to prevent companies from bidding employees away from each other and to keep the costs of production down, the federal government imposed wage controls on the private sector. These controls did nothing to eliminate the pressure behind the shortages, although they may have prevented people from doing things to address it. Companies quickly started to get around the controls by offering nonmonetary benefits, including health care. Later, the Internal Revenue Service (IRS) ruled that these benefits were not taxable as income. Even though they had a clear monetary benefit to workers, they did not have to pay income or payroll tax on their value.

Because the employer generally makes the relevant choices, employee benefits usually cost the employer more than they are worth to the employee. In other words, if employees were given the choice, they would generally choose for the employer to give them a pay raise rather than spend money on additional benefits. For this reason, many employer-provided benefits might have faded out after wage controls were lifted were it not for the fact that the IRS had ruled that they were tax exempt.

A simple example illustrates the economics of tax exemption. Let's assume a worker making ninety thousand dollars faces a marginal tax of 25 percent. In addition, the worker and her or his employer pay 15.6 percent in payroll taxes. What happens if the employer is willing to spend one thousand dollars more per year in order to keep the worker? If the employer raises the worker's salary, the latter will receive only $633 after all taxes. But if the employer spends the money on extra health care for the worker, no taxes are paid. Thus, even if the employee only values the increased benefits at eight hundred dollars, she or he will prefer to receive them over an increase in pay. The employer of course is indifferent. The result, however, is that social welfare is decreased by two hundred dollars.

There are two other problems with the result. First, the employee has an artificial preference for receiving health benefits through work, even though in this example the benefits are worth less than their cost to the employer. If benefits were treated as taxable income, this preference would disappear. Second, as with tax deductions, the tax exclusion benefits the rich much more than it benefits the poor. Once again, the amount of subsidy is directly proportional to the marginal tax bracket, which increases with income. It is true that, unlike a deduction, the exclusion from income benefits all workers who pay income tax, even those who do not itemize deductions. But the middle and upper classes are much more likely to work with employers who offer health benefits, further tilting the advantage toward them. In 2006, these subsidies cost government $225 billion in lost tax revenue.[4]

Linking health benefits to employment has several disadvantages. First, it starves the market for individual health insurance. Given the tremendous tax advantage given to employer-provided benefits, it should be no surprise that the market for individuals purchasing health insurance on their own is small and therefore expensive. As a result, those workers whose employers do not offer health insurance often have a difficult time finding and affording it. They also do not benefit at all from the tax break. Because the market is so thin, individuals with preexisting health conditions and the elderly may find it impossible to get affordable insurance. Yet there is no innate reason an individual market could not work for most people. Although every economic sector has important differences, it is not at all clear that an individual health insurance market could not function as well as fire or auto insurance markets do. In the latter case there is a public mandate to purchase the insurance, but individuals arrange coverage on their own, and few would think of looking to their employer for help.

A second negative effect is that the tax exclusion involves companies in an activity that they are not necessarily very good at. Much of the management efficiency since the 1990s has resulted from companies returning to their core competencies: those activities that they do best. Choosing and administering health benefits is seldom one of them. From the company's standpoint, health benefits often work as a competitive disadvantage because established companies with older workers and retirees tend to have much higher health care costs. They are always vulnerable to new companies that can enter the market without these liabilities associated with past operations. General Motors, for example, paid $5.2 billion in health care in 2004 or $15,000 per car; $4 billion of this cost went to retirees.[5] Toyota, which has a much younger workforce and fewer retirees has a built-in cost advantage, even if it were to offer the exact same benefits.

These costs allocate health care inefficiently, but it is not clear that they place U.S. companies at a disadvantage. Some businessmen have worried that high health care costs hinder their international competitiveness. The president of the Business Roundtable was recently quoted as saying, "Our soaring health care costs put American goods and services at a significant competitive disadvantage, and they slow economic growth."[6] Certainly companies in other parts of the world normally do not pay health care coverage for their workers, but they do pay much higher payroll taxes in order to fund government coverage. But even when compared to countries such as China, where government coverage is rudimentary, American employers are not harmed if they can pass these costs on to workers. There is good evidence that, on the whole, they do. Increases in overall compensation, including benefits, roughly track producer productivity over the medium term, indicating that employers pay workers what they are worth, no more, no less. As health care costs rise, it is employees who bear most of the cost through lower salary increases than they otherwise would get. Since the total cost of compensation to employers is the same, they may not suffer any competitive disadvantage.[7]

The one case in which this is clearly not true is in heavily unionized companies that have already committed to paying expensive benefits and which therefore have heavy fixed costs unrelated to current production or productivity. In these industries, employee strikes can be prohibitively expensive even if the short-term costs of labor far exceed its marginal benefit. The union has no incentive to agree to benefit cuts because they know that the employer cannot afford to stop production or relocate without abandoning a large amount of sunken investments. In these situations, a more rational pay system that preserves the employer's long-term competitiveness is not likely to occur until the company actually goes into bankruptcy and the owners demonstrate a willingness to write off their investment. Such was the fate of the steel and airline industries, and the American automobile industry seems likely to follow course.

It is clear, however, that the linkage between health benefits and work restricts the job mobility of workers, especially those with health concerns. This might not have mattered very much when most workers expected to stay with one employer throughout most of their career. But it does matter in a world where company mergers and dissolutions are common events and where workers can expect to change companies and even careers a number of times during their life. It adds yet another factor to the consideration of whether to take a particular job. The handicapped, seriously ill, or elderly are especially limited in their choices. They must accept a job with an employer that offers good benefits and can only leave for another that also offers comprehensive benefits. The advantage that large companies have in either purchasing insurance or self-insuring translates into an advantage in attracting workers, not necessarily because workers value the insurance more but rather because the benefits are much cheaper than they could get on their own.

The dominance of employer-provided health care also makes workers insensitive to the cost of the services they receive. In a private market, prices are normally determined through a delicate interplay of the supply and demand for all goods. Suppliers always want higher prices and larger profit margins. Consumers want prices as low as possible. For most consumers the list of things they want is much larger than the amount of things they can afford. They therefore trade goods and services off against each other, buying those that give them the most value. The fact that consumers seldom pay the full cost of their health care distorts this balancing act and tilts consumption far more toward "free" health care and away from other goods. This in turn draws more resources into the health care sector and weakens the pressure on suppliers to provide true value.

To some extent, employers have stepped in to exert this market discipline. Because health care costs are rising so rapidly and have already become a large cost item, companies have started to participate directly in efforts to hold down costs.[8] In Minnesota, a coalition of private and public employers has banded together into the Buyers Health Care Action Group in order to get the health care system to focus on increasing the value being delivered to their workers. Working with labor unions, they formed the Smart Buy Alliance to push for better measurement of health quality, wider adoption of best practices, more efficient administration, and better public education. Companies have also subjected workers to higher deductibles and co-payments, thereby making them bear more of the direct cost. Evidence shows that these changes do have an impact on usage, but when employers are still choosing the basic plans and paying most of the costs, and when the individual market for health insurance is so small, consumers still have limited incentives and ability to trade off consumption decisions in the same way that they do for housing or food. Because demand is not accompanied by the normal desire to hold down prices, supply is relatively unconstrained and prices are disconnected from quality.

Demand and prices are further inflated by the fact that the federal government already accounts for 35 percent of all spending on health care, mainly through its two main programs, Medicare and Medicaid, and the purchase of health care for its employees. Since this spending is also not tightly linked to quality or the relative benefit of nonhealth goods and services, it draws additional resources into the medical sector without imposing on them any real requirement that they increase marginal welfare to the same degree that spending on other social priorities might. These programs have also had the deleterious effect of introducing political considerations into decisions about who should get or offer care, at what prices, and with what degree of quality. Because the government is inherently poor at equating marginal cost with marginal benefit, a large percentage of medical spending is wasted, either in the sense that the services associated with one hundred dollars of government spending are worth much less to those who receive them or through outright fraud.

The latter is known to be large. In 2003, the General Accounting Office (GAO) put Medicaid on its list of high-risk programs due to its size, growth, and management weaknesses. Although GAO has conducted dozens of studies on the program, it believes that the total amount of fraud cannot be precisely quantified.[9] A study of the Medicare program estimated dollars paid in error to be $19.9 billion in 2004.[10] Another estimate puts the figure at $35 billion.[11] But even these estimates are likely to understate the level of government waste because they accept all payments made under the rules to be legitimate. Yet many of these payments are almost certain to confer far fewer benefits than they cost the taxpayers. In a normal market, consumers will seldom spend one hundred dollars unless they receive benefits worth at least that amount. But when government is paying for a service, beneficiaries may come to insist that the government provide services even if it costs the government one hundred dollars and even if they would not pay seventy dollars if they had to bear the cost themselves. In this case we can say that, in some sense, at least thirty dollars has been wasted.

Unfortunately, this type of waste is almost certainly large but immeasurable. Among some patients and doctors, government care has become a culture, with patients having multiple visits with multiple doctors and doctors including numerous procedures for each visit in order to increase the reimbursement the government will pay.[12] In order to control this, the government has to develop an elaborate system of controls that add a great deal of administrative cost to the system.[13] Advocates of a single-payer system often point to its low administrative costs, but they seldom include in these costs either the lost value outlined above or the administrative costs imposed upon private parties to learn and comply with the rules. The results of these controls can be perverse. For example, Intermountain Health Care, a network of hospitals in Utah and Idaho, claims that medical practices that it put in place to save lives significantly reduce its revenue because Medicare pays for procedures to cure disease not precautions to prevent them.[14] This delinking of value from payment further inflates both the demand and the price of health care. Inflation is then often pointed to as an example of why a private market will not work.

Any examination of the health care sector should acknowledge its importance to Americans. In many respects there are few things more important than health. Although individuals may be lax about it in normal times, when they suffer from a severe problem, they desperately seek help.

What is not natural is to have almost no link between expenditures and quality. Without this link, a number of things happen. First, health care costs rise more then they would if consumers were insisting on value for their money. Second, there are few incentives to increase either quality or efficiency over time. Over the last few decades, manufacturing industries have undergone a series of revolutions involving restructuring, reengineering, supply chain management, and quality control. These changes have brought about dramatic improvements in both quality and price, pushing back the tradeoffs that normally dominate the two. This type of pressure does not drive continuous improvements in the medical field. Researchers have identified many areas where better management could save large amounts of money.[15] Yet the industry faces little pressure to adopt them.

Instead, as in education, the tradeoff between cost and quality barely exists. Studies show that medical practices and costs differ widely across the country, with some areas routinely performing procedures that are known not to be effective.[16] Another study showed that even experienced doctors vary widely in the number of precancerous polyps they discover in routine colonoscopies, with the main factor seeming to be the amount of time they spend on the procedure.[17] The research on variations in medical care produces three main results.[18] First, variations in resource use are very large: Medicare spending per patient in Miami is about two and a half times what it is in Minneapolis. Second, resource use is sensitive to supply, indicating that hospitals and doctors feel free to bill out equipment whether it is cost justified or not. Normally, more MRI machines in an area would drive down the price of each procedure, but in health care, it seemingly gives doctors an incentive to schedule more MRIs. Third, more aggressive treatment and higher spending does not result in better patient outcomes. In part this is because sicker patients often require more intervention just to get the same result as healthier ones. But a large part of the discrepancy stems from the unique payment structure and incentives associated with health care.

Because patients are used to passing the bills on to someone else, they have developed a sense of entitlement to health care that they do not apply to the quality of their housing, transportation, or college educations. They expect the best, regardless of cost, and resent any decision to deny them care, even if there is no medical evidence that such care is justified. It very well might be that a seventy-five-year-old man who had to pay the full cost of a hip replacement himself would balk at the cost and decide to manage on his own, even if money was no object. But let his HMO or the government tell him that it is not cost effective, and he will truly believe that a gross injustice has been done to him. The path of least resistance is often to allow the procedure and then build it into future costs. This, of course, raises premiums and prices many out of health care. But they cannot sue.

At the same time, doctors usually have a financial incentive to schedule as many procedures as possible, and they are generally able to do this because they know the patient will not bear the cost. These pressures on the doctor's side are increased by the desire to avoid being second-guessed in a malpractice suit.

Although government introduces several inefficiencies into health care, there are two major objections to a totally free market that do point to a need for some boundaries on how the private markets should work. This need for boundaries is not unique; all markets need them, if only to ensure that companies fulfill their contracts once they enter into them. In banking, for instance, few would question the wisdom of some level of federal deposit insurance or the requirement that banks maintain a certain level of capitalization in order to absorb financial shocks. The need for these controls does not automatically justify other constraints such as the old prohibitions on banks selling insurance or paying interest on checking accounts, however. Similarly, in health, the fact that some level of government regulation is likely to be beneficial does not justify a single-payer system in which the government runs virtually all health care.

The first complication with health care stems from society's decision that it will not deny vital care to a person who needs it simply because she or he cannot pay. Homeowners who lose their houses to fire or flood usually have little reason to think the government will cover their loss if they do not have insurance. This provides a strong incentive to purchase it. People who do not purchase health insurance still have good reason to think they will receive a minimal level of care if they suffer a severe injury or illness, whether or not they can pay. As a result, they may be less inclined to purchase insurance. These costs are then borne by either taxpayers or other users of health care. The Federation of American Hospitals claims that hospitals have to absorb forty billion dollars in unpaid bills each year.[19] These costs must either be absorbed by the hospitals, in which case fewer of them are likely to offer emergency room service, or passed on to other patients. If the latter, then the costs of health care will rise further, possibly causing other people to drop insurance or forego care.

In theory, this problem could be solved relatively easily by requiring everyone to purchase an insurance policy as is done in car insurance. In practice, one in seven drivers still does not carry insurance.[20] Any requirement would also force the government to define what the minimum level of insurance is. This inevitably leads to pressure from lobby groups to cover their specific diseases, procedures, and drugs. Drug manufacturers will press for mandated coverage of erectile dysfunction and hair loss drugs. Psychologists and psychiatrists are already pressing for laws that make insurance plans cover mental health. Each of these mandates adds to the cost of insurance without necessarily delivering an equal or greater benefit. Normally, individuals would purchase such plans only if the benefits outweighed the costs. With a mandate, the decision on whether this condition is met is taken away from the individual and given to the government. Adding too many requirements prices many workers out of the market.

The second major problem with a free market in which everyone purchases individual insurance is that future medical costs can often be predicted by past ones. Some medical events, such as automobile accidents and breast cancer, hit suddenly and unpredictably (although to the extent that cancer is genetic, future technology may soon be able to accurately predict the probability of cancer). Many, however, are associated with past and existing health. As a result, individuals with chronic health problems have very high expected future costs. These people can only find affordable health care if the pool of individuals participating in an insurance plan contains a large number of relatively healthy people. If this is the case, then people with good health subsidize those with poor health. The problem is that the former have no incentive to do so. If given other options, such as Medical Savings Accounts, that permit them to pay lower insurance costs, they are likely to do so. This, of course, raises the premiums of those still in the insurance pool, exacerbating the problem of cross-subsidization and making health care unaffordable to the sick.

But forcing everyone to participate in the pool is not necessarily the best result either. For one thing, it is not very clear why a young worker on the bottom of the career ladder should subsidize an older worker who might make two or three times the younger worker's salary. Certain inequalities are inherent in life. We know we cannot restore eyesight to the blind by making everyone else's eyesight just a little bit worse, but some people think that we have an obligation to protect people who happen to have high health care costs by reducing the income of everyone else.

Is there really any inherent injustice in expecting someone with twenty thousand dollars in annual medical costs to pay for them? Shouldn't the real problem be whether they have the ability to make these payments themselves without suffering the type of extreme economic hardship that we would want to protect any deserving person from, regardless of the cause? If the answer is yes, then once again we are faced not so much with a health care problem as with an income problem that in this particular case is linked to health. Since the costs of preexisting conditions are largely predictable, they cannot be spread out among a broader population through insurance unless we force everyone into the same insurance pool and maintain the practice of including most health costs, except those that are relatively minor or predictable, in the insurance policies that everyone buys. We have already seen the complications that this creates.

It is true that purchasers of health insurance might very well wish to purchase policies that not only cover the costs of an unexpected, expensive event but also protect them against the large annual costs associated with a chronic disease. The policy might therefore cover all annual expenses over a set figure such as ten thousand dollars. But this option does not exist for people with preexisting conditions, many of whom are in the lower and middle class and will therefore have difficulty bearing the cost themselves. Protecting these individuals by having someone else pay the cost raises several problems, however, the most important of which is that any protection is likely to remove their incentive to minimize costs or to forego treatment that costs society more than it benefits them. Someone or something else therefore has to impose this discipline.

Nevertheless, some of these individuals will need a subsidy in order to afford health care. It is difficult for private markets to provide this subsidy, however. Insurers may be willing to extend coverage but only if they can charge the proper risk-adjusted premium, which is likely to be too high for many to afford. If insurers are forced to offer the same premium to everyone, then consumers with few health concerns are likely to find that their benefits are not worth the premiums. They will look for cheaper insurance or, if none is available, possibly do without. Another alternative is to have the government subsidize insurance for individuals with preexisting conditions. But this sometimes creates perverse incentives as individuals seek to avoid losing their eligibility as their income rises.

Recent problems in Maine illustrate some of these difficulties.[21] Because the state's insurance plan, DirigoChoice, offers very comprehensive coverage, many individuals cannot afford it. Others who can afford it decide to go without because they do not see the need to pay for coverage that they are unlikely to use. Those who did sign up often needed significant care, often for preexisting problems, which increased the cost of the program. Because the program is means-tested, different people are required to pay different amounts. At least one person interviewed stated that he limited the amount of hours he worked in order to remain eligible for the low premium rate. He still dropped the insurance after rates rose 13.4 percent, however.

For this reason, many people believe that some form of compulsion is needed in order to get younger and healthier individuals to participate in the insurance pool. But forcing the healthy to purchase insurance will not automatically solve the problem of high-cost individuals. Left to themselves, people who expect to use very few health services will form a separate pool with lower premiums. The rules must force them to participate in the same insurance pool as the sick, thereby subsidizing them.

For this reason some observers call for a single-payer program in which the government provides health care to all individuals, similar to what other major industrialized countries such as Japan, Germany, the United Kingdom, and Canada offer their citizens.[22] In theory a centralized system would reduce administrative costs, achieve the greatest savings though standardization and volume purchasing, and rationalize medical care by deciding on the best treatment in each case, thereby eliminating unnecessary procedures. In practice, government administrators can never display the drive toward efficiency, continual innovation, and rapid evolution that a properly designed private sector can.[23] As one article states,

> Everywhere it has been tried, the single-payer model has yielded inefficient service and lower-quality care. In Britain today, more than 700,000 patients are waiting for hospital treatment. In Canada, it takes, on average, seventeen weeks to see a specialist after a referral. In Germany and France, roughly half of the men diagnosed with prostate cancer will die from the disease, while in the United States only one in five will. According to one study, 40 percent of British cancer patients in the mid-1990's never got to see an oncologist at all.[24]

These single-payer systems were started decades ago when medicine was still relatively simple and the national population was young and healthy. As long as health costs were a relatively minor part of the total economy, a relatively large amount of inefficiency could be tolerated, especially if it was possible to maintain current services by avoiding investments in future quality improvements. Now each of these systems is increasingly being forced to deal with the same tradeoffs facing American medicine, except that the single-payer system has far less flexibility to make the necessary changes. Their problems would be even worse if the United States did not continue to originate and subsidize most of the medical advancement and innovation in the rest of the world.[25]

The primary task of medical reform cannot be extending the best quality health care coverage to all Americans. Such a goal is likely to be self-defeating both because of its indeterminate nature and because the vast resources that it would require would likely to have the net effect of pricing more Americans out of health care. The definition of health coverage is likely to expand gradually to cover much more than the necessities of adequate physical health. Already it has been expanded to include remedies aimed at improving one's sex life, baldness, birth control, and hip replacements for eighty-year-olds. This adds to the cost of giving the poor coverage for broken bones, heart attacks, and diabetes.

Even if a narrow definition of health care is maintained, government funding is usually not well linked to quality. When this is the case, costs increase up to whatever threshold is set by the government. After that, quality deteriorates. As in housing and education, increases in funding are unlikely to produce automatic increases in quality. They are likely to create a situation where the real cost of a given level of quality rises, pricing the poor out of the market. Since there will never be enough government funds to provide a sufficient level of service to all who qualify, many are likely to be left without. Unlike in housing, rationing in health care is unlikely to take the form of people being denied any form of government assistance. Instead, everyone will have coverage for basic care, but cost control measures will gradually limit the scope of that care by imposing waiting lines and denying certain medications and procedures. The existence of a private care option will exacerbate this trend as those who can afford it opt out for a better level of service even if they have to pay for it themselves. This trend is already happening in public schools even though local control of school districts protects wealthier neighborhoods from the effects of deteriorating districts. The same pattern in health care is also evident in the fact that more and more doctors are refusing to see Medicare and Medicaid patients because government reimbursement rates are so low.[26] At the same time, richer individuals are paying more in order to get a higher standard of care than most people receive.[27] Although some people have criticized this practice as unethical, it is likely to continue as the quality of government and private programs deteriorates.

There is no magic bullet that will solve the many inefficiencies of health care. In fact, tradeoffs are inherent in any market. But there are strong reasons to think that giving individual patients more control over their own health care and subjecting the sector to greater competition will create an environment in which quality is gradually improved and prices are brought under control.

Before we begin to explore what such a system would look like, it is worth pointing out that there is nothing inherently wrong with the fact that Americans spend a growing proportion of their income on health care. To begin with, the United States is a rich country. Most workers have all of their basic necessities met and can afford to spend more on things that are important, but not vital, to life. Health care certainly qualifies for that. In a country where expenditures on flat screen televisions, pet care, and vacations are rapidly increasing, it should not be surprising that people also devote a growing fraction of their income to physical well-being. And science has certainly made this possible. A growing number of drugs, equipment, and therapies now promise improvements that before were unachievable. Americans have received some benefit from these expenditures. Life expectancy has steadily risen, especially for older individuals, largely because mortality rates associated with causes like heart disease, cancer, and stroke have fallen.[28] This trend is increased by the fact that demographically Americans are getting older as the baby boomers mature. Since medical costs increase with age, it is almost inevitable that health care spending will rise over time.

The challenge therefore is not to slow down the growth in health care spending but rather to make sure that Americans are getting adequate value for what they spend, both in terms of health benefits and in comparison to the benefits that they receive from spending in other sectors such as education, housing, and entertainment. Despite the beliefs of those whose philosophical leanings incline them toward a single-payer system run by government and administered by a bureaucracy of experts, true cost-benefit pressure will only come about by giving individuals both the power and the incentive to make these tradeoffs for themselves. Partly because of the complexities already introduced by government, the transition to such a system will be exceedingly difficult, involving a number of separate reforms. However, there is no reason to think that health care is inherently more complex than other industries in which the government plays a much smaller role. And unless we know the general direction in which we want the system to move, evaluating any single reform is very difficult.

The ideal policy for promoting both flexibility and coverage in health care would involve two reforms. The first is a refundable tax credit of roughly fifteen thousand dollars for each family ($7,500 for single filers) that would be available only if the taxpayer provided the policy number for a qualified health insurance plan that covered catastrophic coverage. The coverage would have to extend to all children for which the couple is responsible. Since the credit would only be available if an individual purchased insurance, every adult would have a strong incentive to do so even absent a government mandate. Making the full fifteen thousand dollars refundable even if the actual policy costs much less would ensure that taxpayers treat the money as their own. This would cause them to use the same type of cost-benefit test that they apply to spending in other parts of their life. This change would be strongly progressive since it would effectively pay uncovered people, many of whom are poor, to obtain coverage while holding harmless most of the people who benefit from the current tax exclusion for employer-provided insurance.

An important part of this reform would be the elimination of the income exclusion for employer-paid benefits, including health care. Employers would have to list the employer's cost of their health care on each employee's W-2 form. This amount would be included as income in the employee's tax return. Employers should also be required to allow each employee to opt out of care, taking the employer's payment share in return. This would give employees the ability to shop for other plans and increase the size of the individual insurance market. This requirement should extend to the federal government's provision of Medicare and Medicaid benefits.

The second major reform would be to allow much greater freedom for individuals and groups to band into insurance pools. The resistance to allowing small business groups to get together to purchase insurance for their members makes no economic sense. Similarly, the efforts of groups like AARP and many labor unions to offer insurance plans to their members and others should be encouraged. Finally, the government should open up the Federal Employee Health Benefits Plan to all individuals. Under the federal plan the government uses its size to negotiate terms with a wide range of health care plans. Employees can then choose whichever plan is best for them. In each pool insurers should be required to offer the same terms to all individuals, regardless of prior history, with one exception. Insurers should be allowed to vary their price by the age and sex of the individual. This reform would keep premiums low for young people, encouraging them to participate in the pool, rather than purchase individual coverage. It would also create a better match between health care premiums and income over one's career. If desired, the size of the refundable tax credit could also vary by age in order to create a better match with expenses.

Other experts have proposed plans similar to this one.[29] The goals are to give people purchasing power and to offer them as many choices as possible. Most individuals will continue to be content to participate in a large pool. While this reduces their sensitivity to price/quality concerns, it protects them from risk. But the freedom to move between pools and to get individual coverage should ensure that competitive pressures are greater than they are now. With large pools, insurers should have greater certainty over the actual costs they will face. A small tax could be levied on each policy and redistributed according to an objective formula to those plans that suffered a disproportionately greater number of adverse events within their pool.

How would such a system evolve? One outcome is that individuals are likely to assume a much greater role in their own health care. A number of people have objected to this, arguing that individuals will always lack the time or information needed to make intelligent decisions about cost and quality. As one writer says, "No matter how much information consumers have, who's to say they will make good decisions?"[30] There is, of course no guarantee. However, we do know that innovations such as the Internet, support groups, and networking software are making it increasingly easy for consumers to obtain detailed personalized medical information.[31] Patients are forming sophisticated virtual communities to inform and support each other. Government agencies and health care providers use software to deliver personalized health messages and alerts. Although consumers will not always make the correct decisions, neither will the doctors whose advice they have traditionally deferred to. Doctors are not infallible; some are young and inexperienced. Others have failed to keep up with advances in their field. And none has the single, self-interested focus that the patient has. For many of the cases in which a clear diagnosis or remedy is not clear, medicine remains as much an art as a science.[32] Where there is doubt about the best path to pursue, who but the client should make an informed decision?

If patients are to make informed decisions, they need information. Over the last decade, the federal government has announced several initiatives to track the quality of care and the effectiveness of alternative treatments. The government should adopt policies that make it much easier for patients to get the information they need. Just as it required gas stations to post their prices, it could require hospitals to provide an all-in cost estimate prior to any medical procedure. At present doctors often bill for their services separately, bills contain multiple itemizations that are not clearly labeled, and the bill arrives several weeks or months after the procedure. The government and employers could also continue with their efforts to collect information on the quality of outcomes, both between individual doctors and hospitals and between different procedures or treatments. This does raise some difficulties: doctors who take the most difficult cases may show higher failure rates, and different patients may react differently to the same treatments. But overall it should allow patients to make more informed choices.

Other improvements could be made in the efficiency with which services are delivered. The Veterans Health Administration has been leading an effort to implement electronic medical records for all patients. Greater use of electronic records could make it easier for doctors to look at a patient's full medical history and could give patients better control over their own records by putting them in the form of a single electronic record that they can carry around, rather than in individual paper records scattered among the various doctors, dentists, and pharmacists that patients see throughout their lifetime.

The use of a single form to submit medical billing would also reduce administrative costs for doctors. The government's large role in Medicare and Medicaid introduces much inefficiency into the market, but it does give the government a critical mass sufficient to impose some sensible changes into the market. By adopting a single form that other insurance agencies could voluntarily use, the government might be able to lead the market toward beneficial standardization. Since use of the form would be voluntary for private insurers, the government would have to make sure that the form met private needs to a great extent; otherwise, companies would continue to use their own forms. But if the government did implement a good form for its own programs, other insurers would face pressure to adopt it as well.

Although specialization has often led to increased costs, it also provides a possible route to greater efficiency. Centers that specialize in a limited number of procedures can often produce better results at cheaper prices due to economies of scale. Among the most important economies is the ability to fully utilize highly trained professionals who, because of their narrow focus, have a much deeper level of experience with a particular illness or procedure than does the average doctor. In India, the Aravind Eye Hospital provides one example of this model in the context of a developing country. The hospital specializes in eye surgery, delivering the world's highest standards at a small fraction of the normal cost. Business practices are designed to make the maximum use of its most skilled professionals, while its services are closely integrated with those of suppliers and complementary products to minimize costs.[33] If such specialized centers demonstrate greater efficiency in terms of either cost or outcomes, government policy should not discourage them in order to protect less efficient general hospitals.

Another innovation that is likely to spread if left to market forces is the emergence of small walk-in clinics that provide routine care in locations and at times that are most convenient to the average patient. Wal-Mart recently decided to place several of these centers in its stores.[34] If the clinics do not provide enough value to individuals, they will fail. But there is no reason we should hope they do not succeed. They are likely to provide much better care for the type of inquires they see. If their nature and location are widely known, they may also attract patients that might otherwise go to the emergency room for lack of a better alternative.

Government should also play an active role in addressing some of the structural rigidities that can reduce competition in the health care markets, thereby keeping costs high. Without strong competitive forces operating in all parts of the market, the drive for innovation and improvement will weaken. One issue involves determining exactly what skills are needed to provide certain treatments. We have seen how licensing requirements can make it more expensive for young people to enter professions by artificially increasing the amount of training needed to perform at a certain level. These requirements can also make professional services unaffordable to many people by giving providers the right to limit the competition they face. Within medicine there have been a number of controversies over allowing professionals with fewer skills to perform designated services. New technology is likely to further this trend by substituting capital, including information technology, for human skills, thereby allowing lower-skilled technicians to deliver services that used to require more specialized knowledge.

Unfortunately, the context in which these disputes are settled is clouded by self-interest. The premise that government should regulate the skills needed to perform certain functions is implicitly based on the assumption that these decisions will be made in the patient's interest, presumably following a subjective study of whether extra training is needed to produce a better outcome and, if it is, whether the improvement in results justifies the higher costs associated with hiring higher-skilled professionals. However, threatened professions usually try to exert political pressure in order to guard their privileges. For example, radiologists have recently expressed concern about general practice doctors reading MRIs.[35] The specialists claim that regular doctors may misinterpret the results. Anesthetists have opposed reforms that would allow nurse anesthetists to substitute for them in the operating room under general supervision.[36] Doctors have also opposed state laws that give nonphysicians the ability to write prescriptions.[37] It is perhaps natural that in each case the threatened professionals would use the interest of patients as a cover. But it is not clear from any of these cases that the political decision of what standard of care is deemed appropriate will be made in the patient's interest rather than on the respective political power of the professions concerned.

Another avenue in which competition is likely to increase is medical vacations. The cost of care is often much lower in developing countries. Yet centers in these countries often have U.S.-trained doctors and facilities that match world standards. In addition, they can offer special amenities that patients cannot afford at home, such as private rooms, higher nurse-to-patient ratios, and special meals. There are of course some legitimate issues to be concerned about. One is the need to ensure that patients receive adequate care. Increasingly, foreign hospitals are seeking U.S. accreditation for both their facilities and their doctors, thereby ensuring that standards are the same as in America. It is also possible to negotiate ways to ensure that patients that suffer from malpractice receive compensation, either by having foreign facilities affiliate with domestic institutions who can be sued or by setting up impartial arbitration boards to hear cases and award compensation. The savings can be significant. Yet, despite the fact that treatment abroad can benefit both the health insurer and the patient, unions have opposed this trend even when willing members would be able to save thousands of dollars of their own money on the procedures.[38]

A final improvement would be to set up an alternative mechanism for resolving disputes about medical care. Although its flaws are often exaggerated, there is little doubt that the current system of medical malpractice imposes significant costs without providing timely recovery to those who are hurt by malpractice.[39]

Under the current system, injured patients must initiate a private lawsuit in order to seek compensation. Unless the case is clear cut, it can often take several years before the plaintiff is able to collect anything. A recent study shows that plaintiffs win only about one-half of the cases that expert reviewers think they should win.[40] In the cases where there is an award, attorneys' fees typically consume 30–40 percent of it, leaving the plaintiff with only a partial recovery. At the same time, the threat of a lawsuit imposes severe costs on all other doctors. Medical malpractice premiums for a general surgeon in Miami can equal $174,000 per year, causing many to move to cheaper states.[41] The result has been a shortage of specialists in some areas of the country. Although doctors frequently claim that lawsuits force them to practice defensive medicine by assigning additional procedures that are not medically indicated, a recent Congressional Budget Office report had a difficult time documenting this.[42] Part of the reason may have been that doctors already have a financial incentive to schedule additional care or that the threat of a suit in some cases causes doctors to avoid extending care, especially to high-risk patients. Neither explanation is a sign of health in the system.

At the same time, it can hardly be said that the medical profession has been vigilant about monitoring the quality it delivers to patients. The profession continues to suffer from a high number of medical accidents and hospital-induced infection rates.[43] Even getting doctors to wash their hands regularly can be a large problem.[44] There is often little pressure to conform to best-known practices. But most important, the profession does a terrible job of weeding out those professionals that are the greatest threat to patients. Even in cases where there is evidence that a doctor or nurse is intentionally murdering patients, hospitals have been slow to reach judgment and often merely dismiss the suspect from the hospital, leaving them free to go elsewhere.[45]

Common Good and the Harvard School of Public Health have proposed setting up independent administrative law judges with medical expertise to decide cases based on liberal standards of recovery, which allow patients to obtain an award if their injury was preventable, without having to prove malpractice. Such a system would be quicker and cheaper and, if truly independent, might result in more frequent awards to patients.[46] Part of the plan calls for the information leading to the injury to be widely disclosed so that the root error causing it could be corrected. Without such a practice, it is much harder to implement a process of continuous improvement across the industry. Moreover, there is some evidence that full disclosure, followed by a quick apology and offer of a fair settlement, can often reduce total malpractice costs. When the University of Michigan implemented such a policy, its medical malpractice suits fell by over 60 percent, and its cost per claim fell by more than half.[47]

The goal of public policy is not to lower total spending on health care, broadly defined. It may well be that in an increasingly affluent society where most individuals can easily afford all of the material goods they need, people choose to spend 50 percent or more of their incomes on ensuring they live several more decades in good health, assuming that new technologies let them. The goals are to make sure all Americans can afford basic health care, to ensure that they receive true value for whatever they spend on health care and to subject the sector to the same competitive pressures that have driven down real costs in other parts of the economy. In other words, while new technologies may come forward and justify new expenditures, we should expect the price of any given medical service to decline over time, even as its quality goes up. This can happen but only if health care spending is forced to compete with the broad range of goods and services available to the average consumer. This in return requires us to trust individuals with both the power and the incentive to make their own health care decisions.

8

HELPING PEOPLE ACHIEVE
FINANCIAL INDEPENDENCE

Life was much simpler when people died young. Few people needed to worry about saving for old age or finding something productive to do in retirement. In 1930 when Social Security was first created, the average life expectancy for a male infant was 57.7 years.[1] Since the retirement age for Social Security was set at sixty-five, the average American could not expect to receive it. In 1940, when the first monthly payments were made, only 6.3 percent of the population was over the age of sixty-five.[2] Five years later, there were 41.9 workers for every Social Security recipient,[3] thus the burden of supporting older Americans was relatively manageable. The total Social Security tax originally amounted to only 2 percent of payroll, and workers were told they only had to pay half of that; their employers would pay the rest.

According to Social Security's Board of Trustees, today's situation is much different.[4] In 2006 the period life expectancy for males at birth was 75 years and for females 79.7 years. Males aged 65 could expect to live another 16.5 years, while females had another 19.1 years to go. Meanwhile, the number of workers per retiree had declined to 3.3. The trustees expect these trends to continue. According to their most likely forecast, by 2050 males are expected to have a period life expectancy of 79.5 years at birth, and females 83.1 years. The number of workers per retiree will decline to 2.0. Some scientists believe technology will produce life expectancies that are much, much longer.[5]

We will discuss what this means for Social Security later. What it means for the nation is much clearer. We now live in a society where individuals should expect to live into their seventies. Most of them expect to spend several years at the end of their life in retirement. To do this they need a source of income that is not connected to current work. This can only take place if either the living standard of nonretirees is reduced or if sufficient savings are put aside now. Because the government serves as the default source of support, it has an interest in ensuring these individuals have adequate income in their old age. The development of sound saving and retirement programs is therefore an important element of any comprehensive social policy.

The retirement of today's workers is increasingly one of choice. In the 1930s, when a far greater proportion of workers were in physically demanding occupations such as agriculture and manufacturing, this meant that most might reach a point where they were physically unable to work. Today, far fewer workers are either on the farm or in the factories. Both proportions are likely to continue to decline in the future. In addition, much of the work in any area is increasingly mechanized, requiring far less physical exertion. A greater proportion of jobs in all sectors involves intellect and experience more than strength and stamina. The decision to stop working is therefore less a matter of pure inability.

In addition to dramatically reducing poverty among the elderly, Social Security helped to create the modern idea of retirement: that at a certain age such as sixty-five workers should expect to cease working and spend the rest of their days in idle leisure. This policy was motivated at least in part by the common belief, now discredited, that the economy could only create a certain number of jobs. By leaving the workforce, retirees therefore opened up their jobs to younger workers. Steady withdrawal at the top also created openings all along the career ladder and ensured that younger workers would receive regular promotions.

We now know that the demand for labor is not fixed. Like any scarce resource, the economy will eventually find a way to make use of productive people, whatever their skills. The process is neither instantaneous nor easy; all individuals have to find their own path toward productive labor that provides them with enough enumeration and personal satisfaction to make life interesting. The good news is that in an increasingly developed and diverse economy, an increased supply of unique and high-skilled jobs should make work an important element of self-expression for a large proportion of the population.

As a greater proportion of the population lives into their seventies and even eighties, neither they nor the nation can afford to have them sit as unproductive members of society. Even as unionized companies seek to downsize in order to reach a more competitive mix of capital and labor, other businesses are increasingly worried about losing some of their most skilled workers to retirement.[6] Half of all federal workers either are or soon will be eligible to retire.[7] Capturing the experience and institutional knowledge of these individuals is extremely difficult. As a result, companies are finding new ways of keeping them engaged in the workforce.[8]

If individuals save enough during their careers to be able to leave the workforce and live lives of self-indulgent leisure, the government certainly does not have the right to force them back to work just because society would be better off. But it is legitimate to question the common philosophy that says after a certain age individuals have no obligation to make any positive contribution to society and simultaneously discounts the prospective worth of many of the nation's most experienced citizens. While the independently wealthy may have a right to separate themselves from the concerns of those around them, they are not right to do so. In fact, many are voluntarily reentering the workforce in order to keep their lives interesting and productive.[9]

It should be remembered that most current retirees are not living on their own savings. Both Social Security and, to a large extent, defined benefit programs are funded from current revenues, not past savings. In other words, recipients did not save up foregone income or consumption in order to afford their current benefits. The payments are instead coming from younger generations who, through higher taxes or lower incomes, have to make good on promises that were made in the past. This fact should impose at least some moral duty on retirees to continue making a contribution to the society that sustains them.

This is especially true of individuals, often in the public sector, who are allowed to retire at age fifty-five. These workers have not paid for their own retirement in the form of wages foregone. As we will see later, state and local retiree benefits are seriously underfunded and are unlikely to be paid in full. To the extent that they are paid, a great deal of the burden will fall on current taxpayers. Many of these workers retire simply to be rehired to their current job as consultants or temporary workers, allowing them to collect both a salary and a pension. In Arizona a company called SmartSchoolsPlus hires retired teachers and then contracts them back to the schools, often in their same job.[10] The propriety of this practice depends on the current status of the pension reserves that fund the retirement payments. If the benefits are fully funded, there is a strong presumption that the workers have paid for their own retirement by receiving lower wages during their careers. In this case, the real problem is that pension systems do not contain enough flexibility to allow workers to defer their pension benefits until the age at which they would prefer to retire.

In many plans, workers lose benefits if they delay retirement. This can significantly reduce the marginal benefit of continuing to work. Let's say that at sixty-five a worker earning seventy thousand dollars is eligible for a pension of thirty thousand dollars per year if he or she retires. In that case, the benefit of working falls to forty thousand dollars. Since most pensions allow the worker to find another job elsewhere, the real benefit of staying at the current job becomes negative. If the worker finds another job that pays sixty thousand dollars, he or she can have a total income of ninety thousand dollars, but only by quitting the current job. Tax laws and the rules of specific pension plans complicate these calculations somewhat but do not change the basic result.

Thus, where pension plans are fully funded, it would make more sense to allow workers to return their pension to the pool and have it continue to grow until they need it. This would give individuals greater control over their own retirement and allow them to trade off additional years of work for a larger pension later in life. Alternatively, workers could move to part-time work at a lower salary and draw on only part of their pension, reserving the rest for later in life. Recently passed legislation that makes it easier for workers with defined benefit plans to have a phased retirement starting at age sixty-two goes partway toward this goal.

But the situation is much different for workers whose plans are under-funded. In these cases workers did not accept lower wages in return for setting aside enough funds to pay for the retirement benefits they were demanding; they merely passed the burden on to younger generations. Most of these cases occur in state or local governments and heavily unionized industries where the employer did not face much competitive pressure to keep wages aligned with productivity. In these cases, workers and employers knowingly created large contingent liabilities that they asked future workers, customers, and taxpayers to pay for. Society has no moral obligation to make these payments, except to the extent they are based on need. And if others are to pay for these benefits, then it should be done in the context of an overall compromise that addresses the structural weaknesses in the pension rules, including those that allow a full retirement at age fifty-five. In these cases it is entirely fair for an employer to raise the retirement age to sixty-five or higher to reflect increased longevity. Workers may still leave their present employment at age fifty-five or any time before or after, but they should not be allowed to earn a salary and take benefits out of a program that already lacks the resources to pay all the benefits it has promised.

This discussion naturally raises the question of just how sound America's pension plans are. The answer is mixed. Unless the growth rate of health care costs can be contained, the nation will be hard pressed to meet the health care promises that baby boomers have committed it to. Pension obligations, however, are more manageable.

The system of retirement income is often said to rest on three legs: Social Security, employer pensions, and personal savings. Each is weak in certain areas, but overall it should be possible to ensure everyone an adequate income through retirement, provided sensible reforms can be made. However, these weaknesses demonstrate the need for a more flexible, individualized system of savings that allows everyone to plan for their own retirement.

PRIVATE PENSIONS

The growth of private pensions was spurred in large part by two forces. The first was the same confluence of wartime controls on wages and preferable tax treatment for nonsalary benefits that encouraged the growth of employer-paid health coverage. During World War II, employers could not offer higher wages in order to attract workers. But they could promise better pension benefits. Better yet, unlike wages, the money needed to fund these benefits did not have to be set aside at the time the benefits were promised. Because companies had relatively few workers with full retirement benefits, they normally paid benefits out of current earnings.

The second major force was unionized labor. Unions have come to favor employer pensions for several reasons. First, they give unions a continuing influence over retirees. Although unions do not formally represent retirees, they have in the past regularly negotiated higher pensions and health care benefits for existing as well as future retirees. Second, in those cases where control of the pension funds was shared with the union, it provided a source of patronage and even graft. Third, by giving workers a collective voice with which to pressure employers, unions have spurred the growth of pension benefits even in companies that are facing severe competitive pressures. When a company is struggling financially, it is seldom able to pay higher wages to its workers. Absent a union, workers might not have much recourse other than to leave for better paying jobs if they can find them. Unions, however, face pressure to obtain continued gains to take back to their members. In the past, they have conspired with companies by agreeing to increase future benefits, even in cases where the pension funds are already underfunded and the company has little prospect of being able to increase its contributions to the plan. A number of companies have agreed to increase the pension benefits of their workers even when they clearly have no prospect of being able to pay the benefits they have already promised.[11]

The government has actually encouraged this practice by providing subsidized insurance for many private pension benefits. In 2008, the federal Pension Benefits Guarantee Corporation (PBGC) guaranteed pension benefits up to a maximum amount of $51,750 for workers who retired at sixty-five.[12] The benefit is much less for workers who retire at a younger age, however. As a result, even with pension insurance, many workers suffer a decline in their benefits when their employer's pension fund fails. The PBGC charges companies an annual premium for each participant for this insurance, but these premiums are below the level that a private company would charge for similar insurance. As a result of federal insurance, unions have felt less need to make sure their company's pensions are adequately funded or that employers are making adequate payments into the fund. And both companies and unions have resisted efforts to increase either the funding requirements or the insurance premiums, arguing they will push companies into terminating their plans, leaving the government to make up the difference.[13]

Although Congress has periodically changed the laws to deal with pension underfunding, it has never addressed the central problem of requiring companies to fully fund the obligations that they make to their employees or requiring employees, especially through their unions, to take responsibility for making sure that employers put aside money when promises are made, even if it comes at the expense of higher pay raises. Since 1974 the federal government has required most private organizations to at least partially fund their pension obligations and to purchase federal pension insurance from the PBGC. In addition, public companies are now required to disclose their pension obligations in their financial statements.

But in many ways the federal government has also encouraged the problem of underfunding. The law gives companies several years to fund new pension benefits, meaning that companies that promise frequent increases in pension benefits may steadily increase their pension fund's liabilities much faster than they increase its assets. On the opposite end, because contributions to pension funds reduce tax revenues, the government has also limited a company's ability to fully fund its obligations even when it wants to. Pension insurance has been priced far too low and has not fully reflected the risk that individual companies pose. Recent changes in the law only partially correct this. Finally, the accounting rules have allowed companies to misrepresent the financial health of their plans. Calculating the value of obligations that extend over several decades and that depend on future salary increases, rates of return, employee retention, and life expectancy can never be exact. But by manipulating assumptions, companies have consistently portrayed their pensions as being better funded than they actually are. This misleads both pension beneficiaries and investors.

Yet reform efforts have often been opposed by the very beneficiaries they are meant to help. Unions have recognized that actually making companies set aside funds as promises are made will reduce their willingness to make these promises. As a result they have often lobbied for weaker funding requirements and against full risk-based premiums for federal pension insurance.

There are no good reasons federal policy should support employer pensions. Although pensions can offer some benefits to employers, they offer few to employees when compared to individual retirement plans that are under the control of the worker. For employers, pension benefits can offer a valuable retention tool. In traditional defined benefit plans, pension benefits are typically based on a worker's final salary and the number of years worked in that firm. As a result, workers earn most of their benefits during their final few years with the firm. A worker who spends thirty years with one firm earns a much better retirement than an identical worker who works ten years with each of three firms. For the employer, such a tool can serve to tie the employee to the firm, thus protecting the employee's expertise and knowledge. The arrangement may actually save the employer from having to pay higher wages at the end of careers, when workers are most productive, because workers will lose significant pension benefits if they leave for another firm. On the opposite side, however, these same pension benefits increase workers' costs of remaining with the firm after they become eligible for full retirement. For this reason some firms will always find it in their interest to offer a defined benefit program as part of the overall package of pay and benefits that they use to attract and retain good employees.

Increasingly, however, defined benefit plans do not even benefit employers. In an increasingly competitive world, firms cannot afford to have high fixed costs or make long-term commitments that are not tied to their actual profitability. In the first three decades after World War II, books like William H. Whyte's *The Organization Man*[14] and John Kenneth Galbraith's *The New Industrial State*[15] described an economy increasingly dominated by a few large permanent oligopolies that faced limited competition and heavy regulation. This vision made it easy to believe that government and unions could saddle these corporations with a variety of long-term fixed obligations, which they could pay for out of future earnings rather than by cutting current production. Capital was less mobile, so the owners had few other places to go. Regulation often protected companies and their profits from competition, so managers could pass extra costs on to consumers. And the pace of innovation was relatively predictable, meaning that adjustments could be planned as needed.

None of these is true now. Many of the largest companies have gone bankrupt or been taken over. New companies, both foreign and domestic, have risen to compete, offering innovative products and lower costs. Government deregulation has brought enormous benefits to consumers but has exposed companies like Pan Am in airlines, Greyhound in passenger bus service, and Pacific Intermountain Express in trucking to new competitors that were not burdened with high average wages and pensions going decades forward. The result was predictable. Firms with large future liabilities to retirees are always subject to a competitive challenge from other firms that start with a new, younger workforce. Firms increasingly need to continually invest in new technology, and they must compete for these funds in global capital markets. Companies in today's environment cannot promise future profitability to either their shareholders or their employees. As a result, promises about future pension or health care benefits are meaningless unless money is put away now to fund them. But if money is put away now, that money largely comes out of workers own paychecks, in which case it makes more sense to leave funds in workers' control so that they are not dependent on the viability of their current employer thirty or forty years from now.

If defined benefit plans make little sense for companies, they make less sense for workers. Until the 1980s the argument could be made that collective pensions at least gave workers the ability to participate in portfolio investment by proxy. Prior to that, most individuals had a limited ability to earn high rates of return on their savings. The federal government prohibited banks from paying interest on many deposits, and few individuals had enough income to compile a balanced portfolio of investments that would sufficiently diversify risk. Those who did buy stocks were therefore dependent on the performance of a few companies. The emergence of mutual funds changed this, however. Individuals with limited means can now create a diversified portfolio managed by experienced professionals for a management fee of less than 1 percent of their balance. Alternatively, they can purchase an index fund that automatically tracks the market for them. Thanks to deregulation, transaction fees for buying and selling stock have plummeted, making individual investing more affordable as well.

Defined benefit plans do protect workers against the risk that they will exhaust their benefits by living longer than expected. But they do so at the cost of making the worker dependent on the firm's future viability. The plans also limit the mobility of workers and unfairly discriminate against individuals who change jobs several times during their career. The economy grows fastest when workers move to the firms where their skills are valued most. Worker mobility has already increased a great deal over the past decades due to the increased pace of economic change, which presents workers with both risk and opportunity. If a new job offers a worker more pay and a better future, she or he should be free to take it without worrying about unrelated factors such as health care or savings. The best way to ensure this is to vest control of both in a portable system under the worker's control.

While some workers have benefited from defined benefit pensions, others have suffered large losses when companies and unions have not fulfilled their promises. The risk has been greatest in those cases where a large portion of the pension fund was invested in the company itself. Workers at Corning had a large part of their pensions invested in the company beyond their control and had to watch as the value of the firm fell from $113 to $1 within a few months.[16] Joy Whitehouse lost her husband's death benefits when Pacific Intermountain Express went bankrupt after trucking deregulation.[17] Workers at Bethlehem Steel watched as their union repeatedly fought for higher wages or job protections rather than for higher contributions to the pension plan, which would have protected the benefits they were already promised. In none of these cases did workers have the ability to control their own destiny by withdrawing the pension funds and investing them on their own.

At the same time, pension laws are often used to give executives far greater pensions than they have actually earned. Drew Lewis, former chairman and CEO of Union Pacific Corp. was awarded a pension based on thirty years of service, when in fact he had only been with the company for eleven years.[18] Without the protection of the pension laws, the board of directors might still have awarded him the money in the form of a lump-sum payment, but Lewis would have at least had to pay tax on the full amount of it.

Over the past several decades, companies have been moving away from defined benefit programs toward either defined contribution programs, in which the employer makes an annual contribution to the employees' account but does not guarantee the final payout, or cash benefit plans, in which the employer guarantees a certain rate of return to the employee's retirement fund, but the employee can transfer the fund if she or he moves to another job. Each has been criticized as exposing workers to more risk, and

leaving them with lower pensions than if they had stayed in a traditional defined benefit plan their whole career. But this comparison ignores the fact
that employees will increasingly move from job to job, especially early in
their career, thus losing any benefits from the traditional plans. It also assumes away the risk of tying the employee's retirement income to the continued competitiveness of a single firm.

The latter risk is especially great. By one estimate, pension funds for
the S&P 500 companies were underfunded by over two hundred billion
dollars in 2003.[19] Many troubled plans are run by companies that are currently facing financial difficulty, making it unlikely that they will be able to
make the future contributions required to pay promised benefits. The
PBGC, which takes over terminated funds, estimates that 90 percent of
beneficiaries receive all the benefits that were promised to them under their
former plan.[20] Although this figure is high, PBGC is currently experiencing its own financial difficulties, raising the possibility that the government
might reduce its guarantee in the future.

State and local pension plans are often in worse shape. Unlike private
plans, benefits are often set according to political influence, not the economic ability to pay. Although unions have repeatedly pressed for new benefits, they have felt little responsibility to ensure that the funds needed to
pay for them are actually set aside. During the Pataki administration, New
York State repeatedly enacted increased benefit levels that its cities could not
afford.[21] According to one estimate, state and local pensions are underfunded by a total of seven hundred billion dollars.[22] The level of neglect is
often shocking. The West Virginia Teachers Pension is only 31.6 percent
funded and has an unfunded accrued liability of $4.7 billion.[23]

There is a common assumption that these benefits are sacrosanct, even
if a city or state declares bankruptcy, because of court opinions and state
constitutions. This complacence is misplaced, however.[24] Governments are
increasingly unable to impose draconian budget cuts or significant tax increases in order to pay for past benefits, even if a court orders them to, and
at some point citizens will refuse to pay higher taxes. Political opposition
can quickly undo assurances that once seemed inviolable. In addition, the
most prosperous businesses and citizens are increasingly able to move to jurisdictions that do not face large liabilities. Jurisdictions can therefore find
that a sudden deterioration in their financial position sparks a negative
cycle where spending cuts and tax increases drive away businesses and residents, leading to a further deterioration in their finances. Financial difficulties can also cause rating agencies to downgrade a jurisdiction's bond rating,
increasing the cost of borrowing funds for necessary investment in schools

and infrastructure. Governments are not immune from the competitive forces that swept away giants in the steel, airline, and automotive industries. As proof, we need only look at the shift in economic growth from the industrial states in New England and the Rust Belt to those in the South and Southwest.

In sum, future pension benefits can only be secured if they are fully funded when promised. But in that case, economic studies show that most of the funding comes out of worker salaries in the near term. So workers are in effect paying for these benefits themselves. And there are some reasons to think that, given the realities of how pay and pension benefits are set, centralized pensions will result in pay being held down most for those workers who have the fewest skills and pensions being highest for those who have the most influence. To the extent that this is true, collective pensions are likely to be regressive, benefiting older and more experienced workers more. In this case, it is wise to give workers control over their own pensions, freeing them of dependence on the decisions of others.

SOCIAL SECURITY

The second leg of the retirement system is Social Security, or more accurately the Old-Age and Survivors Insurance part of the program. This is the part that pays normal Social Security benefits. It is important to distinguish this from the Disability Insurance program, which is also administered by the Social Security Administration. Although the disability program has serious flaws, neither it nor Supplemental Security Income payments are included in most proposals for Social Security reform. Thus, efforts to reform or privatize Social Security do not affect the disability insurance that workers receive. This does not mean that the programs should not be examined. Under an ideal system, neither Disability Insurance nor state Workers' Compensation programs would be needed; injured workers would be completely compensated by a combination of health and life insurance.

Looking at just the Old-Age and Survivors program then, it is becoming increasingly difficult to argue that Social Security benefits the average worker. Part of the difficulty is that the program suffers from the interplay of three conflicting goals. On the one hand, Social Security is meant as a personal savings plan, albeit under government mandate. Thus, each worker is given an account into which she or he must make regular payments from each paycheck. Although half of these payments come directly from the employer, we have seen that almost the entire burden is passed down to employees in the form of lower wages. So, it is only technically incorrect and not at all misleading to say that workers pays roughly 10.8 percent of their salary into a program that is sold as being primarily for their own retirement. For self-employed workers, the fiction that someone else bears half the burden is harder to sustain, as they must pay the full 10.8 percent directly. Yet, as a pension system, Social Security does a very poor job. It is true that past generations received far more in benefits than they paid in taxes, thereby receiving a very high rate of return on their "contributions." But the same is not true of current workers. Under current law, a low-income worker born in 1973 is promised a real rate of return of only 2.99 percent.[25] If the worker is married but his or her spouse does not work, an increasingly rare situation for low-income households, the rate of return rises, but only to 5.1 percent. For medium-income workers the rates of return are even lower. A worker investing in a well-diversified portfolio consisting of stocks and bonds should expect to earn a substantially higher rate of return over the course of her or his career.

Proponents of Social Security will argue that its benefits are risk free, justifying the lower return. This misleads. First, the risk associated with prudent investing over a period of several decades is relatively low. Second, it is well known that under current law Social Security will not be able to pay out all of the claims against it. By the time a worker born in 1985 retires, the program will be able to pay only 75 percent of the worker's benefits, assuming that the government credits all of the interest promised on the Trust Fund.[26] Reforms, whether they are tax increases or benefit cuts, will lower the rate of return that beneficiaries receive even further. Although upper- and middle-income workers will bear most of the burden, even low-income workers are likely to see their rate of return fall.

Opponents of reform often argue that the program is not in crisis. They miss the point. It is true that, according to the Trustee's latest report, Social Security will not exhaust its trust fund until 2041, but beneficiaries are likely to be impacted long before then. Social Security's Trust Fund consists solely of government bonds. If, instead, it contained the stocks and bonds of private companies, these assets could be sold to pay promised benefits without affecting the rest of the government. It is true the value of these assets might fluctuate up or down in value, probably up if invested wisely, but the federal government could bear this risk. There might also be disagreements about whether to spend all of this wealth on Social Security or divert some of it to other pressing national needs.

However, the government bonds currently in the Trust Fund cannot be used without (1) selling debt to the public, (2) cutting spending, or (3) raising taxes. Social Security currently brings in more money than it spends. In 2006 this surplus amounted to over $185 billion. So it is no surprise that the pressure to reform it is relatively weak, and many who see the need for reform are content to wait. Beginning in 2017, however, Social Security will begin contributing to the federal deficit as it tries to spend the bonds in its Trust Fund. At this point, the political dynamics are likely to change, and Social Security is likely to have to compete with every other federal priority, including defense, health care, and income support. The reluctance to run large deficits or raise taxes is unlikely to lessen just because Social Security is now drawing down its reserves, nor is the political support in favor of various other spending programs likely to fall.

A common response to this argument is that the federal government will never default on the bonds issued to the Trust Fund. True enough, but again that misses the point. Although Congress will not default, by cutting benefits it can delay the time when the bonds are cashed in, thereby relieving pressure on the rest of the budget. The question is not whether the bonds will be honored; it is when. Congress could delay retirement by ten years and cut benefits in half without ever reneging on a single bond in the Trust Fund. They would all continue to sit safely in the fund until Congress decides to spend them.

Social Security's weakness as a pension plan is often excused by its need to fulfill a second goal: redistributing income to poorer workers. Any serious reform of the program is likely to tilt it further toward this goal, at the expense of pension fairness. Yet even here Social Security now does a poor job. For one thing, even low-income workers now receive less from Social Security than they could get if they invested the funds in a balanced portfolio. If the concern really is the residual risk from the private sector, the government could collect the money itself but then invest in private equities and at the end of the worker's career present him or her with an annuity equal to the value of the fund. When even low-income workers come off worse than they would with a private account, just who is the program helping?

Even if we look only at the distribution of actual benefits among people born in a given year, the system is less progressive than many people assume. Social Security pays benefits for as long as a retiree lives. Since workers with higher incomes tend to live longer, they will receive benefits for more years. If every worker received the same monthly benefit, this fact would mean that the benefits-to-taxes ratio for the highest-income workers born in 1960 would be about 30 percent more than the ratio for those at the bottom.[27] In fact, Social Security does replace a higher proportion of monthly income for poor workers than it does for middle- and upper-income workers. Does the impact of longevity outweigh the progressivity in the program's monthly benefit levels? Studies differ depending upon the assumptions and populations they use. The Congressional Budget Office determined that, for workers born in 1960, the retired worker benefits were still progressive, with low-income workers receiving a benefit-to-cost ratio that was about three times that of the highest-income workers, although the curve is steepest at either end of the income distribution and close to flat for the middle third of workers.[28] A study by Eugene Steuerle and Jon Bakija found that within-generation redistribution was regressive for most past and current generations but turns strongly progressive for most people retiring in the distant future.[29] A recent survey of the literature finds that studies that take the various factors into consideration "find that Social Security is, at the least, not very progressive and might in fact be regressive—transferring money from the poor to the rich!"[30] Of course, individuals who die prior to retirement have nothing to leave their families. It is true that survivor's benefits pay something, but this function merely duplicates the purpose of private life insurance.

Why has Social Security done such a poor job of fulfilling its two main goals? Largely because of a third, unwritten purpose that the program has largely met: to transfer income between generations. Social Security was set up as a pay-as-you-go system in which payroll taxes from each working generation went, not to save for their own retirement, but rather to pay benefits to preceding generations now in retirement. In return, they could look to their children and grandchildren for their own retirement. The first generations to receive Social Security therefore received far more than they paid in. In addition, benefits were regularly increased by Congress. The rationale was that succeeding generations were likely to be richer than current workers and could therefore afford to share part of their higher incomes with retirees, who presumably had financed their education and helped build the financial, physical, and social infrastructure that made economic growth possible.

Now, however, the assumptions on which the New Deal was built are falling apart. The current workforce is increasing at a slower rate, and the ratio of workers to retirees has fallen. Even if future workers are richer, it is increasingly doubtful they will want to spend 15–20 percent of their income on people they do not know, especially when the benefits are not means-tested. They will know that their prospect of receiving significant benefits from Social Security is much less secure. Most objections to Social Security reform assume that the social contract that held when payroll taxes were relatively modest and benefits were high will continue to hold when the reverse is true.

The basic problem with Social Security can be seen from the fact that even the poorest workers entering the job market today would be better off if they saved 10.4 percent of their income than if they paid into Social Security, even if future benefits are not cut. In fact, if economic growth occurs at the pace that Social Security's trustees predict, saving this proportion of their income is likely to make them self-sufficient by the time they are seventy. Why should their ability to accomplish this be jeopardized by a program ostensibly aimed at helping people like them live a comfortable retirement?

The government has already committed to paying current retirees significant benefits. Any attempt to allow current generations to divert their payroll taxes into private accounts would create further financial difficulty for Social Security. In essence, present workers would be asked to support both current retirees and themselves. But to a large degree this is likely to happen anyway. It is a necessary consequence of moving from a system of intergenerational transfers to one in which workers are allowed to benefit from and control their own savings, without depending on decisions made by the government or their employer. The burden of this transition should fall on those who can bear it best.

PRIVATE SAVINGS

The third leg of traditional savings programs has been private savings. Although the government stresses the importance of individuals saving for themselves, it often makes it difficult to do so. The government should adopt a much simpler approach to private savings that encourages people to put money away, even temporarily.

Over the past several decades, there has been a great deal of concern that Americans are not saving enough. According to the traditional measure of savings, personal savings as a percent of disposable personal income has fallen from 10.0 percent in 1980 to 0.4 percent in 2006. The chairman of the Federal Reserve, Ben Bernanke, has expressed the opinion that a combination of too little saving in the United States and excessive savings in Asia has been a major cause of the nation's balance of payments deficit.[31] Others take it as a sign that many Americans will not have the resources necessary for a secure retirement.

There are some reasons to think that the official savings rate underestimates the degree of asset creation in the country, especially when compared with several decades ago. Most Americans have far less need to save today than in the past. For one thing, incomes are higher, so a smaller percentage of income is needed to afford a modest level of living in retirement. More important, one of the major purposes of savings used to be for the purchase of expensive items such as a house, car, or vacation. The rising sophistication of financial markets makes it possible for almost all Americans to obtain credit for these purchases, paying for them out of future earnings rather than past savings. Although the availability of credit raises debt levels and lowers savings, it is not clear that it reduces national welfare. In addition, individuals may have reasonable expectations of support, such as life and health insurance, outside of their personal savings. Despite the risk of non-payment, individuals may also save less because they anticipate receiving a pension or Social Security. In an early study, Martin Feldstein concluded that the availability of Social Security reduced personal savings by between 40 and 50 percent.[32] Younger workers in the middle and upper classes are likely to inherit large amounts of money from their parents, by some estimates two hundred billion dollars annually, although the size of the average inheritance may not appreciably alter the wealth of the person who receives it.[33] Finally, many workers anticipate receiving assistance from their children, just as they paid for their children's education. In fact, the family, rather than the government, should still be seen as the primary source of support for the elderly poor. Children ought to have a legal obligation, as they do in Singapore, to support their parents in old age, absent a showing of earlier neglect.[34]

The official measure of savings also does not capture all items that people normally associate with the term.[35] For one thing, it does not measure the capital appreciation in company stock or houses. Yet it is the final balance of assets, rather than the annual contributions, that ultimately matters to a retiree.

The federal tax code contains a number of provisions to encourage people to save. Collectively, these cost the federal government over one hundred billion dollars in lost tax revenue in 2006.[36] It is not clear that these subsidies have had a strong effect on encouraging more savings.[37] Federal policy would be more effective, especially in helping low-income individuals save, if it was simpler and gave individuals more flexibility. The largest tax break for savings is the reduced marginal tax rate for capital gains. The provision rewards individuals for foregoing consumption by taxing the appreciation of capital assets at the relatively low marginal rate of 15 percent. Of course, this break does not help the poorest workers, who already have even lower marginal rates. And we shall see in chapter 9 that it distorts important incentives in the financial markets. Other savings incentives also benefit higher-income individuals relatively more than lower-income taxpayers.

Most other tax provisions are unnecessarily restrictive. With a few exceptions, savings in an Individual Retirement Account or a 401(k) can only be used for retirement income; otherwise, individuals must pay a penalty for withdrawing their money. In order to reduce tax losses, the government actually requires workers to begin withdrawing the money at a certain age, whether they need it or not. Similarly, 429 plans can only be used for educational purposes, and Medical Savings Accounts must be used for heath care expenses. Although there is some evidence that individuals naturally compartmentalize savings and investment decisions, it is not clear why these findings should drive government policy. Certainly, there is little excuse for the multiplicity of savings plans or the complicated regulations that surround them.

Government policy should encourage savings by allowing individuals to avoid taxation on any money that they put into an identified savings vehicle and by allowing all earnings in that plan to remain untaxed until withdrawn. Some people have objected that this provision would unnecessarily benefit the rich because they can save more, both in absolute terms and as a proportion of their income. They point out that there is little evidence that tax preferences increase individual savings.

There are two answers to this. The first is that, assuming all savings are exhausted by the time an individual dies, it is quite possible that savings plans increase the long-term tax revenue that the government receives. It is true that the federal government loses revenue in the short term, but it can fill this deficit at a lower cost than anyone else by issuing bonds. Meanwhile, the savings will be earning a rate of return that on average is likely to be significantly higher than the government's cost of borrowing. Assuming the individual faces the same marginal tax rate at all times, the final taxes paid on the account will grow faster than the government's obligation on its debt. Although the government might have to wait decades to collect, as the world's largest financial entity it is well positioned to bridge the time gap.

To prevent perpetual accretions of wealth, savings and assets could be taxed at the normal income rate at death, before passing onto heirs. Rather than a separate tax on estates, the tax would merely represent the delayed payment of regular tax on the income. One of the rationales for an estate tax is that it compensates for the fact that heirs are allowed to avoid paying capital gains taxes on many assets. Without an estate tax, many of the wealthiest families would escape all taxation on most of their wealth since heirs are allowed to substitute the market value at death for the original basis, ensuring that when they sell the asset, tax will be paid on only a fraction of the total rise in value since it was originally acquired. Elimination of the estate tax should be accompanied by a removal of the tax-free step-up in basis, and the death of the owner should be considered a taxable event, ensuring that tax is paid on the full appreciation since purchased. Unlike the death tax, such a policy would be just a special application of regular tax provisions.

The social contract requires individuals benefiting from it to save 15 percent of their income. It is worth remembering that even the poorest worker is now required to pay 10.4 percent of her or his salary into Social Security. Combining privatization of Social Security with the new contract would therefore require an additional savings of less than 5 percent. Eliminating Disability Insurance and Medicare and replacing them with adequate life insurance and the refundable tax credit for health insurance described in chapter 7 would eliminate even this gap. It is therefore possible to allow everyone to set aside 15 percent of their salary without reducing take-home pay from what it already is.

Of course, the transition away from existing programs is not painless. It entails two types of costs. This burden of these costs should be distributed in a progressive manner. Affected individuals can be divided into three groups. The first group is retirees who are already receiving Social Security and Medicare. Most reform proposals call for grandfathering these people in by preserving their benefits untouched. Changing benefits late in a worker's life certainly raises problems. Retirees have become used to a certain standard of living. Any reduction in existing benefits that is means-tested clearly penalizes those who were most frugal during their careers; the opposite of what public policy should normally do. But the transition away from heavy dependence on government-run programs necessarily involves pain, and it is not fair to impose all of this pain on younger generations who had no say in enacting the policies that created the problem. Some reduction in benefits should be made for those retirees who can afford it.

In return, present retirees become eligible for the social contract. As long as they are productively employed and meet the program's other requirements, they would qualify for the regular income subsidy. Of course, the meaning of productively employed can vary according to age and ability. And individuals over the age of sixty-five should be excused from the requirement to save 15 percent of their income. It would also probably be wise to allow an individual to work less than a full workweek in return for accepting a proportionate reduction in the government subsidy. This would ease phased retirements and give all workers greater flexibility in balancing work and other activities.

The second group is poorer workers. These individuals will lose Social Security and Medicare benefits, but unless they are currently very close to retirement, they are likely to lose some of these benefits anyway since both programs are financially unsustainable beyond the next twenty years in their current form. Congress will either cut benefits or raise taxes. Assuming that the transition costs fall mainly on the middle and upper classes, these workers should benefit strongly under the reforms called for in this book. This is especially true for the youngest workers. They will get to save the full portion of their current FICA taxes, while earning a higher return. In addition, the health insurance tax credit will make health care more affordable even before they would normally qualify for Medicare. And for the poorest workers, the benefits of the income subsidy would provide a financial floor that is well above what current programs provide.

For the youngest workers, being allowed to put the full FICA tax into a personal savings account goes a long way toward ensuring fiscal independence in retirement. Provided they saved 15 percent of their income, workers who started working at twenty-five and saw their real salary increase by 2 percent each year would have savings of approximately twelve times their final annual income by the time they were sixty-five provided they received a real rate of return of 5 percent each year. This would allow them to retire and live off their earnings, while still increasing their income after savings by 2 percent each year until they were eighty-one.

Of course, many workers will live into their eighties and nineties, raising the possibility that they will outlast their savings. Several points are important here. First, retirees usually need less income than workers. Second, many workers in this position will decide to transition out of work rather than retire suddenly. If they have control over the decision, they are likely to find themselves working longer than they might otherwise have thought because each year the idea of remaining actively employed, earning more income, and preserving more of their savings is likely to be relatively appealing. Only if they are forced to work longer with no compensation in the form of higher benefits later will they be likely to resent the decision. Third, many of the poorest workers will of course start working before the age of twenty-five and already are likely to work past sixty-five, so the difference in the longevity of their careers is less and the financial impact greater than for others.

The third group of people affected by the transition to a new system is middle- and upper-class workers. The burden of paying for any transition out of Social Security and Medicare will fall largely on them, as it should. According to the Trustees Report, the combined actuarial deficit for both programs in 2007 was $16.6 trillion, or just under 130 percent of the gross national product. For the younger generations, who had no say in creating these liabilities, the cost of transition is indeed unfair, but also largely inevitable. The programs will be reformed; the only question is in what direction and in what time frame. Those who do well in this country strongly benefit from a deep and diverse infrastructure built and maintained by others, including many of those they will be asked to support. There is an important balance between the need to maintain individual incentives and rewards on the one hand and the need to interject nonmonetary considerations into market outcomes on the other. As part of the cost of transitioning to a better system, those who have benefited most should be asked temporarily to bear a greater load. But this burden should not be imposed merely to prop up failing programs.

When combined with the income guarantee, the recommendations in this chapter have three goals. The first and most important is to involve even the poorest workers in the creation of wealth. By imposing the savings requirement as one of the conditions for receiving an income subsidy, the government ensures that each individual will gradually acquire significant assets that are not dependent on the whim of government or charities. Although the value of this wealth will fluctuate over time depending upon economic conditions and investment decisions, it is guaranteed to become large enough to represent a significant stake in how the economy and the nation do. Having wealth will likely change individual behavior. Although individuals should have the right to spend their savings in retirement, they would continue to be eligible for the income supplement as long as they are willing to meet its terms.

The second goal is to introduce the flexibility needed to ease the ongoing transition to a new concept of work and worth in a postindustrial economy. The current concept of retirement is not healthy. It creates an artificial divide between age groups that is largely a creation of government policy based on outdated concepts of the labor market, rather than a true reflection of individual desires. Currently, Social Security and private pensions give individuals a large incentive to retire around the age of sixty-five. In some workplaces, retirement is even mandatory. Yet if people have full control over the financial resources devoted to their retirement, they may well be more reluctant to begin spending their money. The decision to work another year, at least part time, becomes more attractive. Their transition away from work is likely to be more gradual than it is now. Conversely, when people anticipate being employed into their seventies, with an income supplement to ward off poverty, they may decide not to wait until their midsixties to make a career change, take time off, or transition into a much different lifestyle. If the traditional notion of retirement has given people an artificial goal that they can look forward to attaining, it has also kept many on a path ill-suited to them in hopes of crossing the finish line before they collapse.

The third goal is to affirm the essential dignity and worth of people of all ages. The income supplement remains open to all citizens above the age of twenty-one. To qualify, the individual needs to be productively employed. The contract affirms that any person of any age can and should meet this test. If we start with the premise that each human being has innate worth and a capacity to bestow benefit on others, then the challenge becomes finding a way to match this ability with someone else's need.

If the affluent wish to withdraw from life and live for their own purposes they have the right to do so. But that lifestyle should not be held up as the ideal goal any more than the lifestyle led by younger dilettantes such as Paris Hilton or Britney Spears. For others, the price of social support should be continued contribution throughout life. As our means grow, we may find that the need for support diminishes, and we may rely less on current income and more on our savings, giving us greater control over how we spend our days. But to the maximum extent possible, the last decades of our life should be among the most productive, both for us and society.

9

IMPLEMENTING A FAIRER, MORE EFFICIENT TAX SYSTEM

The broad programs described in this book cannot work as marginal additions to the existing structure of government. Each requires significant resources in order to give individuals the purchasing power in housing, education, health care, and savings that are necessary to turn markets toward satisfying the individual needs of all Americans, even those whose skills are not highly valued by the private sector. None can exist if the current structure of government tax and spending policy is kept in place.

Current tax policy is inherently flawed. One of the first principles of any fiscal system is that taxation should seek to provide simple but effective incentives to individual behavior. Current law does not do this.

From an economic point of view, the purest form of a tax would involve some combination of user fees and excise taxes that require individuals to pay for any identifiable government services that they use and burdens that they impose, combined with a uniform poll tax on each person to cover the cost of public services that cannot be easily divided, such as defense. Yet both types of taxes have often faced strong opposition. In the case of poll taxes, this opposition is probably fatal, even though a great deal of progressivity could still be built into the combined pattern of government taxes and spending. User fees, however, show some signs of strength.[1]

User fees hold promise both for placing the burden of specific government services on those individuals that use them and for providing a dedicated revenue stream to fund the services that people want. Thus, commuters might pay a daily fee that depends on how much they use public roads and on the congestion they contribute to when they use them. This would reward drivers that use the roads less or that switch their use to less congested times. It would also give the government resources that can be used to build additional infrastructure.

User fees cause individuals to react gradually, often in subtle ways, to the prices they pay. In this case, commuters might decided to come in fifteen minutes earlier or later to avoid peak time periods, or they might find a partner to ride with in order to split the cost. In general, user fees should be attached to any use of resources that imposes a cost on either government or the general society. If properly set, the fee causes individuals to internalize the cost of using the resource and therefore causes them to avoid overusing it. Fees also provide the government with revenue that it can use to expand the supply of the resource, at least to the point where the marginal cost equals the marginal benefit.

The second component of the ideal tax system is an equal per head tax on every person. The tax is ideal from an economic point of view because it avoids a distortion of economic motives. Linking taxation to a specific activity such as buying gas or owning a car normally causes people to engage in less of it because the cost to them rises. For example, an excise tax on cigarettes reduces smoking, especially among young people.[2] This type of taxation makes sense whenever the social cost of an activity exceeds its market price, causing people to engage in too much of the activity. But for similar reasons, imposing an income tax causes individuals to work less or migrate. Since income is closely linked to value created in a capitalist society, such a tax reduces total social welfare. A poll tax, if ever enacted, would have to wait until society reaches the point where every person has a substantial amount of income or where the burden of government is much lower than it is now. Economic efficiency is only one goal of tax policy. Fairness is another and may often justify some inefficiency. Nevertheless, government revenue should be collected with the twin views of simplicity and minimal economic distortion.

The deadweight loss of taxation imposes a special responsibility on government spending. Even the most ardent conservative would agree that some government spending is necessary, if only for defense and the administration of justice. As a result, some level of taxation is inevitable. But the fact that taxes reduce economic welfare imposes an obligation on government to try to ensure that the way in which the revenue is spent does not harm the economy even further. In some cases, government spending can actually increase national welfare by more than the deadweight loss. For example, government spending on national defense and internal justice provides the foundation upon which individuals can engage in mutually beneficial transactions with some assurance that contracts will be honored, long-term investments will pay off, and accumulations of wealth will not be appropriated by someone with more power. Federal spending on the national highway system, the Internet, and scientific research is also generally credited with creating large social welfare.[3]

As a matter of practicality the ideal tax system has never existed and never will. This is partly because tax policy is motivated by a number of social goals that sometimes conflict. As a result, the pursuit of one goal often comes at the cost of attaining another. Since the identity and weighting of these goals is at least partially subjective, reasonable people can easily differ on how to strike the correct balance. For instance, a fundamental principle of tax policy is horizontal equity, the idea that similar people should be treated similarly. Many people believe that progressivity, having people pay according to their ability, should be another. Yet a third goal is the idea that tax policy should reward people for doing things that benefit society. At first these goals do not seem to conflict, but let's assume that two individuals earn equal amounts at their jobs. If one saves half of what she earns and the other spends everything, how should they be treated? Horizontal equity could argue that, since each started equal except for the personal decisions they made, each should pay the same amount of total tax over their lives. Progressives could argue that, since the person who saved now presumably has a higher income, she should pay more tax, perhaps even at a higher marginal rate. Finally, someone concerned with economic growth could argue that, because the social benefits of saving exceed its private benefits, savings should be encouraged by giving savers a tax break so that they actually pay less tax than nonsavers.

Even the application of a single principle can create uncertainty. Take the principle of horizontal equity. In what circumstances should people be treated equally? If people start equal at birth should their lifetime taxes be equal? If one taxpayer has higher expenses for medical care or child care, should these differences be reflected in different tax payments? The mere principle of equity does not answer these questions.

Another reason tax policy is necessarily complex is that it has to be applied to an increasingly complex world. This is especially true of the corporate tax. Companies increasingly engage in widespread and complex transactions across different jurisdictions as part of their normal business. A computer manufacturer may operate in several countries in order to manufacture a computer sold in yet another country. Since most of the operations may be done within the same company, it is difficult to determine how much of the total income from the sale is earned in any one country. Companies also engage in increasingly complex financial transactions to raise capital and hedge risk. Tax law must then necessarily determine the value of and income from these varied instruments.

The problem is made worse when the government seeks to pursue social policy through the tax code. This is usually done by treating some income or transactions differently from others. Both corporations and individuals are quick to use differences in tax treatment for their own purposes, adding further complexity to their operations. For example, the tax exemption for charities requires the Internal Revenue Service (IRS) to issue lengthy regulations about what constitutes a charitable activity, the degree to which leaders of a charity can personally benefit from the organization's activities, and the activities an organization can engage in without losing its status. In addition, the IRS often has to take enforcement action against organizations that seek to disguise regular businesses as charities. For example, in recent years the IRS has investigated several credit counseling agencies for abuse of their tax status. In many cases, these organizations were providing little education, enriching officers, and resulting in very little social benefit to the broader community.

The regular practice of inserting special provisions into the tax code in order to promote social policies also makes it much easier for special interests to use political power to pursue their own agenda. The tax code is necessarily complex and so there are inevitably instances where the broad application of a simple provision might not reflect material differences in the real circumstances to which it is applied. From one perspective this can cause an injustice. However, the complexity of tax law ensures that few people understand it in any depth or follow the intricacies of tax regulation. Washington contains a whole industry of lobbyists whose main purpose is to insert technical language into tax legislation that will benefit their clients by either reducing their taxes or increasing those of their competitors. It is all but impossible for the average citizen to separate out those provisions that have some semblance of a legitimate financial or social purpose from those that exist solely because of the political power, privileged connections, or campaign contributions of the beneficiary. Opening up the tax code to this type of special interest pleading is likely to create far more injustice in how it is applied. Moreover, this injustice is likely to fall hardest on those with the least political power and the fewest financial resources.

If tax law is complex, its effects on the economy are even more difficult to measure. Certain things are known to a rough degree. The first is that the current system imposes enormous costs on the American economy. As explained above, taxes cause individuals to engage in less of whatever activities are taxed and to do more of whatever activities receive a subsidy. Although society is neither poorer nor richer when an individual transfers money to the government, it is poorer if the system of taxes causes people to engage in less productive behavior or if the government spends the money less efficiently than the taxpayer would. If we assume that people have a pretty good incentive and ability to engage in whatever action is optimal for them, then taxation, by changing this behavior, reduces social welfare. This burden increases as more taxes are raised. One study estimated that the marginal deadweight loss of raising another dollar through a proportional rise in all income taxes was nearly two dollars.[4] *In other words, for every dollar that the government collects in revenue, national income is reduced by two dollars.*

Taxes also impose large transaction costs on the economy. According to one estimate, Americans spend roughly $110 billion complying with the tax code, or about ten cents for every dollar raised.[5] This burden is spread very unevenly, however. Many lower-income Americans either do not have to file a tax return or can get by with a simple form. Individuals and corporations, especially those with complex finances, must often spend large sums simply to document, calculate, and file their taxes. One study estimated that the typical Fortune 500 Company spent $4.6 million on tax matters.[6] In 2006 the federal tax return of Berkshire Hathaway totaled 9,386 pages.[7] In many cases these businesses have no complete assurance of accuracy because the tax laws leave a great deal of room for interpretation. Not all compliance burdens fall on the rich, however. Many low-income individuals qualify for the Earned Income Tax Credit (EITC), which is ruled by complex regulations, requiring many beneficiaries to pay someone else to prepare their taxes. This reliance in turn has given the tax preparation industry an opportunity to target a variety of financial products such as refund anticipation loans to these people. Some consumer groups have criticized these products as predatory.[8]

Another issue with tax law is that the actual burden of a tax does not necessarily fall on the person who pays it. An excellent example of this is American citizens who are employees of the World Bank or International Monetary Fund. Employees of these two organizations are normally exempt from their national income taxes. Although the exemption does not apply to Americans, the organizations make a separate payment to Americans that compensates them for the taxes they pay. The payment is based on average tax rates, but if employees can demonstrate that their actual taxes were higher, the organizations will compensate them for the full amount. Raising income taxes on these individuals therefore has no effect on their personal finances. They will merely pass the additional payments on to their organization, which bears the cost of the tax.

Although few cases are this clean cut, others are pretty clear. For example, the owners of a corporation have several avenues through which they can try to pass on the cost of any tax imposed on them. They can attempt to slow the growth of pay raises for their employees or raise the cost that consumers must pay for their product. They can shift production to lower-cost states or countries, often using subsidiaries or joint ventures. Or they can demand compensating payments from another level of government in order to continue doing business in their jurisdiction. As has been discussed above, there is a strong consensus that most of the burden of the employer's share of Social Security taxes actually falls on employees as a group.

In general, it is likely that most of the burden of any tax will ultimately fall on those with the fewest choices or the least power. If the government raises the tax liability of a CEO by one hundred thousand dollars, how likely is it that the next year the compensation committee of his board of directors will raise his pay by an equal amount to compensate him? Conversely, if the government requires the employer of a worker making twenty thousand dollars to pay more payroll taxes on the worker's existing salary, how likely is the worker to get a raise of any kind the next year?

Determining the burden of taxes is equally important in corporate taxes. Obviously, the total burden of taxes ultimately falls on individuals, not fictional legal entities such as corporations. In some way, shareholders, consumers, and workers must collectively pay whatever tax we assign to any organization. Of course, some of this burden may fall on foreign individuals through their dealings with the corporation. The common assumption is that the burden of the tax falls on shareholders, since they are the ultimate owners of the company. But this need not be true, especially in the long run. Companies increasingly compete in a global market for capital, meaning that, once they are adjusted for the risk of the business, long-run rates of return cannot depart very much from the global average. If returns are too low, either the company will have a hard time attracting the capital it needs to stay competitive or it will shift production to more favorable areas. If returns are too high, additional capital will flood into the market, depressing returns. Granted, capital is not completely mobile, but to the extent that it is, investors are likely to escape the burden of taxes. In this case, either revenue will not be collected because there is less productive investment, or the burden of the tax will be shifted to consumers and workers.

TAXATION IN THE UNITED STATES

The American tax system has been described by one expert as broken.[9] Rather than a simple and fair way to collect needed revenues as efficiently as possible, the system has become a quagmire of social engineering and special interests, encouraging a type of competition that brings out the worst in lobbyists and politicians alike. Special tax provisions now account for one-fourth to one-third of the total benefits and subsidies granted by government.[10] In Eugene Steuerle's words, "To understand housing, welfare, health, energy, or almost any government policy, you have to look at what is going on in the tax code."[11]

Both Democrats and Republicans should be largely dissatisfied with current tax policy. From a Democratic perspective, the tax is barely progressive, especially with regard to payroll taxes, which are the main source of revenue for those parts of the government that are growing the fastest. As figure 9.1 shows, the tax system as a whole is not obviously progressive, except in the grossest sense. The figure shows the total marginal tax faced by a couple with two children at each income level. Although the lowest-

Figure 9.1   Effective Marginal Tax Rates for a Married Couple With Two Children in 2005

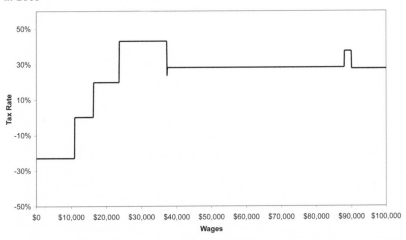

Source: Congressional Budget Office, *Effective Tax rates on Labor Income*, Washington D.C., November 2005

income individuals receive a net subsidy from the EITC and certain refundable tax credits, marginal tax rates rise steeply at relatively low levels of income, largely because many of the tax benefits phase out as a worker's income rises. At certain points, the marginal rate actually falls with higher income, most significantly when individuals hit the earnings cap on Social Security taxes. If the impact of benefit reductions in spending programs such as housing vouchers that are not administered through the tax code are taken into account, the marginal rates on the poor would be even higher. Finally, as we have discussed, economic realities associated with burden shifting may mean that the graph actually understates the lack of progressivity.

The tax code also fails to capture a large portion of the nation's income. Joel Slemrod and Jon Bakija estimate that roughly 18 percent of all personal and income tax is not paid due to tax evasion, resulting in $223 billion in unpaid taxes in 2002, not including taxes not paid on illegal income.[12] Even without deliberate avoidance, the system is very inefficient at capturing all income, especially capital gains. Slemrod and Bakija estimate that the personal income tax covered only 16 percent of the total capital gains realized by individuals and nonprofit organizations between 1985 and 2001.[13] On the other hand, some capital gains are taxed twice, first as income to the corporation that originally earns them and then as income to the individual who holds the stock. Other gains represent compensation for inflation and, from a purely economic perspective, should never be taxed. Overall, the authors conclude that the total amount of capital gains that was taxed during that period was slightly larger than what should have been taxed looking at economic income.[14] But the result represented massive compensating errors, with some capital gains facing too much taxation and others facing none or very little.

Tax law also does a poor job of achieving horizontal equity, or treating similar people similarly. Again, to some extent this is the result of deliberate policy choices. As Slemrod and Bakija point out, "Even among families of the same level of affluence, the tax burden can differ widely depending on whether family members are married, how many dependent children they have, how much they give to charity, whether they own or rent housing, and whether their income is mostly from wages or salaries or from capital gains."[15]

To a large extent the inequality is an unintended consequence of the tax code's complexity. Different provisions interweave in such unpredictable ways that unintended consequences are inevitable. Another expert concludes that "government seems to have limited ability to prevent new 'tax shelters' born of complex forms of arbitrage. . . . Tax professionals' growing skillfulness in exploiting every differential in the tax system, the computerization of tax accounting, and the emergence of split-second electronic transfers of billions of dollars all perpetuate the tax shelter crisis."[16]

Liberals have also become caught in a trap. The demand for higher government spending of all kinds creates a need for greater revenue, which in turn must of necessity reach down to the lower and middle classes. Although higher taxes on the rich will bring in a few more billions of dollars, it will not substantially change the financial structure of the federal government. The current size of government and the flexibility of global markets prevent a tax system that is dramatically progressive. The dilemma is most clear in the case of Social Security, where the Democratic Party by itself created a regressive tax system and is now left arguing for a marginal tax hike of over 10 percentage points on a large section of the middle class in order to partially address the program's long-term deficit. At the same time, the high marginal tax rates faced by low-income Americans serve as a strong impediment to economic advancement.

Taxes and spending need to be viewed as a whole when progressivity is measured. A tax that on its surface looks slightly regressive may be preferable from a liberal standpoint if it is clear who the ultimate burden falls on, if it minimizes collection costs and economic distortions, and if it supports spending programs that are clearly progressive. But making these judgments is extremely difficult when both tax and spending policy is riddled with special provisions that benefit one narrow group or another and when policy decisions are made one bill at a time, in isolation from any broader policy goals.

Figure 9.2 shows that, despite periodic tax cuts and tax hikes, overall federal revenue has remained surprisingly level over the last five decades, averaging around 18 percent of gross domestic product (GDP). Significant departures either way have quickly been reversed by a combination of policy changes and economic forces. The composition of taxes has changed, however. The individual income tax rose sharply during World War II and has remained high since then. It reached a high point of 10.3 percent of GDP in 2000 but then declined to 7.0 percent by 2004 before rising back to 8.0 percent in 2006. Corporate taxes also rose significantly after World War II but have since declined. In 2004 they amounted to only 1.2 percent of GDP. Strong corporate profits have since caused them to rebound to 2.7 percent of GDP, a level not seen since 1978. It is unlikely they will stay at this level, however. Excise taxes have declined in importance as a source of revenue. The most dramatic growth in recent decades has come from payroll taxes, which rose steadily every decade until 1990. Since then they have usually

Figure 9.2   Composition of Federal tax Revenues as a Percent of GDP

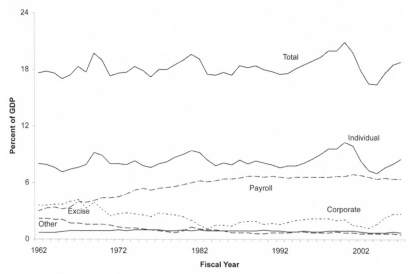

Source: Office of Management and Budget

hovered between 6.6 and 6.7 percent of GDP. Again, the regressive nature of the payroll tax and its explicit linkage to the government's two largest spending programs significantly complicates the task of collecting and distributing federal funds in a way that is both progressive and efficient.

Conservatives have cause to dislike the tax system because of the many ways in which it discourages economic growth. These include the large distortions in economic efficiency associated with deadweight losses and heavy compliance costs. In many ways the tax code penalizes people who do the right thing. Unless they use a specific savings plan, individuals who save money can end up paying the same tax as those who spend it freely, and they often end up paying additional tax on the income earned from their savings. Individuals who stay in school and work hard earn more money and consequently pay more taxes than those who do not, even when the extra income is merely compensation for the cost of tuition and time spent learning.

Conservatives also ought to object to the social engineering contained in the tax code. The ability to craft additional taxes or tax breaks for specific interest groups expands the role of government and interferes with market forces. Yet in many cases, conservatives have wholeheartedly embraced tax preferences. For example, most Republican politicians support the continued tax subsidies that keep corn-based ethanol competitive with regular gasoline. This support has more to do with the fact that many Republican senators come from corn-producing states and Iowa holds an important presidential caucus every four years than with the economic or environmental merits of corn-based ethanol, which are few. Similarly, conservatives seem enamored with the research and development tax credit, which rewards certain companies for a portion of their research and development expenditures. This reflects a conservative bias for greater economic growth, even at the expense of equality. Although conservatives may privately hold this preference, it is not clear why government policy rather than market forces should set the balance between these two goals.

Some tax preferences can be justified on economic grounds because the activity they encourage creates large social benefits. But it is dangerous to enact even these. For one thing, the identification and measurement of social benefits is a very inexact science. But even if measurement was more precise, once the principle of government involvement is legitimized, the correct balance becomes a valid topic of debate, opening the way for all other types of government intervention.

COMPREHENSIVE TAX REFORM

What would a better tax system look like? Ideally, it would be built on three major changes: (1) the elimination of most exclusions and deductions from the individual income tax, (2) elimination of the corporate and payroll taxes, and (3) greater use of user fees and excise taxes to deal with activities that clearly involve social costs, especially a comprehensive energy tax.

This combination would accomplish three major goals. First, it would focus and simplify the task of collecting revenue from those on whom it ultimately lands, individuals. The new system is likely to be at least as progressive as the current one, albeit much simpler, imposing a lower deadweight loss and fewer compliance costs. Second, the reform would reduce the government's role in picking winners and losers and with it the lobbying and political fund-raising industry that surrounds the Senate Finance and House Ways and Means Committees. This in turn should increase the public legitimacy of the tax system. Third, the increased use of selective excise taxes will allow the government to steer economic growth and technological change more efficiently, by adjusting the relative prices that businesses and consumers face.

CHANGING THE INCOME TAX

Tax reform should move us toward the elimination of all exemptions, credits, and deductions, except for the few exceptions discussed elsewhere in this book. Those exceptions are refundable credits for education, housing, and health care and the exclusion for all savings segregated in an identifiable account. Of these, the credit for health care is the most important because healthy individuals may not have a strong enough incentive to purchase health insurance on their own, and without it, society will bear the risk of having to pay their bills if they become seriously ill or hurt. The credit for education is meant primarily to ensure that displaced workers have the resources needed to retrain for new jobs and to give parents the ability to save for their children's college education. The credit for housing replaces the existing mortgage interest deduction, even though individuals normally have a sufficient incentive to purchase adequate housing. Similarly, although an exemption would encourage personal savings, evidence shows that existing provisions do not have a large effect on net savings.[17]

There will always be close calls around the margins. For instance, the determination of when and how much income is realized from a grant of stock options that cannot be exercised unless an employee remains with a company for four years has more than one legitimate answer. At the extremes, it could be partially counted as income as soon as the individual receives it since it has some economic value. The value would have to be estimated, but there are ways to do this that produce reasonable values. Additional income could be taxed if and when the options are ever exercised or when the stock is sold. Alternatively, all income could be deferred until one of the latter two events. The specific decision does not matter so long as politics is kept out of it. The best way of doing this is to let the Internal Revenue Service make the decision guided by general principles that Congress lays out in the tax code.

For the most part, however, special provisions that inappropriately benefit one group or another will be easy to recognize. The cleaner the rest of the tax code is, the easier it will be to keep new provisions out. This general trend of reform follows the 1986 tax reform, which most observers believe was a success. It has been criticized by some for raising taxes on capital, an issue discussed next, but few people criticize the general effort to reduce marginal tax rates by broadening the tax base through the elimination of special provisions. The problem is that almost everyone who supports this general concept has one or two special exceptions that they are unwilling to part with. For the real estate industry it is the deduction for mortgage interest. Charities will insist on keeping the deduction for charitable giving. Others will argue that there needs to be a continued credit for child care beyond allowing it as a legitimate business expense. In the end, little reform gets done.

The taxation of capital gains raises a slightly different issue. The tax proposals in this book, if pursued together, would almost certainly involve a significant decrease in the tax paid on productive investment. The elimination of the corporate income tax would reduce total taxes on capital earnings, and the elimination of tax expenditures would allow an increase in the tax base and hence a reduction in marginal rates. This would be offset by equalizing the marginal rates for all forms of income and by eliminating both the payroll and corporate tax since the lost revenue would require an increase in income taxes that would have to be spread among all forms of income.

From a purely economic point, there is little reason to distinguish between income that comes from capital gains and income that comes from labor, especially when most wage income now represents a return on investments in human capital. In other words, if a twenty-five-year-old spends seventy-five thousand dollars on an MBA, why should government tax the extra income he or she earns after graduating any different than the income that someone else earns from investing seventy-five thousand dollars in stocks? Both choices involve the deferment of immediate gratification for a larger reward, both presumably confer positive economic externalities on the rest of society, and it is not immediately clear that government should prefer one over the other.

There are several arguments for taxing capital gains at a lower tax rate than regular income, beyond the 15.3 percentage point benefit it already receives from being exempt from FICA taxes. The first is that some portion of the income represents compensation for inflation and therefore does not increase the recipient's real income. This is especially true in times of high inflation and for assets that are held a long time. But this argument applies to all long-term investments, including those in human capital.

A second reason is the general feeling among many conservatives that government should help encourage investment. By lowering the marginal tax rate on capital gains, the government raises the rate of return to Americans who decide to save their money rather than spend it. Liberals are often suspicious of this policy goal because they believe that the only people who are in a position to save more are the rich; others are too close to the margins to be able to save. This was never true and is even less so now. Nevertheless, given the low official marginal tax rates that lower-income workers already face on regular income, a lower rate on capital gains means much less to them, so any tax differential again benefits mainly the wealthy.

A final rationale is that high taxes on capital gains trap investment in unproductive uses. The theory is that individuals have investments that are earning low rates of return that could be used more productively elsewhere. Normally, the promise of a higher rate of return elsewhere would be enough of an incentive to switch investments, but proponents of lower capital gains taxes argue that investors remain trapped because a sale of underperforming assets would trigger a tax on any capital gains realized since they were purchased. This rationale makes little economic sense, however. Assuming that tax will have to be paid on the gains at some point, the owner is much better off getting them into more productive areas sooner rather than later, even if this triggers tax payments. More to the point, in order for the investor to realize his capital gains, she or he must find a buyer, in which case the asset is still tying up investment capital, just that of a different person. There may be investors who would like to cash out but are reluctant to face a tax bill for the capital gains they have realized. Reducing the taxes they have to pay on any gains does not imply that capital overall will be better allocated, however.

In sum, it is hard to think of compelling reasons that income from investments should be taxed at a different rate than income from labor. It is true that reducing the tax on savings should increase investment, which is likely to spur economic growth and make society richer. Vestiges of our Protestant heritage still attach moral implications to the decision to forego immediate gratification for later rewards. But technology and consumer demand will ensure that the economy continues to grow anyway. In fact, some believe that society is poised for a period of unprecedented wealth in the next few decades.[18] It is not at all clear that maximizing total national income should be the primary goal that tax policy pursues, especially when no inquiry is made into the distribution of that income. Society may well decide to accept a lower rate of growth in return for greater consumption and equity now. It is not obvious that government should tip this balance by subsidizing investment at the cost of higher taxes on labor. Perhaps just as important, admitting the propriety of government favoring some forms of income over others in order to achieve social goals provides legitimacy to a host of other tax provisions that clearly have little economic value. If government can discriminate against some taxpayers in order to promote the goal of raising national income, then it is difficult to argue that it should not also be free to discriminate against others in order to promote goals such as greater income equality.

On the other hand, there are good equity arguments against differential taxation. Especially if society is going to ask every individual to bear at least some tax burden, it is unfair to allow richer individuals to pay lower taxes simply because they have structured their lives so that a large portion of their income comes from investments. There is some justification for the liberal view that, if they did save, it is to some extent because they had the means to save, and having a larger share of America's wealth, they have a larger stake in its well-being and at least a proportional duty to contribute to its continued strength. This is especially true for the very rich, where a great deal of family income represents the work of individuals other than the immediate beneficiary. If estate and corporate taxes are to be done away with in order to avoid double taxation, the other side of equity demands that capital gains then be treated on par with other income and that inheritance be treated as a taxable event so that income tax is paid on any capital gains before assets are received from others. There are always equity arguments for treating some cases differently than others. But some equity arguments outweigh others, and even if they did not, our current political system seldom makes such judgments based on the merits. It is better not to give it the power to make such judgments.

A number of politicians have argued in favor of switching to a consumption tax in which people are taxed not on a measure of what they contribute to society (income) but rather on what they take from it (consumption). In fact, the difference between a true consumption tax and the reforms argued for here is relatively minor, since each individual can shelter income from taxation merely by saving it in designated accounts. If no caps are placed on this ability the distinction between the two systems mainly comes down to the application of normal taxes to accumulated wealth at death, something that cannot affect investment decisions and is needed to prevent the emergence of large concentrations of wealth that are never taxed as income.

CORPORATE TAX

Although corporate taxes do not raise a great deal of revenue, they do impose large economic costs and influence the decision of whether to base economic activity in this country or in others. The first point to remember is that all taxes are eventually paid by individuals. The corporate income tax is no exception. Although the corporation ultimately writes the check to the IRS, the entire burden falls on one of three main groups: shareholders may pay through lower returns on their investment in the corporation; consumers may suffer because the company raises its prices in order to pass along the increased cost of doing business; and workers may see lower salaries because the corporation has less money or fewer sales. There is a great deal of evidence that much of the burden is passed on to consumers. A natural implication is that eliminating the corporate income tax would benefit consumers by reducing the price of most of the goods and services they purchase. While it is likely that high-income individuals pay a higher proportion of this tax than others, it is possible that making up the lost revenues through an increase in the income tax would be at least as progressive.

Elimination of the corporate income tax would dramatically lower the cost of doing business in the United States. This should attract more investment, strengthen the country's position as a base for both domestic and export production, and stem the flow of corporate activity to low-tax jurisdictions. It would also eliminate many of the current debates over corporate policy, such as expensing timetables and the research and development tax credit. Because elimination of the corporate tax rate also eliminates the possibility of double taxation of profits, the case for treating capital income on par with wages is also strengthened. Although part of the benefit would be passed on to foreign consumers in the form of lower prices on the products companies produce, the growth in export production is itself a positive development. Eliminating the tax would also end the government's influence over the degree to which companies borrow instead of issuing stock to raise capital. This should lead to greater efficiency and stability in the equity markets.

Phasing out the corporate income tax would create a large windfall for current shareholders. This could be partially recouped by a one-time tax on the average increase in stock price during the year in which the corporate tax was eliminated. In fact, if policy makers were concerned about significant wealth being tied up for long periods of time without being taxed, they could have individuals include the increase or decrease of average daily prices as income on their tax returns. For publicly traded companies this information is easily accessible, and the use of yearly averages would smooth out sudden increases or decreases that are unrelated to changes in fundamental value. Stock held in savings accounts would continue to build up tax free until funds were withdrawn from the account.

THE NEED FOR AN ENERGY TAX

One of the most powerful tools available to government is the ability to change relative prices through subsidies and taxes. Both individuals and businesses respond quickly to prices. In fact, corporations over the past few decades have become much more efficient in measuring their costs and passing any increases on to their customers. Whereas regulatory systems impose large administrative and compliance costs that firm managements have difficulty measuring and allocating to specific products, changes in relative prices appear to them as natural costs of doing business. Because they disappear into the total price of the good or service and are passed on to others, taxes that change relative prices also affect the behavior of everyone further down the supply chain. Yet the government has made limited use of excise taxes so far. In total they accounted for only 0.6 percent of GDP or seventy-four billion dollars in 2006.

Several policy reasons argue for imposing a broad energy tax on the economy, but only if it is revenue neutral; in other words, whatever revenues the tax is expected to bring in must be used to reduce existing taxes, preferably the corporate income or payroll tax. Given that the federal government alone already collects over 18 percent of GDP in tax revenue and that much of this goes to spending programs that are poorly managed or not in the national interest, the case for additional net taxes is extremely weak. Using new revenues to reduce existing taxes would also reduce the negative effect any energy tax would have on the economy.

A broad energy tax would have important benefits for technology, national security, and the environment. Starting with technology, there is a wide range of new technologies being developed to increase energy efficiency, make other sources of energy more competitive, and limit the environmental impact of existing technologies. Increasing the price of existing technology by raising the price of the energy it consumes would aid this development in a number of ways. First, it would increase the price of using energy, thereby reducing demand. Second, it would make energy-saving technologies more competitive with existing ones. This would shift demand toward them and reduce the need for a range of inefficient subsidies. Third, it would significantly increase the potential value of any new technology that promised to either produce energy more efficiently or reduce consumption, thus attracting new capital into the discovery and application phases of technology development. A significant energy tax could advance the timetable for introducing workable new technology by several years. This in turn would have a large impact on America's economic competitiveness, since world demand for these technologies is likely to be very high. Past experience demonstrates that over the period of a few years, energy use is quite responsive to prices.

An energy tax would also strengthen national security. The United States now depends on oil for 40 percent of its total energy use. Every day, the country uses twenty million barrels of oil, and over 50 percent of this comes from outside the country. Such heavy dependence on foreign imports increases the nation's trade deficit. More importantly, a great deal of these purchases go to countries that are either politically unstable or have governments that are strongly hostile to America's way of living. These governments include the following: Iran, which sponsors terrorism in the Gaza Strip, Lebanon, and Iraq and which is currently pursuing the acquisition of nuclear weapons with the avowed purpose of sharing the technology with other Muslim groups; Saudi Arabia, whose government still sponsors Wahhabism, a radical form of Islam that inspires groups like Al-Qaeda; Nigeria, whose government is impoverishing its oil-producing regions, leading to armed opposition that threatens continued production; Venezuela, whose populist leader seems determined to prove once again that Peronist policies lead to higher inflation, unemployment, and internal crime and less investment and growth, only this time wasting much more money in the process; and Sudan, which is practicing genocide on a large fraction of its people.

None of these governments could pursue these policies for long without the constant windfall that oil revenues provide. Their economic policies are incapable of generating enough internal value to support their political ambitions. Without oil, they would either have to radically change their policies to pursue the kind of wealth-generating economic activity that has raised living standards in countries such as Chile, South Korea, Taiwan, and China or wallow in continued poverty and insignificance like Zimbabwe, Somalia, and Egypt, depending on a continued flow of assistance from others.

An energy tax would have a strong effect on total oil consumption over the medium term. It would do so by reducing total demand for energy and shifting some demand away from petroleum toward alternative sources. Although other countries may not impose their own taxes, U.S. policy would also have an effect on their usage as new technologies spread to their economies.

Although they often seem to pursue irrational policies, oil-producing countries have a firm understanding of the importance of continued oil demand to both their economies and their ability to stay in power. Any change that threatened to make a significant dent in the link between global economic growth and demand for oil would quickly get their attention. Policies that cut into their future oil revenues would strongly encourage a moderation of their foreign policies.

Finally, an energy tax would have broad environmental benefits. Combustion of coal, natural gas, and oil products leads to emissions that have negative health and economic effects. These pollutants include ozone, sulfur dioxide, and fine particulates. These emissions impose significant economic costs aside from the issue of climate change. These costs take the form of damaged buildings, polluted water, reduced visibility, and poorer health. A tax that reflected these costs would reduce pollution over time. There is broad agreement that lower levels of pollution, if achieved at a modest cost, would bring both economic and health benefits.

A tax would be much more efficient and effective than current environmental policies. In order to control emissions, the United States has resorted to a variety of regulatory schemes including permitting requirements for generating plants and Corporate Average Fuel Economy (CAFE) standards for automobiles. Because these regulations are relatively inefficient mechanisms for controlling pollution, a tax should be able to achieve the same environmental benefits at a lower cost. And unlike current policies, it would create a permanent economic incentive for continued improvement. For instance, an increase in CAFE standards would only be effective if accompanied by a significant level of bureaucracy to decide issues like how to measure fuel efficiency and enforce compliance. Once manufacturers had met new standards they would have no further incentive to increase fuel efficiency, so further legislation would be needed. A broad tax on hydrocarbon fuels is much simpler to administer and imposes a continuous incentive to improve efficiency whenever the cost of doing so is lower than the tax.

At present there are enough environmental benefits to justify a significant tax without considering climate change. That is important because the threat of climate change is still too remote to justify major expenditures to prevent it. In a recent project known as the Copenhagen Consensus, prominent economists, including several Nobel laureates, gathered to consider how the world could best increase total welfare if it had an extra fifty billion dollars to invest. The group ranked the benefits and costs of several dozen potential investments and concluded that combating climate change ranked very low on the list in terms of the net benefits it would bring to the world.[19] Nevertheless, the issue continues to gain political momentum. The Democratic Party sees it as more politically promising than some of the other issues identified by the group, including combating HIV/AIDS, controlling malaria, and developing supplements for micronutrients such as Vitamin A and iodine. As a result, it is increasingly likely that the United States will enact policies to control carbon emissions. Although most economists believe a carbon tax would have the greatest benefit at the least cost, the most likely policy is some form of tradable carbon permits, accompanied by another bureaucracy to determine what constitutes an emission or offset, who can trade emission permits at what cost and when, and how many permits should be handed out. Democrats are likely to use any government revenues from selling permits to fund additional spending programs rather than to reduce taxes. A properly structured energy tax could prevent this wrong turn by achieving the same result at far less cost.

Two final points need to be made about any energy tax. The first is that if the primary purpose is to change the long-term behavior of the economy, then the amount of the tax can be increased slowly in the first few years. The real purpose is to send a credible signal about what the tax will be five, ten, or more years out. If this is done, companies will begin to change their decisions now, perhaps by building fewer coal-fired generating plants or ensuring that the ones they do build are more efficient. The long-range signal also gives investors assurance that the market for new technology will be there. It is much less important what the tax is in the first few years. Although it may not hurt the long-term effectiveness of the tax, a slower introduction does minimize any negative economic impact by giving the economy time to anticipate and adjust to higher energy prices.

Second, if an energy tax is effective in achieving its main goals of spurring the development of alternative sources of energy, increasing energy efficiency, and reducing our dependence on oil from governments that are fundamentally hostile to our way of life, then it may not raise a lot of revenue, especially in the long term. As the economy adjusts to the higher prices, the activity subject to tax should decline, reducing tax revenues. Declining revenues would represent a success, but they would enable fewer cuts in other tax revenues. Nevertheless, any broad-based tax on fossil fuel consumption capable of gradually shifting the economy to healthier energy markets is likely to raise substantial revenues for the foreseeable future, even if the annual amount declines over time. In fact, if the market turns out to be more responsive than forecast, the amount of the tax could be increased to turn the economy even further in the desired direction.

A central problem with current tax policy is that it is constantly subject to the political influence of thousands of special interests. To some extent this is inevitable in a democracy, where all laws, including tax legislation, should be responsive to social needs and flexible enough to respond to changes in the economy. More than most laws, however, tax law needs to be stable over the long term. It is most effective when the signals it sends affect both short-term and long-term behavior in ways that increase social welfare. Its effectiveness in doing this is reduced when it is subject to annual changes. More disturbingly, the law's legitimacy is weakened when changes are seen mainly as a method of raising campaign contributions by the members of the committees that write tax law. When the law hinges on barely disguised bribes from special interests to Congressmen rather than on the national interest, and when it tries to micromanage the outcome of competition that should be left to the private sector, then the right of government to tax Americans is brought into question.

One reform that would help change the dynamic of tax law would be a constitutional amendment that delays the effective date of any change to government tax law until two years after it is enacted into law. This would force Congress to focus on what tax policy should be over the long term and reduce both the ability and the incentive to try to craft tax policy according to short-term pressures. It should also discourage the passage of annual tax bills that become loaded with special favors. Without better discipline from Congress, any future broad tax reform such as the 1986 act is likely to be quickly undone as soon as the normal process of special interest lobbying begins its work.

The federal government's role in the economy and society needs to undergo a fundamental change if it is to address the needs of its citizens in an increasingly fluid world. It cannot accomplish this without significant reforms in the way that it collects revenue and spends money. Absent these reforms, its leaders will have neither the resources nor the integrity needed to embark on such a radical redesign of its role in the economy. The new programs cannot be added on to the existing structure of government policy; they must substitute for it. And, if ever enacted, they must be protected against the insidious creep of special interest legislation that has dampened the effectiveness of so many other reforms. Public policy will always require flexibility and change, but institutional changes are needed to make sure that the outcome of the legislative process reflects the national interest, not just the power of one or two lawmakers seeking favor with a special interest lobby.

10

REFORMING GOVERNMENT
SPENDING PROGRAMS

The type of income support contract described in this book represents a significant departure from the current plethora of government programs. In order to work, it requires radical reform of the rest of the federal government's budget. It would be a great mistake to add something like the income guarantee onto existing programs. Doing so would only represent an unwarranted increase in an already bloated bureaucracy and would ensure that the new approach lacks the resources to make a meaningful change in the way workers relate to government and the broader economy.

For the program to have meaning, it must have enough resources to ensure that those who abide by the behavioral requirements are guaranteed enough income to escape poverty. In fact, in order to work as intended, it must provide all Americans with an assurance that, if they contribute to the society around them and expose themselves to the uncertainties of globalization, deregulation, competition, and technological change, they are assured of at least a comfortable life. To do this the program must have significant resources. To get these resources, the rest of government must be pared back drastically. The reforms advocated in the book represent a different approach to government. It cannot be combined with the current approach. It must be substituted for it.

Briefly, what is this approach? The argument is simple. First, it starts with the premise that all citizens have worth and that, if they contribute to society according to their abilities, government should guarantee them a morally fair income even if those abilities are limited. Second, once this income is guaranteed, the rationale for most other government programs is severely weakened. These programs should therefore be eliminated, freeing up the resources needed to increase the income floor.

Why does the guarantee of a fair income weaken the rationale for most other government programs? The basic reason is that a major part of the justification for most government spending is the need to increase the purchasing power of the beneficiaries. If this purchasing power is already sufficient, then the need and proper role for government is much different. We can look at three examples.

In 2006, the federal government spent twenty-one billion dollars on farm support payments of various types. Farm policy includes a diverse set of separate programs that include supports for the price of certain crops, subsidies for crop insurance, payments to farmers in exchange for not planting land, tariffs to increase the price of sugar, and legal backing for farmers groups that set limits on the amount of crops farmers can sell and the minimum price they can charge consumers. Supporters justify each of these programs as needed to raise the income of farmers. Yet their existence has sped the decline in family farms by giving more money to larger growers, making it easier for them to outcompete and buy out neighboring farms. These programs have raised the price of food to consumers by artificially restricting production. By increasing the price of farm land and capital, they have made it harder for the next generation of farmers to enter the industry. And they continue to exist despite the fact that many recipients have incomes that are much higher than that of the average shopper. If farmers who tilled a minimum number of acres were guaranteed the same minimum income as other Americans, agricultural programs would not be needed as income supports. Farmers would have enough income to purchase crop insurance if they wanted it. And farm policy would have to be justified on other grounds.

Medicare and Medicaid exist largely to help individuals afford health care. To the extent that market failures in health care are addressed by a refundable tax credit, these two programs are no longer needed to address a health problem. Instead, they address an income problem: individuals who cannot purchase the health care needed in private markets. But if the combination of the refundable credit and the income guarantee ensure that everyone can afford insurance, then Medicare and Medicaid are no longer needed. There may continue to be market failures in health care, but these can be dealt with by the normal regulatory process.

Similarly, Food Stamps and Temporary Assistance for Needy Families (TANF) are designed primarily to provide poor individuals with a minimum level of nutrition and income. Food Stamps do not address a market failure in the economy's ability to grow the food that people need and deliver it to them in a safe and convenient manner; they address a perceived inability of certain people to buy enough food even when it is offered at a reasonable price. But if everyone is guaranteed enough income to make these purchases, then Food Stamps become superfluous.

This chapter will examine how many resources would be available within the current budget if the federal government terminated all programs that have as their primary purpose ensuring that certain individuals have enough purchasing power to afford a decent standard of living. These resources would then be available to support the income guarantee contract and tax provisions discussed elsewhere in this book.

THE FEDERAL BUDGET IN BRIEF

Total spending by the federal government has also fluctuated over the past several decades. As figure 10.1 shows, the federal government played only a minor role in the economy until World War II. In 1930, the year after the stock market crash, federal spending totaled only 3.4 percent of gross domestic product (GDP). Spending rose sharply as a result of the Great Depression and the New Deal, amounting to 10.7 percent by 1934. But that was the high point. In 1940, four years after Roosevelt first entered office and one year before the United States entered World War II, federal outlays were only 9.8 percent of GDP.

Figure 10.1   Federal Outlays as a Percent of GDP

Source: Office of Management and Budget

During the war, government spending rose quickly, reaching an all-time high of 43.6 percent of the economy in both 1943 and 1944. Although outlays quickly fell below 15 percent of GDP after the war, Americans' expectations of the federal government had dramatically changed. Most of the dominant political movements of the time, such as Progressivism, Socialism, and Communism, asserted that government could and should solve most of the problems inherent in a modern economy. Encouraged by these philosophies, Americans increasingly looked to the government for the solution to the country's economic and social ills. Legislation such as the Social Security Act of 1936 and the Agricultural Adjustment Act of 1938 constituted major encroachments of the federal government into sectors that had formerly been left to private initiative or the states. Federal spending began to rise slowly in each succeeding decade until it hit a postwar high of over 23 percent of GDP in 1982 and 1983. Since then it has fluctuated with the economy and the success of repeated deficit cutting legislation, falling to 18.4 percent of GDP in 2000 before rising back over 20 percent in the most recent years.

Although the total level of federal spending may not have changed dramatically since 1980, its composition has (see figure 10.2). The two most significant changes have been the role of military spending and the rise of entitlements. Military spending rose to a high of 9.5 percent of GDP at the

Figure 10.2   Composition of Federal Outlays as a Percent of GDP

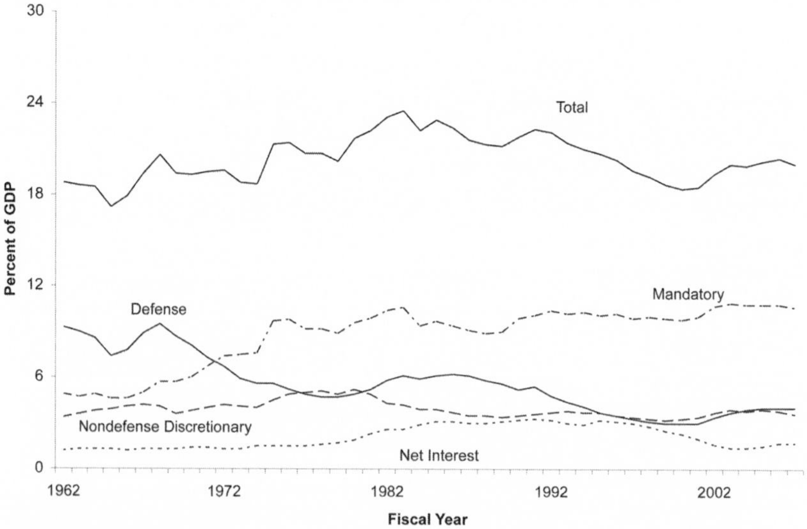

Source: Office of Management and Budget

height of the Vietnam War in 1968. It fell back after the war but was still close to 5 percent when President Ronald Reagan took office. His emphasis on building up the nation's defense capability produced defense budgets that averaged about 6 percent of GDP per year in the late 1980s. After the collapse of the Soviet Union and the end of the Cold War, military spending underwent a dramatic decline, falling steadily to 3 percent of GDP in 1999–2001. The fall in military spending was accompanied by a corresponding fall in total federal spending as a percent of GDP, partly due to a strong economy, which lifted GDP, and to fiscal restraint on the part of Congress and President Bill Clinton.

It is unlikely that defense spending can be cut much further. In fact, military spending has increased to meet the challenge of terrorism, including the wars in Iraq and Afghanistan. By 2006, military spending had risen to 4 percent of GDP and, although Democrats are strongly against the Iraq war, both of their main candidates in the 2008 presidential election advocate increasing the military's capability, indicating that outlays are not likely to fall much even if the United States withdraws from Iraq.

Even more significant than the fall in defense spending has been the rise in mandatory spending since 1980. Because of its importance, it is worth spending some time to explain the concept of mandatory spending. Ultimately, all federal spending is under the control of the administration and Congress. Although it would threaten the stability of the nation's financial markets, the government could conceivably renege on all of its agreements, including repayment of the federal debt. Although holders of bonds would have a legal recourse, the Supreme Court has already decided that beneficiaries of government spending have no property interest in continued payments.[1] In creating programs like Social Security and Medicare, Congress implicitly reserved the right to reduce or even end them at any time. But the way in which spending is appropriated matters. For almost all defense spending and many poverty programs such as Food Stamps and TANF, Congress appropriates money for one year at a time. If, by the end of the year, Congress has not acted to provide more money, the program shuts down automatically. These discretionary programs are therefore under the immediate control of policy makers. Longer-term authorizing legislation, such as the No Child Left Behind Act, may set out the program's structure and the goals that it should try to achieve, but the actual allocation of resources is done on an annual basis. Although some have advocated moving to a two-year appropriation cycle, doing so would not substantially change the government's ability to move resources around to balance immediate priorities.

Other programs, however, have received permanent appropriations. These so-called mandatory programs operate on autopilot. Legislation, usually without any expiration date, sets out the circumstances under which recipients are entitled to federal funds, and the money automatically flows according to the formula unless Congress passes new legislation changing the underlying law. The political bias toward the status quo ensures that it is much easier to stop legislation from being passed than it is to pass new legislation. As a result, these programs acquire strong momentum, including the rise of political lobbies, which acquire a vested interest in seeing them continue and make radical change all but impossible and even gradual change very difficult.

The problem might seem like a technical matter of interest only to federal budget experts, except for the fact that mandatory spending is dominating the rest of the budget. In 1962, net mandatory spending amounted to only 4.9 percent of GDP, less than half the size of all discretionary programs. By 2006, however, it had grown to 10.8 percent of GDP. Spending on all other domestic discretionary programs, including housing assistance, Food Stamps, and government services, totaled only 3.5 percent of GDP. The Congressional Budget Office (CBO) recently estimated that, by the year 2015, mandatory spending will grow by another full percentage point, to 11.7 percent of GDP.

This growth is driven largely by three programs, Social Security, Medicare, and Medicaid. The growth of these programs in turn is driven by a limited number of demographic and economic forces. The majority of benefits from Social Security and Medicare go to individuals who are over the age of sixty-five. This group of individuals has been rising over the last several decades and is likely to rise even faster over the next thirty years. One reason is that advances in income and health care have enabled a much larger portion of the population to reach the age of sixty-five, and once they do, they tend to live a lot longer. In addition to this there is the baby boom. Between 1945 and 1947 the birth rate per one thousand women rose from 20.4 to 26.6 and remained above 24 until 1960.[2] The first of these individuals will be sixty-five in 2011. During the next three decades, this cohort will produce a large increase in the number of retirees who are eligible for both Social Security and Medicare.

A second driver is the sustained increases in the cost of health care. With few respites, these costs have been increasing significantly faster than inflation. Chapter 7 discusses some of the reasons for this increase and policy changes that might help moderate it. Absent any changes, however, CBO estimates that by 2050 spending on Medicare and Medicaid could grow to over 20 percent of GDP, while spending on Social Security will grow to 6.5 percent of GDP.[3] Unless health care costs are brought under control, these two programs will begin to dominate the budget after 2015. As chapter 7 explains, it will be very difficult to control health care inflation without structural changes to the two programs, which together accounted for 35.1 percent of all health spending in the country in 2005.[4]

Most observers believe that, if nothing is done, growth in mandatory spending will result in a severe imbalance in federal priorities. Spending on the elderly, especially the elderly poor, is important, but it is not necessarily more important than assistance to the working poor, national defense, support of education, the elimination of homelessness, or strengthening the nation's infrastructure. Yet all of the latter have become second thoughts when determining how government spends taxpayers' money. Each year Congress engages in fierce debates about how much money the government should spend and how that money should be allocated among a large number of diverse programs. But these debates apply to less than 25 percent of all domestic spending. Mandatory programs are never subject to these discussions. Instead, every year the government sends out over half of all the money it spends to a few programs according to predetermined set formulas, and the rest of government then fights over the declining remainder.

Spending on all programs should be subject to the same appropriations rules, and these rules should make it easy for Congress to shift money between programs at the margins as priorities and needs shift. Once tax law is devoted to the purpose of raising a set proportion of revenue at a minimum cost to the economy instead of to implementing social policy through tax breaks, it is important to give the tax code some permanency so that taxpayers can plan their activities around it and to reduce Congress' ability to use annual tax bills as a tool to raise money for reelection campaigns. But all spending, including interest on the national debt, should require the same periodic appropriations from Congress. Every individual and business must set an annual budget that includes all spending. Although some payments, including repayment of debt and rent, may have a higher priority than others, they all compete at the margin. The same should be true of the nation's budget.

Some may worry that subjecting all spending to regular appropriations may introduce too much uncertainty into the programs. However, Congress, despite all of its weaknesses, is capable of the challenge. In over two hundred years, it has never defaulted on the national debt, even when Congress and the administration were deadlocked over legislation to increase the debt ceiling—nor have fierce budget debates ever jeopardized the nation's defense even though the vast majority of defense spending must be renewed each year. When budget stalemates have led to brief government shutdowns, leaders ensured that the most important functions would continue uninterrupted. It is extremely unlikely that subjecting Social Security, Medicare, and Medicaid or even debt repayment to annual appropriations would lead to any significant delays in the operation of the programs. What it would do is increase the nation's ability to balance the importance of those programs with its other needs. It would also make it politically easier to control the rapid growth in entitlement spending that is projected to occur over the next decades. Although the authorizing legislation would remain the same unless changed by Congress, it no longer would automatically drive spending; this would be a separate decision by each Congress, not bound by its predecessors. It would address one economist's complaint that "never in the nation's history have dead and retired officials been able to exert such control over current and future budgets,"[5] by making it easier for current officials to control spending.

But even this change will not be sufficient to ensure that the majority of government spending truly serves the public interest. That is because most spending today is heavily influenced by special interest groups. Even programs that were created to meet a legitimate public need, such as transportation or homelessness, must deal with the interests of powerful beneficiaries such as unions or landlords whose interests often diverge from those of the intended beneficiaries or the general public. For instance, unions may press for artificially higher wages or unnecessary construction projects in order to create more jobs, even if it produces more expensive roads that do not address an area's real transportation needs. Similarly, landlords may oppose changes that would link continued subsidies to minimum quality standards even if these would ensure that the government was not paying above-market rents for below-market living conditions.

WHY FEDERAL SPENDING IS
SO DIFFICULT TO CONTROL

Four decades ago, Mancur Olson explained why government spending often caters to narrow special interests rather than the broader public welfare.[6] Basically, it is costly for individuals to participate in the political process. They must educate themselves about the issues and then spend time and often money trying to influence policy makers. Even if it would be profitable for a group of individuals to incur these costs, they must still overcome one additional hurdle, free riding. Assuming a group effort is started, all members of the group have an incentive to resist doing their own part and hope that the rest of the group incurs the costs of organizing for them. Since their own personal effort is unlikely to make the difference between winning and losing, their total expected reward is not altered if they choose to free ride.

Smaller groups have an easier time overcoming the free rider problem and organizing joint action to influence government. They also have an inherent advantage over the public interest. Every member of the group usually has a much stronger interest in legislation that benefits it than does the average citizen. Take sugar imports. American tariffs on sugar imports raise domestic sugar prices and grower profits. In 2000, the General Accounting Office (GAO) tried to estimate the benefits and costs. It found that, in 1998, the program had benefited sugar farmers about one billion dollars or about one hundred thousand dollars for each sugar beet farm.[7] The tariffs reduce overall national welfare by close to two billion dollars.[8] But this loss is spread over roughly 120 million voters. As a result, the average citizen has only a small incentive to learn about how the program works and lobby against it. When measured against other concerns and interests this issue is likely to rank very low. The average sugar farmer had a strong interest in defending the program, however, which explains why the industry was willing to pay Representative Carolyn Maloney (D-NY) $9,500 in campaign contributions to influence her vote.[9] In fact, it may very well be sugar farmers' primary concern. Another example of the power of these interests can be seen from the fact that in 2002 Senator Mary Landrieu (D) narrowly won reelection in Louisiana largely by inventing the claim that President George W. Bush had a secret deal with Mexico to double sugar imports from that country.[10]

In politics, such narrow, focused interests will often win out over the national interest, especially when defending programs that already exist. Although it is often awkward to argue against the public interest, when push comes to shove, few groups sacrifice their own interests for the broader public well-being. Economists have described this behavior as rent-seeking.

Normally, individuals and businesses have to compete against each other in the free market. If consumers want to purchase a particular item, they have to convince a producer to make and sell it to them. Companies can't force customers to buy their products. And if another firm makes a better product for a lower price, consumers are allowed to switch to the new firm, putting the incumbents out of business. Although government is involved in the market, its main role should be as a neutral enforcer of laws that are designed to maximize total welfare over the long term, usually by protecting competition and freedom of choice.

But the government's ability to set rules opens up another path to competition: get the government to change the rules in a way that helps you and hurts your competitors. Thus, the dairy industry successfully sought legislation that burdened an independent producer who was selling milk at lower prices than they were.[11] In addition to changing the rules, private interests can also work to get public subsidies or have taxes placed on others.

A great deal of time and effort goes into diverting public spending to private causes. Some of this, such as fraud in Medicare, does not reflect the wishes of policy makers. But much of it does. Almost all economists agree that current farm programs are wasteful and counterproductive: they are not needed to ensure a steady supply of cheap food, and they hasten the demise of the family farm. Yet the federal government spends tens of billions of dollars every year to subsidize a small proportion of farmers. From 2003 to 2005, 66 percent of all subsidy payments went to only 10 percent of the country's farmers.[12] The distribution of payments reflects the way the law was written and should not come as a surprise to any of the lawmakers who voted for it.

Because of the constant pressure to devote public monies to private interests, real spending reform is unlikely to occur without changes to the rules that govern how Congress makes spending decisions. Several changes might make a difference. The first is a change in the way Congress includes earmarks in spending legislation. An earmark is a specific directive by Congress to spend money on a particular project, purchase a specific product, or give money to a certain individual or group. A famous example is the "bridge to nowhere" in Alaska where Congress initially planned to spend $450 million to build two bridges in rural Alaska.[13] One of the bridges would have served a town of less than fourteen thousand people.

Although earmarks account for a small proportion of total government spending, they have an extremely corrosive effect on Congress. To begin with they monopolize a large portion of congressional staff time every spring when a long line of supplicants besiege senators and representatives with their requests for money. Second, because appropriations earmarks escape much of the normal legislative scrutiny, they account for a disproportionate share of the insidious practice of linking special favors with campaign contributions.

One solution would be to ban earmarks. Besides being tough to enforce, a complete ban would deprive Congress of much of its constitutional power to regulate spending. The specifics of spending should not be left totally to unelected officials within each agency. A strong case can be made that, at least within their district, members of Congress have a better sense of the nation's needs than do the heads of government departments. Particular areas of the country may feel strongly about a specific local project for reasons that outsiders cannot understand. As a result, even when such projects do not qualify under the impartial formulas set out in authorizing legislation, they may still deserve funding. Although it is nice to think that all spending can be determined by an objective weighing of the national interest, much of politics involves compromise to ensure that each region or group feels that it is getting a fair share of the national wealth. Elected representatives are often in the best position to make these decisions.

Such needs could be accommodated by allowing each representative and senator to control the designation of a specific sum of money within appropriation bills. Each earmark should then include the name of the legislator submitting it. This would give all members the ability to ensure that their jurisdiction's most important needs are met, even if the agency controlling the funds in Washington does not appreciate them. It would also ensure that all members remain accountable for the projects they select. Public disclosure would ensure that wise projects were lauded while poor projects were criticized. Because each member would only have a limited amount of money, they would be likely to choose those that mattered most to their constituents. Disclosing which member designated each earmark would increase the scrutiny of any campaign contributions, special favors, or other ties linking the recipient to the lawmaker. Giving all members the same allocation would also have the beneficial purpose of diminishing the importance of seniority and committee membership in securing funding. It would, however, force members to take personal responsibility for projects that are not funded. At present, members can appease constituents by pressing even poor projects on the Appropriations Committees and then blaming the committees when the projects do not receive funding.

Other reforms involve amending the Constitution. Many conservatives have pressed for a Balanced Budget Amendment, which would prohibit the federal government from running deficits unless a supermajority of Congress approves them. The common rationale is that deficits are bad for the country because they contribute to higher government spending and reduce national saving. Many proponents also feel that it is wrong for one generation to pass its debts onto future generations. The fact that many states currently operate with balanced budget requirements indicates that the constraint is workable, although applying it to the federal government increases the magnitude of the complexity. There is also a strong danger that a Balanced Budget Amendment would lead to more manipulation of economic assumptions in order to game the numbers. Finally, it is not clear how the amendment could be enforced.

Then-representative John Kyl (AZ) proposed a simpler approach during the 103rd Congress. His amendment would have limited government spending to 19 percent of GDP, slightly more than the long-term average of tax receipts as a percentage of GDP.[14] The amendment allows a supermajority to override this constraint so that the nation can respond to national emergencies. Kyl's amendment does not address enforcement. But linking spending to the prior year's GDP would give Congress a firm ceiling within which to fit all spending. And making each member jointly responsible for any excess spending would ensure that the total appropriated stays within the cap. If all spending must be appropriated, exceeding a cap takes a conscious act of Congress. The exact percentage chosen is less important than the decision to link the size of government to the nation's total income. If the majority of spending then goes to funding programs like those advocated in this book, public support for policies such as free trade that foster economic growth might increase.

One of the running battles between conservatives and liberals involves the tradeoff between policies that increase the size of the pie and those that distribute the existing pie more evenly. Carving out a large section of the pie for income support programs aimed at those who truly need assistance, but firmly linking the size of this section to the nation's ability to support it, would hopefully give both parties an interest in policies that would enhance the nation's long-term prosperity.

Placing a cap on public spending does not necessarily reduce the impact that government has on the economy. Legislators can still impose laws and regulations that affect the competitive marketplace, thereby favoring one group or another. Some government involvement is inevitable, and even desirable, in order to correct market imbalances and set common rules that help coordinate behavior. Although management of the electromagnetic spectrum could be substantially improved, a total absence of federal involvement would cause confusion over what rights individuals had to use it. This confusion would probably lead to a multiplicity of uses that interfered with each other. This in turn would diminish the total value of the spectrum and deter the private sector from investing in new technologies and infrastructure. The key challenge is to make sure that policy decisions are made in the public interest rather than those of narrow groups such as broadcasters or cable companies.

Giving workers greater protection against forces like globalization, new technology, and social change requires a significant transformation in the individual's relationship to the government. Recently, a number of commentators have called for taxing some of the gains that the wealthy have derived from the economic growth of the last two decades in order to share it with low- and middle-class workers. This book argues that even greater redistribution can be accomplished without increasing the overall size of government. If redistribution is really the ultimate goal of progressives, then perhaps some of these measures ought to be tried before engaging in yet more taxing and spending of the traditional variety.

But, assuming that a transfer of wealth like this would be beneficial, it should only be attempted if three conditions are met. First, existing programs should be cut wherever they do not add value equivalent to that of supporting workers against an increasingly uncertain world. It is likely that this would include a significant part of current spending. Second, government should first focus on changing policies that inhibit the equalization of incomes. These include laws that increase the minimum quality and therefore price of products and services, accreditation and licensing standards that limit access to training and professional services, and zoning and other governance laws that enable those with more power to restrict the activity of others and protect themselves from the strong leveling forces that markets normally exert.

Last, there must be assurances that extra revenues would in fact help stabilize workers' incomes. Otherwise, it is far more likely that the benefits will go to other interests, including nonprofits and government workers, to run programs that benefit very few people. The justice of imposing significant new taxes on the rich is inseparably linked to both the overall efficiency of existing government programs and the effectiveness with which the new resources will be used. Yet most proponents of new taxes take responsibility for neither. Partly for that reason, and also to contain any increase in the overall size of government, using any additional tax revenues to reduce corporate income taxes, which will translate to lower prices and more jobs, or payroll taxes on low-income workers, is preferable to creating new spending programs.

How much could be freed up if government eliminated all programs that do not provide a clear generalized social benefit or are not needed once a fair income is guaranteed? One option is to take a de novo approach and ask what existing programs might need to be created if every individual was entitled to the income guarantee contract and if specific market imperfections were addressed by the refundable tax credits discussed in earlier chapters.

Looking at the rough totals in the budget, the three largest entitlement plans would not be needed. Both of Social Security's two main goals would be achieved; every elderly person would receive a minimum income provided they adhered to the contract; and the mandatory savings requirement would ensure that workers accumulate sufficient savings. In fact, the safety net now has some redundancy because the need for retirement savings is greatly reduced by the continued income guarantee, whose work component requires only that the elderly find *some* positive contribution to make to society.

Also, Medicare and Medicaid would not be needed. The combination of an income guarantee and the refundable tax credit would ensure that almost all individuals have enough income to afford basic health care, and the latter would ensure that they purchased adequate health insurance.

Continued funding for programs specifically targeted to the poor would also be unnecessary. Programs like Food Stamps, welfare payments, Section 8 vouchers, farm supports, and energy assistance all exist primarily to address a lack of income on the part of recipients. Ensure a sufficient minimum income and individuals no longer need these supports. With the income guarantee, most programs that serve primarily low-income individuals are no longer necessary.

How many resources could be freed up for an income support program? The Office of Management and Budget divides federal spending into a number of functions. Spending within each function is largely, though not exclusively, devoted to a common general purpose. Five of these functions are clearly related to income support in one way or another: agriculture, health, Medicare, Income Security, and Social Security. Spending on these programs totaled over $1.5 trillion in 2006 or just over 12 percent of GDP. Community and regional development and education accounted for another $173 billion. Even if one hundred million adults signed up for the income support contract, the federal government could guarantee an income of fifteen thousand dollars per year. This would be in addition to anything earned in the workforce. It would also be in addition to any support that local and state governments chose to provide. Once an income guarantee is in place, the rationale for many programs at lower levels of government is similarly reduced, freeing up resources to add to pure income support.

Other parts of government include a number of programs that offer marginal benefits to the overall public, at least when measured against the imperative of reducing poverty. For example, the federal government subsidized public broadcasting by $460 million in 2006. Public radio and television undoubtedly offer a wide range of quality programming. But should that be the test of public support? It is hard to argue that the stations are incapable of supporting themselves in the private markets. Indeed, individual donations and corporate sponsorship already make up a large portion of station revenues. If the general public is unwilling to pay public stations the full cost of continuing their operations, either in the form of direct donations or through advertising, as is done with regular broadcasting, then why should government divert tax dollars toward making up the difference? Looked at a different way, who exactly does public broadcasting support? Although stations have tried hard to reach a broader audience in recent years, it is not clear that their operations primarily benefit those who need the most help.

Another example is the continued subsidy that government provides for air transportation to rural areas. On a broader level the government should refrain from tilting the balance between cities and rural areas. On the one hand, greater rural development would ease the continued decline of family farms and could help alleviate urban congestion. There are some good reasons to think that evolving toward a more decentralized geographical economy would lead to an improvement in the work and leisure balance, stronger neighborhoods, and lower concentrations of pollutants. On the other hand, some have argued that cities, for all of their problems, impose less of an environmental burden on the planet as a whole.[15]

But surely the practice of subsidizing continued air service to rural areas should rank low on most people's list of priorities. As with most programs of this type, the cost per individual served is extremely high. The main beneficiary tends to be the airline rather than the rural resident. And the mere existence of the subsidy to established companies inhibits the rise of small carriers who might otherwise establish service.

A third example of government spending that is more supportive of special interests than its intended beneficiaries is the Universal Service Fund. The fund is supported by a tax on all interstate phone service in the United States. Its purpose is to subsidize the delivery of telephone and Internet service to both high-cost and low-income areas. Separate programs within the fund also support telecommunications and Internet service to both rural hospitals and schools and libraries. Total outlays for the fund were $6.3 billion in 2005. Although set up to accomplish a worthwhile goal, there is little evidence that the program accomplishes much in the way of service. Two independent studies recently concluded that the program's main effect was to prop up incumbent service providers against new competition.[16] Areas targeted by the fund did not enjoy higher service levels than other areas. The result is not atypical. Once a program is created, it quickly becomes the object of competition among a host of special interests. Those interests with the most political power and specific knowledge of how the program works and who makes the decisions about it have a strong advantage. These are usually not the most needful or deserving.

Conservatives and liberals ought to agree that government spending needs to accomplish a clear and important public purpose. For conservatives this belief supports the concept of limited government and the continued need to resist government encroachment on market forces.

But for liberals, the principle should be equally important for two reasons. First, spending that is not absolutely necessary diverts resources from what is truly important and clouds the difference between a government that sets the necessary conditions within which private enterprise can flourish and a government that serves mainly as a battleground in which powerful interests use their influence to protect themselves and appropriate resources from the least powerful. Second, for all of the good intentions and noble pronouncements, there is surprisingly little evidence that most programs deliver great benefits to those that they are intended to serve, especially when one looks at the significant resources devoted to them and the deadweight loss associated with collecting the taxes necessary to support them as well as the diversion of resources that goes into rent-seeking. Instead, most of the benefit ends up going to the groups, such as teachers' unions, contractors, landlords, broadcasters, and nonprofits organizations, that are paid to deliver products and services. Seldom is the quality of services that the poor receive anywhere near what the resources should support or what the recipients deserve.

Even functions that clearly justify a federal role are subject to corruption. There is a clear need for national coordination of the nation's transportation infrastructure. The ability to move products and people quickly across the country is a key aspect of our national competitiveness. Ideally, each local part of the infrastructure fits into the national whole. Because of the need for coordination and the fact that the most important parts have regional and national benefits, some level of funding at the national level is wise. Yet much of the current spending is politically motivated. Now that most of the infrastructure is in place, the periodic transportation bills have become an exercise in funding projects that do little to further any national purpose. If some of these are desirable from the state or local level, that is where they should be funded. Instead, the national government collects the money itself and then forces local officials to beg to get it back. In many cases the economic justification for projects does not extend much beyond creating jobs for workers and profits for the construction companies.

Of course, any effort to divert significant resources from Social Security and Medicare will entail significant transition costs. While accompanying reforms in health care might alleviate some of the problems that Medicare was set up to address, a large number of the nation's elderly heavily depend on Social Security payments, and workers who are nearing retirement have built their plans around the program. It would be neither fair nor politically wise to eliminate all of these payments, especially when the principal rationale for the taxes needed to fund the program was that individuals were creating their own accounts. Yet it is also impossible to continue funding Social Security within the present budget without crowding out other programs.

The transition could be financed through a onetime increase in the federal debt. The actuarial deficit of Social Security's trust fund over the next seventy-five years is $4.7 trillion.[17] In 2006 total debt held by the public outside of the Federal Reserve System was 31.1 percent of GDP. In the past it has been much higher (see figure 10.3). In 1945 and 1946, it was over 96 percent of GDP due to wartime spending. Yet, within a decade the percentage had fallen by half, due to a combination of budget surpluses and economic growth. More recently, the debt ratio was over 44 percent in 1993–1995 but by 2001 had fallen back to 27.7 percent, and some observers were anticipating paying the entire debt off within the medium term. During that time, the United States ran budget surpluses in some years, but it was mainly continued economic growth, combined with the absence of any significant new borrowing, that produced the decline.

Issuing enough debt to temporarily return to 100 percent of GDP would create almost nine trillion dollars in onetime revenue. This is almost double the entire underfunding in Social Security and should be more than sufficient

Figure 10.3   Publicly-Held Federal Debt as a Percent of GDP

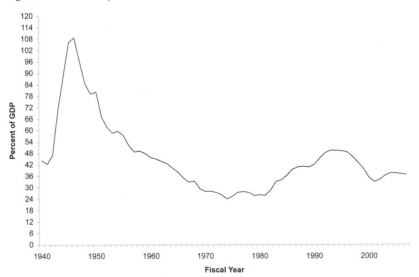

Source: Office of Management and Budget

to pay for the transition costs of switching to an alternative system. The determination of each individual's compensation should be guided by several considerations. First, compensation should be heavily means-tested. Individuals with large incomes and significant wealth should not receive compensation, while those on the margins should receive the full actuarial value of lost benefits. Second, compensation should vary by age. Current retirees should receive more compensation than those whose retirement is more distant. For the youngest workers the fact that they can now divert their payments to their own accounts should be compensation enough. Third, compensation should largely be for Social Security benefits, not other lost entitlements. Finally, because compensation would substitute a certain benefit for one that is likely to be cut in the future, most recipients are likely to prefer the former even if it does not fully reflect the actuarial value of payments under current law.

By issuing a sufficient number of bonds, the federal government could provide individuals with a lump sum compensation for the termination of Social Security benefits while still keeping total debt at a far lower proportion of GDP than it was right after World War II. Although the rise in debt would be dramatic, several aspects bear emphasizing. First, the federal government could issue compensation in the form of government bonds with set due dates. This would help the government match its cash flows better and ensure that actual revenues would only be needed on the same schedule that they would otherwise have been. It would also lower the need for interest payments on the newly issued debt. From the recipients' view, these bonds would have clear value because any change in their terms would now constitute a formal default with all of its consequences, whereas a cut in benefits under current law does not.

Second, accomplishing this transition would remove the largest causes of future deficits. As a result, balanced budgets should be much easier to accomplish. Continued economic growth would then lower the debt-to-GDP ratio significantly within a generation. And the implementation of a better safety net should allow the adoption of policies such as free trade and tax reform that promote faster growth.

There are good reasons to think that financial markets would react favorably to this development. Under current law, Social Security, Medicare, and Medicaid will create unsustainable demands on the federal budget in about a decade (see figure 10.4). Some radical reform is inevitable. Although future entitlement benefits do not constitute a formal obligation of the United States, no one believes the government will totally eliminate them without any compensation. They represent a large, but indeterminate, future liability that significantly affects the long-term financial environment

Figure 10.4   CBO Projections for Federal Spending on Major Programs

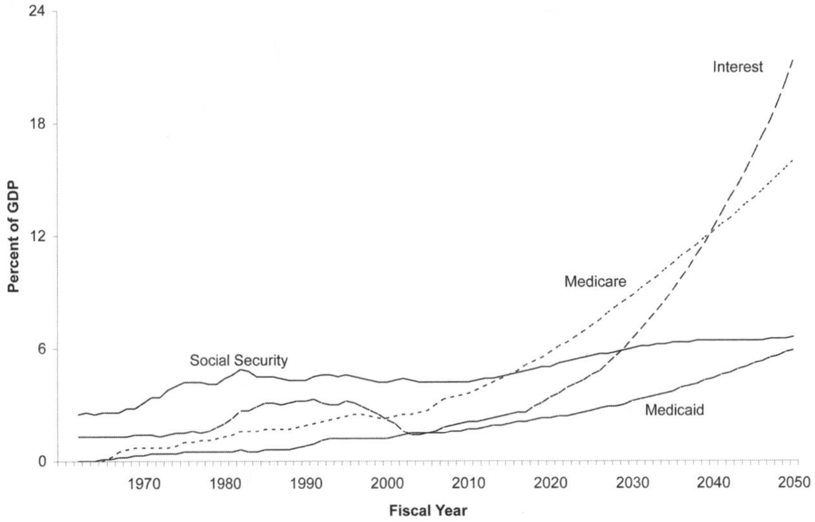

Source: Congressional Budget Office

of the United States and casts doubt on future tax legislation, interest rates, competitiveness, and fiscal policy. Financial markets would welcome legislation that reduces and caps the liability, and if the reduction in total liabilities was significant enough, changing them from indeterminate to definite liabilities could actually improve the fiscal health of the government.

The onetime nature of a transition to a different program justifies a onetime increase in the national debt. It is important to acknowledge that the United States would face some financial vulnerability once this was done because it would be less free to run significant deficits if needed to respond to a war or severe recession. In addition, the increase in debt would have to be followed by a period of balanced budgets to reassure markets that the higher debt-to-GDP ratio represented a ceiling. But if balanced budgets did occur, economic growth should produce a swift reduction in the debt ratio over the next decade.

The government has an obligation to ensure that the taxes it collects from citizens are spent wisely. It is not living up to this duty. Even without considering the deadweight economic loss associated with interfering with mutually profitable transactions as well as the compliance and enforcement costs, taxes represent a confiscation of individuals' personal wealth and a limitation on their freedom. This obligation holds even if officials are only considering a tax on the "rich" because, at a minimum, the revenue could be used to reduce taxes on others. More importantly, even taking from those who have the most should carry with it a strong moral obligation on the government to use the revenues to better society.

Government is necessary in a civilized society. Although there is much greater scope for implementing user fees both as a means of raising the revenue needed to provide services and as a market mechanism to ensure that only government services of value are provided, general taxes are also necessary. But a quick glance at the budget shows many programs that exist only because they were useful decades ago or because a powerful interest group fights to maintain them.

Some might argue that spending in a democracy should reflect public demands. Yet the force driving much of the budget is seldom an informed debate about what best serves the public interest. It is instead a combination of money and privileged access, a refusal to insist on results, and adherence to obsolete political philosophies about what works and what people want. Listen to today's debate about raising taxes and spending. Seldom do you hear a commitment to make sure that the money goes to those who need or deserve it. Seldom do you hear a plan for measuring results to ensure that spending delivers the benefits promised. Instead, the impetus is mainly to transfer money from one group to another simply because the latter supports the party advocating the transfer.

These politics have cheapened government and weakened the social ladder that helps the poor develop their innate capacities. The powers of spending and regulation often are used to help entrenched interests maintain their power and prevent new entrants from offering better services at cheaper prices. In doing so, they are too often aided by those who claim to care most about the poor.

Government cannot fund the programs needed to create a new relationship between individuals and the state while maintaining the old system built on paternalism and parochialism. It must clear away the latter in order to free up the resources needed to credibly guarantee a minimum income and to restore the transparency and degrees of freedom that the economy needs in order to adapt to future changes.

CONCLUSION:
PURSUING MORE THAN GDP

CRAFTING THE RIGHT INSTITUTIONS

A central premise of this book is that the current economic wealth of American society allows for the elimination of what might be called preventable poverty—that which is not the result of deliberate and self-defeating decisions by or insurmountable handicaps of individuals—within one or two decades. This can be done by conditioning a guarantee of adequate income on an obligation to engage in a few behaviors widely acknowledged to influence personal success.

This will be possible only if the programs put in place to achieve it are well designed. In order to command the necessary resources, the programs must be designed with the need to attract and maintain public support. This requires that they advance the public good, not just that of private individuals, even if the latter are poor. Otherwise, support will wane as people see the programs as being ineffective or view themselves as being taken advantage of by rewarding individuals who do not clearly deserve support.

In order to accomplish this, the programs should embody a set of institutional principles. The first is that they should focus on the average person, keeping the rules as clear and simple as possible. There will inevitably be exceptions in the form of individuals who need additional help or specific cases where equity seems to demand an exception to the general rule. But insisting on a standard of simplicity allows the majority of cases to be handled with a minimum of effort and frees up the resources needed to give exceptions the attention that they deserve.

Second, the programs must be transparent so that both recipients and the general public can understand how they work both in theory and, even more important, in practice. This allows society to see whether the programs are making a difference. It also limits the opportunities for rent-seeking by denying the possibility of creating specific programs for powerful interest groups and reducing the level of detailed knowledge needed to fairly evaluate the merit of legislation.

Finally, in addition to transferring resources directly, government policy should strongly focus on regulations that minimize the cost of purchasing the goods and services most important to life without destroying the market discipline that ensures that buyers get the best service for the least amount of money. In public policy, government should be firmly on the side of the consumer rather than the producer, and it should trust the former to make informed decisions. The persistence of exploitive markets should be seen for what it is: the lack of sufficient choice among providers abetted by artificial regulations or insufficient income rather than an inability to pursue one's best interests.

GETTING THERE FROM HERE

This relationship between the individual and society is radically different from that which now prevails. The book has not dwelt at length on finances or the method of transitioning from the current system to the one proposed. This is not because such issues are not important. It is because the issues do not stand in the way of making the switch. The resources are there if the decision is ever made. If the decision is not made, it will not be because the way could not be found.

Given current politics, it may seem unrealistic to expect such a radical change to ever take place. But even if the proposals called for in this book are never fully enacted, they still serve the purpose of pointing out the direction in which society should evolve. It is difficult, if not impossible, to evaluate the wisdom of marginal changes to the status quo unless we have an idea of the direction in which we want to go. With such a goal in place, changes that take us toward the ideal gain a preference over ones that take us further away.

Whether society can move in this direction is an open question. Many years ago Mancur Olson hypothesized that the governments of stable nations would gradually be captured by an accumulation of special interests, leading to slower growth. Because of the growing power of special interests, society would become unable to implement the rules and conditions that would benefit society as a whole.[1] America is now faced with the emergence of large nations whose governments are increasingly determined to challenge it for economic and social, if not military, primacy as well as a technological environment that demands constant change. If it is incapable of making the necessary changes to accommodate these forces, events will overtake it.

WHAT REMAINS TO BE DONE

Implementation of a more decentralized public policy does not solve all problems, however. As already mentioned, the biblical reminder that the poor will always be with us will remain true. For one thing, individuals will continue to make unwise and self-destructive choices that make it impossible for them to live a decent life. Addiction, crime, early pregnancy, and other self-defeating behaviors will always take hold of a segment of society. Increasingly, however, poverty will become the symptom signaling an underlying search of meaning in misplaced sources rather than the result of external forces limiting the individual's ability to join society as a productive member.

Second, no policy can eliminate all unhappiness in society. As societies become richer, individuals have both the resources and the desire to fulfill their higher needs. But, whereas the path to solving basic needs like hunger is relatively straightforward, the prescription for satisfying the needs for esteem and self-actualization is much less clear. Not only are many paths open, but also the "right" path differs for each person. Yet it is increasingly toward these higher needs that both society and individuals must turn.

In pursuing them, two false avenues must be resisted. The first is the belief that these higher needs can ever be fulfilled merely by the acquisition of more material goods. The second is the pursuit of perfect justice or equality in human relationships. Both are doomed to failure.

Government can accomplish a great deal if it focuses on what is most important. An attempt to solve all possible problems, including tangential and minor ones, is extremely destructive to efficiency and legitimacy of government. Individual and collective self-government requires maturity. Not every want, nor even every need, can be satisfied by government, and successful societies will increasingly have to rely mainly on individual efforts in order to advance.

Government based on decentralization and greater personal autonomy is needed in order to respond to a rapidly changing world. But it is also vital to the evolution of advanced societies into a postmaterialism in which all people are allowed to pursue their own self-actualization, even if they follow a path that others cannot recognize. This is likely to require a greater, but different bond between the individual and society.

Modern societies are rapidly approaching the point where further economic growth by itself will not result in greater personal well-being. In recent years, a great deal of research has focused on what makes people happy. Although happiness should not be taken as a full substitute for self-actualization, it is usually likely to be a large part of it. We can imagine special circumstances in which a fully self-actualized person may be temporarily unhappy, for example, while making a significant personal sacrifice in pursuit of a more compelling higher virtue. But it is difficult, if not contradictory, to imagine a society in which most people are self-actualized yet still unhappy.

Increasingly, this research shows that individuals, both within society and across societies, do not associate improvements in happiness with improvements in income once they get beyond a relatively low income.[2] As one survey summarizes, "Happiness is thus not given and immutable, but is constructed within the person concerned and largely depends on the social environment within which each person has been socialized and within which he or she lives."[3] Individuals who suddenly experience a large change in income or other circumstances do experience a temporary change in self-reported happiness. But they gradually revert back to their previous level. Certain events, however, are associated with more permanent changes in happiness: an optimistic personal outlook and marriage tend to increase it, whereas involuntary unemployment decreases it.

F. Scott Fitzgerald wrote, "The test of a first-rate intelligence is the ability to hold two opposed ideas in the mind at the same time, and still retain the ability to function. One should, for example, be able to see that things are hopeless and yet be determined to make them otherwise."[4] An advanced society must increasingly possess this function as well, for certain oppositions can never be reconciled. One is the tension between the individual and the society in which she or he lives. The fact that we cannot now see a clear way to implement changes that would redress this balance does not mean that we should not try.

TOWARD A POSTINDUSTRIAL SOCIETY

The challenge for advanced economies is twofold. The first is to help create the conditions by which the vast majority of the world's citizens can join in the benefits of a life in which basic needs are fulfilled. Advancement in developing countries will largely depend on the economic and social policies pursued by their governments and on the political and social views of their individuals and societies. No nation can ever advance as long as its government is pursuing populist policies such as those of Hugo Chavez in Venezuela or authoritarian principles such as those of Gurbanguly Berdimuhamedov in Turkmenistan. But societies built largely around tribalism such as Afghanistan or religious orthodoxy such as Iran are also doomed to economic failure absent large outside flows from either foreign assistance or oil because they are incapable of generating the amount and variety of productive effort needed to sustain an advanced society.

Other nations such as India and China show more promising signs. To the extent that they succeed, there is a moral obligation to accept the economic and political dislocations associated with their rise. Despite the changes it brings, the emergence of strong economies with stable and open governments is a strong benefit to the United States. American policy should seek to make this rise in global living standards as quick and easy as possible.

The second major challenge is to transform further economic and technological advancement into higher social welfare through the development of higher needs. Higher incomes alone are unlikely to accomplish this. They can bring with them advancements that are clearly linked to better personal conditions such as safer food, better health care, and greater access to education. These possibilities are more likely to be realized if government ensures that the underlying markets are decentralized and open. But they can also enable a movement away from activities designed solely to increase material well-being and toward those that aim at a spiritual renewal. This process, if it occurs, will happen gradually, person by person. To some extent it is already happening, and the fresh outlook of each new generation is likely to speed it. Government can assist the transfer by making it easier for people to make individual tradeoffs between work and leisure and to pursue alternative forms of adding value to society.

The fallacy of today's liberals is their belief that individuals can have economic rights without reciprocal obligations. In an economy that relies on voluntary transactions to generate the vast majority of its wealth, the coercive powers of government are increasingly limited. Unlike political rights, which usually impose little cost on others and often create social benefits, every forced transfer of economic assets involves an equal and offsetting loss to someone else, and the net result is often a loss in total social welfare. Even if economic rights were granted the status of political rights, there is no reason to think that the government can continue to sensibly manage the large bureaucratic programs that lie behind much of the current approach to education, housing, hunger, and other social ills without a further deterioration in quality.

But there is an equal fallacy among many conservatives. It is that an individual's worth can and should be measured largely by market forces. This would not be true even if the individual's purpose was largely to contribute to the material well-being of society. When we assert that the primary purpose of each individual lies outside of the economy, it is clearly false. As Alasdair MacIntyre pointed out, there is no pristine, original distribution of rights and goods from which today's inequality can be traced as being merely the fair application of previously agreed upon rules.[5] Today's distribution is no more fair or inevitable than many others that could have been arrived at by alternative rules, and if it is not a violation of political rights to insist that the poor adhere to laws that support an inequality that they never agreed to, it is also not a violation of the economic rights of the rich to insist on some minimum standard of living that all citizens are entitled to as a consequence of their humanity and their participation in society.

There is another issue on which each side is wrong. Today's liberals are mistaken when they assert that individual morality is purely a matter of personal choice, to be selected as one selects clothing or occupations. Clearly, no one believes that as it applies to their own personal position. Yet on fundamental issues like abortion and embryonic stem cell research we repeatedly hear that society has no right to enforce even a common and strongly held position on those who dissent from it.

But conservatives are also mistaken to the extent that they insist morality and virtue exist as static concepts to be applied rigidly to all societies at all times. Both society and the individual have a teleological purpose that defines the virtue and morality that must govern their lives. Economic advancement, by making it possible to supply the bulk of people's material needs with a small fraction of society's total effort, makes it possible to make the search for that purpose: that which gives life meaning, the main focus of human energy. But the relationship between these purposes is circular. The individual cannot be evaluated outside of her or his role in society. If the pursuit of one's own individual pleasure outside of its effects on society were the sole criterion for morality, we could not distinguish between Gandhi and Hitler. But the purpose of society must also refer back to the fulfillment of the individuals in it. Individuals are ends in themselves, not means by which the perfect society can be created. Communism, Nazism, and Islamic fundamentalism are abhorrent not only because they constitute a threat to alternative ideologies. We are just as repulsed by their treatment of their own adherents as cogs in a larger system to be used solely for its advancement and to find satisfaction only in its glory.

Society will not voluntarily return to its primitive state, nor should it. But it also cannot go on merely pursuing individual or social wealth as an end result. The way out is to use the material wealth of society as a means with which to pursue the higher purposes for which people and society exist. All individuals must discover these purposes for themselves, but their search must be rooted in the broader purpose of the society around them. This reconciliation can only be accomplished through a social dialogue within which each individual has a basic level of security and respect. The income contract delivers this. The purpose of government should be to organize and further this mutual search for greater meaning, not to divvy up the spoils of wealth according to a system in which there is no higher purpose than holding political power and in which the moral claim on government assistance is determined largely by the votes one can deliver or the political contributions one can make.

Signs of this individual need are everywhere, in the renewed rise of religion from benign forms of evangelism to the growth of radical Islam and in the increased ability of the young to take advantage of the Internet in order to chart their own search for careers, friends, entertainment, and expression. In all of this a sense of belonging and common ethics are important elements of meaning toward which life can be directed. Those who attack religion[6] run a terrible risk because they mistakenly believe that social norms and ethical principles can be justified purely on a rationale basis. In fact, they cannot: there must be some reference to something outside of ourselves. Take away the reference that many people rely on, and you may find that either adherence to the common good falls or the reference is replaced by something different and more malevolent.

Each individual's sense of purpose must contain at least a component of the social purpose, and the latter can only be arrived at collectively. For politics to once again play a meaningful role in this search for common meaning it must advance beyond today's static debate. The New Deal approach to government problems was never as effective as its proponents claimed, and, in any case, it has run its course. It is incapable of creating a place for each person in society. This place must largely be found by each individual. On the other hand, economic growth and capitalism increasingly need some deeper foundation in order to have meaning. In advanced societies, they cannot be ends in themselves. Progressives must give up on the need to control the conditions within which individuals receive services. Conservatives must increasingly ensure that there is a place for each individual in society and that this place reflects social and political, not just economic, measures of fairness.

By creating a voluntary and reciprocal relationship between the individual and society, a new contract makes explicit the concrete obligations that each person owes his or her neighbors. The contract does not require the individual to rise above those obligations, but it is likely that many, if given the chance, will endeavor to do so. If Abraham Maslow is right, the higher needs are an innate desire of most human beings. They may be superseded by material poverty or retarded by abuse, but in healthy individuals they will assert themselves over time. If those who believe in the future are correct, technology will deliver to people increasingly greater control over their environment and themselves. Control does not imply the ability to use it wisely, but it does open up possibilities. If Democrats can give up their desire for greater government involvement in the daily lives of individuals and if Republicans can support a fairer basic share of society's material prosperity, there is hope that we can begin to embark on a grand discourse about the possibilities before us and, in doing so, set a better example for those nations that wish to join us.

NOTES

INTRODUCTION

1. American Pet Products Manufacturers Association, "Pet Pampering and Pet Health Insurance Drive Pet Industry Sales to Another All Time High," press release, February 11, 2008, at www.appma.org/press_releasedetail.asp?id=118 (accessed February 29, 2008).

2. Entertainment Software Association, "Facts and Research: Top 10 Industry Facts," at www.theesa.com/facts/top_10_facts.php (accessed February 29 2008).

3. U.S. Department of Labor, U.S. Bureau of Labor Statistics, "Consumer Expenditures in 2005," February 2007, at www.bls.gov/cex/csxann05.pdf, 3.

4. International Consumer Electronics Show, "2006 Is the Year of DTV, Forecasts CEA," press release, January 4, 2006, at www.cesweb.org/press/news/rd_release _detail.asp?id=10913 (accessed February 29, 2008).

CHAPTER 1

1. Kenneth Arrow, *Social Choice and Individual Values*, 2nd ed. (New Haven, Conn.: Yale University Press, 1963).

2. "Detroit Teachers Go on Strike, Wait out Better Contract but Could Face Fines," *USA Today*, August 28, 2006, at www.usatoday.com/news/education/2006-08-28-detroit-teachers_x.htm (accessed March 1, 2008).

3. Friedrich A. Hayek, *The Road to Serfdom* (Chicago: University of Chicago Press, 1944).

4. Abraham H. Maslow, *Motivation and Personality*, 3rd ed. (New York: Harper & Row, 1987).

5. Maslow, *Motivation and Personality*, 22.

6. Richard A. Posner, *Economic Analysis of Law*, 6th ed. (New York: Aspen Publishers, 2003), 263.

7. For an interesting case study of market integration see, Pietra Rivoli, *The Travels of a T-Shirt in the Global Economy: An Economist Examines the Markets, Power, and Politics of World Trade* (Hoboken, N.J.: John Wiley & Sons, 2005).

8. See Marc Levinson, *The Box: How the Shipping Container Made the World Smaller and the World Economy Bigger* (Princeton, N.J.: Princeton University Press, 2006).

9. "Voting with Your Trolley," *Economist*, December 9, 2006, 73.

10. Milt Freudenheim and Mary Williams Walsh, "The Next Retirement Time Bomb," *New York Times*, December 11, 2005, sec. 3, 1.

11. Congressional Budget Office, *The Long-Term Budget Outlook* (Washington D.C.: December 2005).

12. Although the Congressional Budget Office projects that revenues under current law will rise to 23.7 percent of GDP by 2050, such a scenario is unlikely. First, it assumes that none of the tax cuts enacted under President George W. Bush will be extended, even though there is wide bipartisan support for some of them. Second, it assumes no changes to the Alternative Minimum Tax (AMT). Yet both parties agree on the desirability of preventing the AMT from affecting millions of middle-class Americans. Although current spending projections are also unlikely to be realized, the political pain associated with spending reductions is much higher than that accompanying tax cuts.

13. Grant D. Aldonas, Robert Z. Lawrence, and Matthew J. Slaughter, *Succeeding in the Global Economy: A New Policy Agenda for the American Workers*, Financial Services Forum, Washington, D.C., June 26, 2007.

14. Joellen Perry, "Exodus of Skilled Workers Leaves Germany in a Bind," *Wall Street Journal*, January 3, 2007, A2.

15. Doreen Carvajal, "Tax Leads Americans Abroad to Renounce U.S.," *New York Times*, December 18, 2006, A6; Robert Lenzner and Phillipe Mao, "The New Refugees," *Forbes*, November 21, 1994, 131.

16. Joel Millman, "Developing Nations Lure Retirees, Raising Idea of 'Outsourcing' Boomers' Golden Years," *Wall Street Journal*, November 14, 2005, A2.

17. Jan Tinbergen, *Economic Policy: Principles and Design* (Amsterdam: North-Holland Publishing, 1956).

18. Congressional Budget Office, *Is Social Security Progressive?* Economic and Budget Issue Brief (Washington, D.C.: December 15, 2006).

19. See Peter F. Drucker, *Management: Tasks, Responsibilities, Practices* (New York: Harper Colophon, 1985), 220–22.

CHAPTER 2

1. Russell L. Lamb, "The New Farm Economy," *Regulation* 26, no. 4 (Winter 2003–2004): 10–15.

2. 1 Timothy 6:18–19.

3. Luke 16:1–13.

4. Mark 12:41–44.

5. See, for example, Tob. 4:7–11; Sir. 4:36; Prov. 11:24–25; Deut. 15:8–11; Luke 6:30–31; Acts 30:35; and James 2:15–17.

6. Peter Barnes, *Capitalism 3.0: A Guide to Reclaiming the Commons* (San Francisco: Berrett Koehler Publishers, 2006).

7. James M. Buchanan and Gordon Tullock, *The Calculus of Consent* (Ann Arbor: University of Michigan Press, 1962).

8. John Rawls, *A Theory of Justice* (Cambridge, Mass.: Harvard University Press, 1971), 302–3.

9. James M. Buchanan, "A Hobbesian Interpretation of the Rawlsian Difference Principle," *Kyklos* 29, fasc. 1 (1976): 16.

10. See Gordon Tullock, "The Welfare Costs of Tariffs, Monopolies, and Theft," *Western Economic Journal* 5 (March 1967): 228. A few pages later Tullock notes that income transfers inflict welfare losses only to the extent that they lead people to employ resources in attempting to obtain or prevent them (231). It follows that transfers that reduce the need for defensive expenses or that encourage productive activity by reducing individual risk could actually increase social welfare.

11. Mancur Olson, *The Logic of Collective Action: Public Goods and the Theory of Groups* (Cambridge, Mass.: Harvard University Press, 1965).

12. See Philip K. Howard, *The Death of Common Sense: How Law Is Suffocating America* (New York: Random House, 1994).

13. "The Mountain Man and the Surgeon," *Economist*, December 24, 2005, 24–26.

14. Nicholas Eberstadt, "Why Poverty Doesn't Rate," *Washington Post*, September 3, 2006, B1.

15. Eberstadt, "Why Poverty Doesn't Rate."

16. Friedrich A. Hayek, *The Constitution of Liberty* (Chicago: University of Chicago Press, 1960).

17. See Bruno S. Frey and Alois Stutzer, *Happiness and Economics: How the Economy and Institutions Affect Human Well-Being* (Princeton, N.J.: Princeton University Press, 2002), 74–81. The authors note that although per capita income has risen rapidly over the last several decades, the proportion of people who consider themselves "very happy" has fallen.

18. Thomas W. Hazlett, "'Universal Service' Telephone Subsidies: What Does $7 Billion Buy?" June 2006, at www.senior.org/Documents/USF.Master.6.13.06.pdf (accessed March 1, 2008).

19. See Richard Vedder, "Economic Growth, Economic Justice, and Public Policy," testimony before the Joint Economic Committee of Congress, hearing on Ensuring our Economic Future by Promoting Middle-Class Prosperity, 110th Cong., 1st sess., January 31, 2007.

20. Adam Smith, *The Wealth of Nations* (New York: Random House, 1994 [1776]).

21. William A. Henry III, *In Defense of Elitism* (New York: Doubleday, 1994), 18, 26.

22. Bethany McLean and Peter Elkind, *The Smartest Guys in the Room:The Amazing Rise and Scandalous Fall of Enron* (New York: Portfolio, 2003), 406.

23. Brookings Institution, *From Poverty, Opportunity: Putting the Market to Work for Lower Income Families* (Washington, D.C.: 2006).

24. Paul Blustein, "The Tariff Mismatch," *Washington Post*, December 11, 2005, F1.

25. Gary Burtless and Christopher Jencks, "American Inequality and Its Consequences," in *Agenda for a Nation*, ed. Henry J. Aaron, James M. Lindsay, and Pietro S. Nivola (Washington, D.C.: Brookings Institution Press, 2003), 86.

26. Burtless and Jencks, "American Inequality," 77.

27. Burtless and Jencks, "American Inequality," 62.

28. Burtless and Jencks, "American Inequality," 71.

29. Gianmarco I. P. Ottaviano and Giovanni Peri, "Rethinking the Gains from Immigration," National Bureau of Economic Research Working Paper No. 11672, Cambridge, Mass., October 2005; David Card, "Is the New Immigration Really So Bad?" National Bureau of Economic Research Working Paper No. 11547, Cambridge, Mass., August 2005.

30. Burtless and Jencks, "American Inequality," 74.

31. Burtless and Jencks, "American Inequality," 85.

32. Anna Bernasek, "A Poverty Line That's out of Date and out of Favor," *New York Times*, March 12, 2006, sec. 3, 6.

33. Charles A. Murray, *Losing Ground: American Social Policy 1950–1980* (New York: Basic Books, 1984).

34. Isabel Sawhill, "Families at Risk," in *Setting National Priorities: The 2000 Election and Beyond*, ed. Henry J. Aaron and Robert D. Reischauer (Washington, D.C.: Brookings Institution Press, 1999), 107.

35. Sawhill, "Families at Risk," 98.

36. Robert I. Lerman, "The Impact of Changing U.S. Family Structure on Child Poverty and Income Inequality," *Economica* 63 (Supplement 1993): S119–39.

37. Hilary W. Hoynes, Marianne E. Page, and Ann Huff Stevens, "Poverty in America: Trends and Explanations," *Journal of Economic Perspectives* 20 (Winter 2006): 49.

38. Hoynes, Page, and Stevens, "Poverty in America," 60–61.

39. Hoynes, Page, and Stevens, "Poverty in America," 49.

40. Current Population Survey, "Annual Demographic Survey," 2003, at http://pubdb3.census.gov/macro/032004/pov/new29_100_01.htm (accessed March 2, 2008).

41. David Wessel, "In Poverty Tactics, an Old Debate: Who Is at Fault," *Wall Street Journal*, June 15, 2006, A1.

42. Adam Smith, *The Theory of Moral Sentiments*, ed. D. D. Raphael and A. L. Macfie (Indianapolis: Liberty Fund, 1982); James Q. Wilson, *The Moral Sense* (New York: Free Press, 1993).

43. Sawhill, "Families at Risk," 110.

44. James T. Patterson, *America's Struggle against Poverty in the Twentieth Century*, 4th rev. ed. (Cambridge, Mass.: Harvard University Press, 2000).

45. Marvin Olasky, *The Tragedy of American Compassion* (Washington, D.C.: Regnery Publishing, 1992).

46. Murray, *Losing Ground*.

47. Glen G. Cain, "The Issues of Marital Stability and Family Composition and the Income Maintenance Experiments," in *Lessons from the Income Maintenance Experiments*, ed. Alicia H. Munnell (Boston: Federal Reserve Bank of Boston, 1986), 60–93. The effect on black families was statistically significant, however.

48. Gary Burtless, "The Work Response to a Guaranteed Income: A Survey of Experimental Evidence," in *Lessons from the Income Maintenance Experiments*, ed. Alicia H. Munnell (Boston: Federal Reserve Bank of Boston, 1986), 22–52.

49. Dennis J. Coyle and Aaron Wildavsky, "Social Experimentation in the Face of Formidable Fables," in *Lessons from the Income Maintenance Experiments*, ed. Alicia H. Munnell (Boston: Federal Reserve Bank of Boston, 1986), 167–84.

50. Rebecca M. Blank, "Evaluating Welfare Reform in the United States," *Journal of Economic Literature* 40 (December 2002): 1108.

51. Blank, "Evaluating Welfare Reform," 1127–45.

CHAPTER 3

1. Rebecca M. Blank, "Evaluating Welfare Reform in the United States," *Journal of Economic Literature* 40 (December 2002): 1143.

2. Paul Tough, "The Harlem Project," *New York Times Magazine*, June 20, 2004.

3. Martin Anderson, *Welfare: The Political Economy of Welfare Reform in the United States* (Stanford, Calif.: Hoover Institution Press, 1978), 34.

4. Ray Boshara, "Every Baby a Trust Fund Baby," in *Ten Big Ideas for a New America* (Washington, D.C.: New America Foundation, February 2007), 1–4.

5. Dennis J. Coyle and Aaron Wildavsky, "Social Experimentation in the Face of Formidable Fables," in *Lessons from the Income Maintenance Experiments*, ed. Alicia H. Munnell (Boston: Federal Reserve Bank of Boston, 1986), 176.

6. David Neumark and William Wascher, "Minimum Wages and Employment: A Review of Evidence from the New Minimum Wage Research," National Bureau of Economic Research Working Paper No. 12663, Cambridge, Mass., November 2006.

7. Blank, "Evaluating Welfare Reform," 1146.

8. Blank, "Evaluating Welfare Reform," 1159.

9. Deborah Solomon, "For Welfare Clients, Temporary Jobs Can Be a Roadblock," *New York Times*, December 15, 2006, A1.

10. Lou Ann Walker, "A Place Called Hope," *Parade*, July 7, 2002, 10; Rachel Smolkin, "Mixing with Care," *Washington Post*, May 14, 2002, F1.

11. Isabel Sawhill, "Families at Risk," in *Setting National Priorities: The 2000 Election and Beyond*, ed. Henry J. Aaron and Robert D. Reischauer (Washington, D.C.: Brookings Institution Press, 1999), 98.

12. U.S. Bureau of Labor Statistics, U.S. Department of Labor, *The Employment Situation: September 2007*, Release USDL-07-1492, October 5, 2007, tab. A-4.

13. Current Population Survey, "Annual Social and Economic Supplement: Years of School Completed," 2006, at http://pubdb3.census.gov/macro/032007/pov/new29_100_01.htm (accessed March 3, 2008).

14. *Marchwinski v. Howard*, 60 Fed. Appx. 601, 2002 WL 1870916 (6th Cir., April 7, 2003).

15. Sawhill, "Families at Risk," 120.

16. Sawhill, "Families at Risk," 123.

17. Blank, "Evaluating Welfare Reform," 1154. See Rebecca Maynard et al., "Changing Family Formation Behavior through Welfare Reform," in *Welfare, the Family, and Reproductive Behavior*, ed. Robert A. Moffitt (Washington, D.C.: National Research Council, 1998), 134–76.

18. Ted R. Miller, Mark A. Cohen, and Brian Wiersema, *Victim Costs and Consequences: A New Look*, Research Report NCJ 155282 (Washington, D.C.: U.S. Department of Justice, National Institute of Justice, January 1996). See Mark A. Cohen, "Measuring the Costs and Benefits of Crime and Justice," in *Criminal Justice 2000, Volume 4: Measurement and Analysis of Crime and Justice*, ed. David Duffee (Rockville, Md.: National Institute of Justice, 2000), 263–315.

19. Associated Press, "U.S. Prison Population Sets Record," *Washington Post*, December 1, 2006, A3.

20. William J. Sabol, Todd D. Minton, and Paige M. Harrison, "Prison and Jail Inmates at Midyear 2006," U.S. Department of Justice, Office of Justice Programs, Bureau of Justice Statistics, Bulletin NCJ 217675, June 2007.

21. See Marshall B. Reinsdorf, "Alternative Measures of Personal Saving," *Survey of Current Business* (February 2007): 7–13.

22. Orlo Nichols, Michael Clingman, and Alice Wade, "Internal Real Rates of Return under the OASDI Program for Hypothetical Workers," Actuarial Note 2004.5, Social Security Administration, Office of the Chief Actuary, March 2005, at www.ssa.gov/oact/notes/ran5/an2004-5.html (accessed March 3, 2008).

23. Brookings Institution, *From Poverty, Opportunity: Putting the Market to Work for Lower Income Families* (Washington, D.C.: 2006), 20–34.

24. Tax Foundation, *Putting a Face on America's Tax Returns* (Washington, D.C.: 2005), 8–9.

25. Tax Foundation, *Putting a Face*, 18.

CHAPTER 4

1. Peter F. Drucker, *Managing the Non-profit Organization: Principles and Practices* (New York: HarperCollins, 1990), xiii–xiv.

2. Drucker, *Managing the Non-profit Organization*, xvii.

3. See, for example, Christine W. Letts, William Ryan, and Allen Grossman, "Virtuous Capital: What Foundations Can Learn from Venture Capitalists," *Harvard Business Review* (March–April 1997): 36–44.

4. Bill Bradley, Paul Jansen, and Les Silverman, "The Non-profit Sector's $100 Billion Opportunity," *Harvard Business Review* (May 2003): 94–103.

5. Matthew Bishop, "The Birth of Philanthrocapitalism," *Economist*, special supplement on the Business of Giving, February 26, 2006.

6. Tracy Thompson, "Profit with Honor," *Washington Post Magazine*, December 19, 1999; William P. Ryan, "The New Landscape for Nonprofits," *Harvard Business Review* (January–February 1999): 127–36.

7. See Reed Abelson, "Health Plan Used by U.S. Is Debated as a Model," *New York Times*, October 30, 2007, B1.

8. Ben S. Bernanke, "GSE Portfolios, Systematic Risk, and Affordable Housing," speech before the Independent Community Bankers of America's Annual Convention and Techworld, Honolulu, Hawaii, March 6, 2007, at www.federalreserve .gov/newsevents/speech/bernanke20070306a.htm (accessed March 3, 2008); Alan Greenspan, "Regulatory Reform of the Government-Sponsored Enterprises," testimony before the Committee on Banking, Housing and Urban Affairs, U.S. Senate, April 6, 2005, at www.federalreserve.gov/boarddocs/testimony/2005/20050406/ default.htm (accessed March 3, 2008).

9. See John R. Wilke and Patrick Barta, "Firms Report Fannie Mae, Freddie Mac Threats," *Wall Street Journal*, March 8, 2001, A3. When the Congressional Budget Office issued a 1996 report critical of Fannie and Freddie, David Jeffers, Fannie Mae's vice president for corporate relations, responded, "This is the work of economic pencil brains who wouldn't recognize something that works for ordinary home buyers if it bit them in their erasers." Richard W. Stevenson, "Report Is Skeptical of U.S.-Backed Home Mortgages," *New York Times*, May 30, 1996, D1.

10. Paul, Weiss, Rifkind, Wharton, & Garrison LLP and Huron Consulting Group Inc., *A Report to the Special Review Committee of the Board of Directors of Fannie Mae: Executive Summary*, 4, at http://download.fanniemae.com/execsum.pdf (accessed March 3, 2008).

11. Paul et al., *Report to the Special Review*, 5.

12. Paul et al., *Report to the Special Review*, 5.

13. Paul et al., *Report to the Special Review*, 23.

14. Wayne Passmore, "The GSE Implicit Subsidy and Value of Government Ambiguity," Finance and Economic Discussion Series No. 2003-64, Board of Governors of the Federal Reserve System, December 2003.

15. Congressional Budget Office, *Updated Estimates of the Subsidies to the Housing GSEs* (Washington, D.C.: April 2004).

16. U.S. Department of Housing and Urban Development, "HUD Data Shows Fannie Mae and Freddie Mac Have Trailed the Industry in Providing Affordable Housing in 44 States," News Release No. 04-066, July 6, 2004, at www.hud.gov/ news/release.cfm?content=pr04-066.cfm&CFID=1184198&CFTOKEN =48003960 (accessed March 3, 2008).

17. "Re-Competition of MEP Centers Is Cancelled: Manufacturing Extension Program Is Whipsawed by Changing Political Winds," *Manufacturing and Technology News*, August 13, 2004.

18. Unionstats, "Union Membership and Coverage Database from the CPS," February 8, 2008, at www.unionstats.com/ (accessed March 3, 2008).

19. Daniel Akst, "A New Idea for Unions: Forget the Past," *New York Times*, December 5, 1999, sec. 3, 4.

20. Samuel Leiken, "New Jobs for Labor Unions," *New York Times*, August 31, 2002, A23.

21. Aaron Bernstein, "Look Who's Pushing Productivity," *Business Week*, April 7, 1997.

22. Greg Ip, "Union Advances as Key Source of Skilled Labor," *Wall Street Journal*, October, 4, 2005, A17.

23. See Steven Pearlstein, "To Survive, Unions Must Head Back to Their Roots," *Washington Post*, July 22, 2005, D1; "Adapt or Die," *Economist*, June 7, 2003, 13; Akst, "A New Idea for Unions."

24. Steven Greenhouse, "Labor Union, Redefined, for Freelance Workers," *New York Times*, January 27, 2007, A8; "Freelancers of the World, Unite!" *Economist*, November 11, 2006, 76.

25. C. K. Prahalad, *The Fortune at the Bottom of the Pyramid: Eradicating Poverty through Profits* (Upper Saddle River, N.J.: Wharton School Publishing, 2005).

26. William Foster and Jeffrey Bradach, "Should Nonprofits Seek Profits?" *Harvard Business Review* (January 2005): 92–100.

27. "Life Beyond Pay," *Economist*, June 17, 2006, 73; Loretta Chao, "For Gen Xers, It's Work to Live," *Wall Street Journal*, November 29, 2005, B6; Kirstin Downey, "Setting Their Own Schedules: More Boomers Are Fitting Jobs around Other Pursuits," *Washington Post*, December 8, 2002, H1.

28. Steve Lohr, "How Is the Game Played Now?" *New York Times*, December 5, 2005, C1.

29. William McDonough and Michael Braungart, *Cradle to Cradle: Remaking the Way We Make Things* (New York: North Point Press, 2002), 75–76.

30. Kerry Hannon, "More Employers Are Offering Pet-Insurance Benefits," *Wall Street Journal*, November 12, 2005, B3.

31. M. P. McQueen, "Employers Expand Elder-Care Benefits," *Wall Street Journal*, July 27, 2006, D1.

32. Adam Lashinsky, "Search and Enjoy," *Fortune*, January 22, 2007, 70.

33. Alexis de Tocqueville, *Democracy in America, Vol. II* (New York: Vintage Classics, 1990), 106–10.

CHAPTER 5

1. Current Population Survey, "Annual Social and Economic Supplement: Educational Attainment," 2006, at http://pubdb3.census.gov/macro/032007/perinc/new04_001.htm (accessed March 5, 2008).

2. Jay Belsky et al., "Are There Long-Term Effects of Early Child Care?" *Child Development* 78 (March/April 2007): 681–701.

3. Belsky et al., "Are There Long-Term Effects?"

4. Benedict Carey, "Survey Finds Rise in Behavior Problems after Significant Time in Day Care," *New York Times*, March 26, 2007, A14.

5. National Commission on Excellence in Education, *A Nation at Risk* (Washington, D.C.: U.S. Department of Education, 1983), 5.

6. National Research Council, *Rising Above the Gathering Storm: Energizing and Employing America for a Brighter Economic Future* (Washington, D.C.: National Academy Press, 2007).

7. Peter Schrag, "The Near-Myth of Our Failing Schools," *Atlantic Monthly* (October 1997): 72–80.

8. Michael Alison Chandler, "'Nation's Report Card' Shows Improvement," *Washington Post*, September 26, 2007, A11.

9. Karen Arenson, "SAT Math Scores at Record High, but Those on the Verbal Exam Are Stagnant," *New York Times*, August 31, 2005, A7.

10. Joel Slemrod and Jon Bakija, *Taxing Ourselves: A Citizen's Guide to the Debate over Taxes*, 3rd ed. (Cambridge, Mass.: MIT Press, 2004), 44.

11. Robert Gordon, "Class Struggle," *New Republic* (June 6/13, 2005): 24.

12. Paul Ciotti, *Money and School Performance: Lessons from the Kansas City Desegregation Experiment*, Policy Analysis 298 (Washington, D.C.: Cato Institute, March 16, 1998).

13. See, for example, E. D. Hirsch Jr., *What Your Fifth Grader Needs to Know: Fundamentals of a Good Fifth-Grade Education* (New York: Dell Publishing, 1995).

14. Eliyahu M. Goldratt and Jeff Cox, *The Goal: A Process of Ongoing Improvement*, 2nd rev. ed. (Great Barrington, Mass.: North River Press, 1992).

15. U.S. Department of Education, National Center for Education Evaluation and Regional Assistance, *Effectiveness of Reading and Mathematics Software Products: Findings from the First Student Cohort* (Washington, D.C.: 2007); Harold Wenglinsky, *Using Technology Wisely: The Keys to Success in Schools* (New York: Teachers College Press, 2005).

16. Diana Jean Schemo, "Federal Program on Vouchers Draws Strong Minority Support," *New York Times*, April 6, 2006, A1.

17. Paul E. Peterson and William G. Howell, *The Education Gap: Vouchers and Urban Schools* (Washington, D.C.: Brookings Institution Press, 2006); Caroline M. Hoxby, "School Choice and School Competition: Evidence from the United States," *Swedish Economic Policy Review* 10, no. 2 (2003), at www.economics.harvard.edu/faculty/hoxby/papers/hoxby_2.pdf.

18. Hoxby, "School Choice"; Rajashri Chakrabarti, "Can Increasing Private School Participation and Monetary Loss in a Voucher Program Affect Public School Performance? Evidence from Milwaukee," *Journal of Public Economics* 92 (June 2008): 1371–1393. An earlier version of the Chakrabarti paper is available at www.newyorkfed.org/research/staff_reports/sr300.pdf (accessed March 5, 2008).

19. Henry Braun, Frank Jenkins, and Wendy Grigg, *Comparing Private Schools and Public Schools Using Hierarchical Linear Modeling* (NCES 2006-461), U.S. Department

of Education, National Center for Education Statistics, Institute of Education Science (Washington D.C.: Government Printing Office, 2006).

20. Matthew Miller, "Education: A Bold Experiment to Fix City Schools," *Atlantic Monthly* (July 1999): 15–31.

21. Miller, "Education," 31.

22. Jonathan D. Glater and Alan Finder, "In New Twist on Tuition Game, Popularity Rises with the Price," *New York Times*, December 12, 2006, A1.

23. Glater and Finder, "In New Twist."

24. U.S. Department of Education, *A Test of Leadership: Charting the Future of U.S. Higher Education* (Washington, D.C.: 2006), 10.

25. Jay Matthews, "Better than Famous," *Washington Post Magazine*, April 8, 2001; Jeremy Kahn, "Is Harvard Worth It," *Fortune*, May 1, 2000.

26. Anne Marie Chaker, "Lessons in Financial Aid," *Wall Street Journal*, March 27, 2006, R4.

27. Daniel Golden, *The Price of Admission: How America's Ruling Class Buys Its Way into Elite Colleges—and Who Gets Left outside the Gates* (New York: Crown Publishers, 2006); Jerome Karabel, *The Chosen: The Hidden History of Admission and Exclusion at Harvard, Yale, and Princeton* (New York: Houghton Mifflin, 2005).

28. Sharon LaFraniere, "Ivy League Schools Agree to Halt Collaboration on Financial Aid," *Washington Post*, May 23, 1991, A3.

29. U.S. Department of Education, *A Test of Leadership*, 14.

30. U.S. Department of Education, *A Test of Leadership*, 11–12.

31. U.S. Department of Education, *A Test of Leadership*, 11–12.

32. Julie Bosman, "Colleges Relying on Lenders to Counsel Students," *New York Times*, April 21, 2007, A1; John Hechinger, "Financial-Aid Directors Received Payments from Preferred Lender," *Wall Street Journal*, April 10, 2007, A3.

33. Glater and Finder, "In New Twist."

34. John Hechinger, "When $26 Billion Isn't Enough," *Wall Street Journal*, December 17, 2006, P1.

35. Sam Dillon, "Troubles Grow for a University Built on Profits," *New York Times*, February 11, 2007, sec. 1, 1.

36. Christine Lagorio, "Pepperdine in a Treehouse," *New York Times, Education Life*, January 7, 2007, 22.

37. Marcus Stanley, Lawrence Katz, and Alan Krueger, "Developing Skills: What We Know about the Impacts of American Employment and Training Programs on Employment, Earnings, and Educational Outcomes," unpublished paper, October 1998, at www.economics.harvard.edu/faculty/katz/files/stanley_katz_krueger_98.pdf (accessed March 5, 2008).

38. Doreen Carvajal, "Lawyers Are Not Amused by Feisty Legal Publisher," *New York Times*, August 8, 1998, D1.

39. Adam Liptak, "Nonlawyer Father Wins Suit over Education, and the Bar Is Upset," *New York Times*, May 6, 2006, A8.

40. Caroline E. Mayer, "Challenges Beset Low-Cost Paralegal Aid," *Washington Post*, May 30, 2004, F1; Adam Liptak, "Preparing Petitions: It Irks the Lawyers, but

Is It Lawyering?," *New York Times*, August 13, 2002, A1; Crystal Nix Hines, "Without a Lawyer: Chain of Legal Self-Help Centers Is Expanding," *New York Times*, July 31, 2001, C1.

41. Bureau of National Affairs, "FTC, DOJ Support Continued Use of Non-lawyers to Do Real Estate Closings," *Daily Report for Executives*, April 3, 2002, A-27.

42. Adam Liptak, "U.S. Opposes Proposal to Limit Who May Give Legal Advice," *New York Times*, February 3, 2003, A11.

43. Sandra G. Boodman, "Turf Battle in the Operating Room," *Washington Post*, May 5, 1998, Health Section, 12; Milt Freudenheim, "As Nurses Take on Primary Care, Physicians Are Sounding Alarms," *New York Times*, September 30, 1997, A1.

44. Gloria Lau, "A Hair-Brained Scheme," *Forbes*, October 20, 1997, 220.

45. "Skipping Law School: Lincoln Did It, Why Not the Valoises?" *New York Times*, September 9, 2005, A21.

CHAPTER 6

1. For a good discussion of the respective merits of regulation and the common law, see Richard A. Posner, *Economic Analysis of Law*, 6th ed. (New York: Aspen Publishers, 2003), 383–404.

2. John M. Quigley and Steven Raphael, "Is Housing Unaffordable? Why Isn't It More Affordable?" *Journal of Economic Perspectives* 18 (Winter 2004): 191.

3. Millennial Housing Commission, *Meeting Our Nation's Housing Challenges: Report of the Bipartisan Millennial Housing Commission* (Washington, D.C.: Government Printing Office, 2002).

4. Quigley and Raphael, "Is Housing Unaffordable?" 198.

5. Quigley and Raphael, "Is Housing Unaffordable?" 198–99.

6. Office of Management and Budget, *Budget of the United States Government: Fiscal Year 2008, Analytical Perspectives* (Washington, D.C: Government Printing Office, 2007), 288.

7. James R. Hagerty, "Housing Sector Seeks No Tax Remodeling," *Wall Street Journal*, January 31, 2005, A2.

8. Quigley and Raphael, "Is Housing Unaffordable?" 196.

9. Philip Shenon, "Home Exemptions Snag Bankruptcy Bill," *New York Times*, April 6, 2001, A1. In 2005 Congress passed legislation that partially limited debtors' ability to take advantage of this exemption by moving to states where it is particularly high.

10. Lori L. Taylor, "Does the United States Still Overinvest in Housing?" *Economic Review*, Federal Reserve Bank of Dallas (Second Quarter 1998): 10–18.

11. N. Edward Coulson, "Housing Policy and the Social Benefits of Homeownership," *Business Review*, Philadelphia Federal Reserve Bank (Second Quarter 2002): 7–16.

12. Harvey S. Rosen, Kenneth T. Rosen, and Douglas Holtz-Eakin, "Housing Tenure, Uncertainty, and Taxation," *Review of Economics and Statistics* 66, no. 3 (1984): 405–15.

13. Andrew Nieland, "Unwise Wisdom: Buying a House Is Better than Renting," *Wall Street Journal*, January 29, 2001, R12.

14. President's Advisory Panel on Federal Tax Reform, *Simple, Fair, and Pro-Growth: Proposals to Fix America's Tax System* (Washington, D.C.: Government Printing Office, 2005).

15. William A. Fischel, *The Economics of Zoning Laws: A Property Rights Approach to American Land Use Controls* (Baltimore: Johns Hopkins University Press, 1985).

16. Edward L. Glaeser, Joseph Gyourko, and Raven Saks, "Why Have Housing Prices Gone Up?" *American Economic Review* 95 (May 2005): 329–33.

17. Edward L. Glaeser, Joseph Gyourko, and Raven Saks, "Why Is Manhattan So Expensive? Regulation and the Rise in Housing Prices," *Journal of Law and Economics* 48, no. 2 (October 2005): 331–69.

18. Leef Smith, "Affordable Shelter for a Church, and People," *Washington Post*, July 22, 2004, T14.

19. Quigley and Raphael, "Is Housing Unaffordable?" 205.

20. Quigley and Raphael, "Is Housing Unaffordable?" 210.

21. Brendon O'Flaherty, *Making Room: The Economics of Homelessness* (Cambridge, Mass.: Harvard University Press, 1996).

22. Stephen Malpezzi and Richard K. Green, "What Has Happened to the Bottom of the U.S. Housing Market?" *Urban Studies* 33, no. 10 (December 1996): 1807–20.

23. Ned Levine, "The Effects of Local Growth Controls on Regional Housing Production and Population Redistribution in California," *Urban Studies* 36, no. 12 (November 1999): 2047–68; James A. Thorson, "The Effects of Zoning on Housing Construction," *Journal of Housing Economics* 6, no. 1 (March 1997): 81–91; William A. Fischel, *Do Growth Controls Matter? A Review of Empirical Evidence on the Effectiveness and Efficiency of Local Government Land Use Regulation* (Cambridge, Mass.: Lincoln Institute of Land Policy, 1990).

24. Quigley and Raphael, "Is Housing Unaffordable?" 210.

25. Kris Hudson, "Houston's Twilight Zone: Projects Rise in Odd Spots," *Wall Street Journal*, October 17, 2007, B1.

26. See Lawrence J. Vale, *From the Puritans to the Projects: Public Housing and Public Neighbors* (Cambridge, Mass.: Harvard University Press, 2000).

27. Arthur O'Sullivan, *Urban Economics*, 3rd ed. (Chicago: Irwin McGraw-Hill, 1996).

28. Pam Belluck, "Razing the Slums to Rescue the Residents," *New York Times*, September 6, 1998, sec. 1, 1.

29. Martha Burt, *Over the Edge: The Growth of Homelessness during the 1980s* (New York: Russell Sage Foundation, 1992); Peter H. Rossi, *Down and Out in America: The Origins of Homelessness* (Chicago: University of Chicago Press, 1991).

30. Jim Myers, "Requiem for Kentucky Courts," *Washington Post Magazine*, July 1, 2001.

31. Laurie P. Cohen, "Some Rich and Famous of New York City Bask in Shelter of Rent Law," *Wall Street Journal*, March 21, 1994, A1.

32. Deborah Sontag, "For Poorest, Life 'Trapped in a Cage,'" *New York Times*, October 6, 1996, 44.

33. Deborah Sontag, "A Weak Housing Agency Seems to Be a Step Behind," *New York Times*, October 7, 1996, A1.

34. Lizette Alvarez, "Down from Poverty: Mexico to Manhattan," *New York Times*, October 9, 1996, A1; Deborah Sontag, "Behind a Suburban Façade in Queens: A Teeming Angry Urban Arithmetic," *New York Times*, October 8, 1996, A1.

35. "Tap the Treasure in Rent Control," *New York Times*, April 9, 1991, A24.

36. Paul Krugman, "A Rent Affair," *New York Times*, June 7, 2000, A31.

37. John Tierney, "At the Intersection of Supply and Demand," *New York Times Magazine*, May 4, 1997, 40.

38. Evelyn Nieves, "In San Francisco, Renters Are Supplicants," *New York Times*, June 6, 2000, A14.

39. Nieves, "In San Francisco."

40. Judith Havemann, "Mass. City Gets a New Lease on Life," *Washington Post*, September 19, 1998, A1.

41. Havemann, "Mass. City."

42. Havemann, "Mass. City."

43. Lawrence F. Katz, Jeffrey R. Kling, and Jeffrey B. Liebman, "Moving to Opportunity in Boston: Early Results of a Randomized Mobility Experiment," *Quarterly Journal of Economics* 116, no. 2 (May 2001): 607–54. See also Jon E. Hilsenrath and Rafael Gerena-Morales, "How Much Does a Neighborhood Affect the Poor?" *Wall Street Journal*, December 28, 2006, A1.

44. Todd M. Sinai and Joel Waldfogel, *Do Low-Income Housing Subsidies Increase Housing Consumption?* National Bureau of Economic Research Working Paper No. W8709, Cambridge, Mass., January 2002.

45. Frederick Kunkle, "Housing Vouchers No Magic Key," *Washington Post*, August 5, 2002, A1.

46. Ann O'Hanlon, "Boom Times a Bust for Housing Subsidy," *Washington Post*, July 25, 2000, A1.

47. Kunkle, "Housing Vouchers."

48. Quigley and Raphael, "Is Housing Unaffordable?" 211.

49. Howard Husock, "Back to Private Housing," *Wall Street Journal*, July 31, 1997, A18.

50. Husock, "Back to Private Housing."

51. Alan Finder, "In Housing Battle, Faint Hopes and Few Bright Spots," *New York Times*, October 11, 1996, B4.

52. John Norquist and Bret Schundler, "Saving Main Street," *Washington Post*, June 5, 1999, A21.

53. Raul A. Barreneche, "Build Me a Bargain," *New York Times*, July 7, 2005, D1.

54. Ray A. Smith, "From 'Project' to Palace," *Wall Street Journal*, April 21, 2004, B1.

55. Amy Virshup, "Designer Houses for the Poor," *New York Times Magazine*, September 21, 1997, 70.

56. Lynette Holloway, "With New Purpose and Look, S.R.O.'s Make a Comeback," *New York Times*, November 10, 1996, A1.

57. Ann Cameron Siegal, "Housing for Working People," *Washington Post*, April 29, 2000, I3; Judith Evans, "Striking a Balance between Budgets and Beauty," *Washington Post*, December 14, 1996, E1.

58. Dan Darby, "For Landlords, Hard Numbers and Obligations," *New York Times*, October 10, 1996, B6.

59. See Andrew Caplin et al., *Housing Partnerships: A New Approach to a Market at a Crossroads* (Cambridge, Mass.: MIT Press, 2007).

CHAPTER 7

1. Joseph R. Antos and Alice M. Rivlin, "Rising Health Care Spending—Federal and National," in *Restoring Fiscal Sanity 2007: The Health Spending Challenge*, ed. Alice M. Rivlin and Joseph R. Antos (Washington, D.C.: Brookings Institution Press, 2007), 14.

2. Aaron Catlin et al., "National Health Spending in 2005: The Slowdown Continues," *Health Affairs* (January/February 2007): 142–52.

3. Joseph R. Antos and Alice M. Rivlin, "Strategies for Slowing the Growth of Health Spending," in *Restoring Fiscal Sanity 2007: The Health Spending Challenge*, ed. Alice M. Rivlin and Joseph R. Antos (Washington, D.C.: Brookings Institution Press, 2007), 34.

4. Antos and Rivlin, "Strategies for Slowing," 34.

5. Amy Joyce, "GM's UAW Retirees Face Health Care Costs," *Washington Post*, October 21, 2005, D1.

6. Christopher Lee, "Universal Health Coverage Attracts New Support," *Washington Post*, January 7, 2007, A3.

7. See Linda J. Blumberg, "Who Pays for Employer-Sponsored Health Insurance?" *Health Affairs* 18, no. 6 (1999): 58–61.

8. M. P. McQueen, "Look Who's Watching Your Health Expenses," *Wall Street Journal*, September 25, 2007, D1; Marilyn Werber Serafini, "Taking Matters into Their Own Hands," *National Journal*, September 30, 2006.

9. Leslie G. Aronovitz, "Medicaid Integrity: Implementation of New Program Provides Opportunities for Federal Leadership to Combat Fraud, Waste, and Abuse," statement before a hearing of the Subcommittee on Federal Financial Management, Government Information, and International Security, Committee on Homeland Security and Government Affairs, U.S. Senate, March 28, 2006, 1.

10. General Accounting Office, *Medicare Payment: CMS Methodology Adequate to Estimate National Error Rate*, GAO-06-300 (Washington, D.C.: March 2006), 8.

11. Greg Allen, "Medicare Fraud Acute in South Florida," National Public Radio Broadcast, October 11, 2007, at www.npr.org/templates/story/story.php?storyId=15178883 (accessed March 7, 2008).

12. Gina Kolata, "Patients in Florida Lining Up for All That Medicare Covers," *New York Times*, September 11, 2003, A1.

13. Laurie McGinley, "Behind Medicare's Decisions: An Invisible Web of Gate-keepers," *New York Times*, September 16, 2003, A1.

14. Reed Abelson, "Hospitals Say They're Penalized by Medicare for Improving Care," *New York Times*, December 5, 2003, A1.

15. Steven J. Spear, "Fixing Health Care from the Inside, Today," *Harvard Business Review* (September 2005): 78–91; Clayton M. Christensen, Richard Bohmer, and John Kenagy, "Will Disruptive Innovations Cure Health Care?" *Harvard Business Review* (September–October 2000): 102–12.

16. See Reed Abelson, "In Health Care, Cost Isn't Proof of High Quality," *New York Times*, June 14, 2007, A1; David Leonhardt, "Health Care as If Costs Didn't Matter," *New York Times*, June 6, 2007, C1.

17. Gina Kolata, "Study Questions Colonoscopy Effectiveness," *New York Times*, December 14, 2006, A23.

18. Antos and Rivlin, "Strategies for Slowing," 35–36.

19. Milt Freudenheim, "Hospital Group Offers Plan on Health Coverage for All," *New York Times*, February 22, 2007, C2.

20. John R. Graham, "Filet Mignon, Pinot Noir and an MRI," *Washington Post*, December 21, 2006, A29.

21. Pam Belluck, "Maine Learns Expensive Lesson As Universal Health Plan Stalls," *New York Times*, April 30, 2007, A1.

22. See Physicians' Working Group for Single-Payer National Health Insurance, "Proposal of the Physicians' Working Group for Single-Payer National Health Insurance," *Journal of the American Medical Association* 290, no. 6 (August 13, 2003): 798–805.

23. Elena Cherny, "Universal Care Has a Big Price: Patients Wait," *Wall Street Journal*, November 12, 2003, A1.

24. Eric Cohen and Yuval Levin, "Health Care in Three Acts," *Commentary* (February 2007): 48.

25. Tyler Cowen, "Poor U.S. Scores in Health Care Don't Measure Nobels and Innovation," *New York Times*, October 5, 2006, C3.

26. Richard Pérez-Peña, "At Bronx Clinic, High Hurdles for Medicaid Care," *New York Times*, October 17, 2005, A1; Robert Pear, "Many Doctors Shun Patients with Medicare," *New York Times*, March 17, 2002, sec. 1, 1.

27. Abigail Zuger, "For a Retainer, Lavish Care by 'Boutique Doctors,'" *New York Times*, October 30, 2005, sec. 1, 1; Bill Brubaker, "Doctoring at Your Service," *Washington Post*, March 21, 2004, P1; Avram Goldstein, "Doctors on Call—for a Hefty Retainer," *Washington Post*, January 24, 2003, B1.

28. Brad Rodu and Philip Cole, "Here's to Your Health," *Washington Post*, January 26, 2007, A21.

29. Committee for Economic Development, *Moving beyond the Employer-Based Health-Insurance System* (Washington, D.C.: Author, October 2007); Ezekiel J. Emanuel and Victor R. Fuchs, "Health Care Vouchers—A Proposal for Universal Coverage," *New England Journal of Medicine* 352, no. 12 (March 24, 2005): 1255–60.

30. Jonathan Cohn, "Crash Course," *New Republic* (November 7, 2005): 22.

31. Laura Landro, "Social Networking Comes to Health Care," *Wall Street Journal*, December 27, 2006, D1; Sarah Rubenstein, "Patients Get New Tools to Price Health Care," *Wall Street Journal*, June 13, 2006, D1; Jan Hoffman, "Awash in Information, Patients Face a Lonely, Uncertain Road," *New York Times*, August 14, 2005, A1.

32. John Carey, "Medical Guesswork," *Business Week*, May 29, 2006.

33. C. K. Prahalad, *The Fortune at the Bottom of the Pyramid: Eradicating Poverty through Profits* (Upper Saddle River, N.J.: Wharton School Publishing, 2005), 265–86.

34. Grace-Marie Turner, "Customer Health Care," *Wall Street Journal*, May 14, 2007, A17; Jane Spencer, "Getting Your Health Care at Wal-Mart," *Wall Street Journal*, October 5, 2005, D1.

35. David C. Levin, "Me and My M.R.I.," *New York Times*, July 6, 2004, A19.

36. Cindy Skrzycki, "Who Should Put the Zzzz's in the O.R.?" *Washington Post*, February 20, 1998, G1.

37. Jane Spencer, "Getting Drugs without the Doctor," *Wall Street Journal*, June 1, 2004, D1.

38. Jennifer Alsever, "Basking on the Beach, or Maybe on the Operating Table," *New York Times*, October 15, 2006, sec. 3, 5; Saritha Rai, "Union Disrupts Plan to Send Ailing Workers to India for Cheaper Medical Care," *New York Times*, October 11, 2006, C6; Sonya Geis, "Passport to Health Care at Lower Cost to Patient," *Washington Post*, November 6, 2005, A5.

39. Philip Aspden et al., eds., *Preventing Medication Errors* (Washington, D.C.: Institute of Medicine, National Academies Press, 2006).

40. Philip G. Peters, "Doctors and Juries," *University of Michigan Law Review* 105, no. 7 (May 2007): 1453–95.

41. Antos and Rivlin, "Strategies for Slowing," 68; Ralph Blumenthal, "After Texas Caps Malpractice Awards, Doctors Rush to Practice There," *New York Times*, October 5, 2007, A21.

42. Congressional Budget Office, *Medical Malpractice Tort Limits and Health Care Spending*, background paper (Washington, D.C.: April 2006).

43. Janet Corrigan, Linda T. Kohn, and Molla S. Donaldson, eds., *To Err Is Human: Building a Safer Health System* (Washington, D.C.: Institutes of Medicine, National Academy Press, 2000).

44. Didier Pittet et al., "Hand Hygiene among Physicians: Performance, Beliefs, and Perceptions," *Annals of Internal Medicine* 141 (July 2004): 1–8.

45. See James B. Stewart, *Blind Eye: The Terrifying Story of a Doctor Who Got Away with Murder* (New York: Simon & Schuster, 2000).

46. Common Good, *Windows of Opportunity: State-Based Ideas for Improving Medical Injury Compensation and Enhancing Patient Safety* (Washington, D.C.: 2006); see also David B. Kendall, *Fixing America's Health Care System*, policy report (Washington, D.C.: Progressive Policy Institute, September 2005).

47. Laura Landro, "Doctors Learn to Say 'I'm Sorry,'" *Wall Street Journal*, January 24, 2007, D5; Rachel Zimmerman, "Doctors' New Tool to Fight Lawsuits: Saying 'I'm Sorry,'" *Wall Street Journal*, May 18, 2004, A1.

CHAPTER 8

1. Elizabeth Arias, *United States Life Tables, 2003*, National Vital Statistics Reports (Washington, D.C.: Centers for Disease Control and Prevention, April 19, 2006), 30.

2. U.S. Congress, House Ways and Means Committee, *The Social Security Bill*, Report on the 1935 Act, H.R. 7260, 74th Congress, 1st Sess., Report No. 615, at www.ssa.gov/history/reports/35housereport.html (accessed March 8, 2008).

3. Board of Trustees of the Federal Old-Age and Survivors Insurance and Federal Disability Insurance Trust Funds, *2007 Annual Report* (Washington, D.C.: Government Printing Office, 2007), 48.

4. Board of Trustees, *2007 Annual Report*, 48.

5. See Ray Kurzweil and Terry Grossman, *Fantastic Voyage: Live Long Enough to Live Forever* (Emmaus, Pa.: Rodale Books, 2004).

6. "Turning Boomers into Boomerangs," *Economist*, February 18, 2006, 65; Scott Thurm, "Companies Struggle to Pass on Knowledge that Workers Acquire," *Wall Street Journal*, January 23, 2006, B1; Kelly Greene, "Bye-Bye Boomers," *Wall Street Journal*, September 20, 2005, B1.

7. Leonard Wiener, "Brain Drain," *U.S. News and World Report*, November 22, 2004, 54.

8. Peter Coy, "Old. Smart. Productive," *Business Week*, June 27, 2005; Anne Fisher, "How to Battle the Coming Brain Drain," *Fortune*, March 21, 2005.

9. Claudia H. Deutsch, "For Love and a Little Money," *New York Times*, October 23, 2007, H1; Martha McNeil Hamilton, "Embarking on a Second Act," *Washington Post*, April 19, 2003, D12; Stacy Forster, "Heeding the Call," *Wall Street Journal*, March 24, 2003, R5.

10. "Retire to be Rehired," *Economist*, March 31, 2007, 83.

11. Albert B. Crenshaw, "Deficit Strains Pension Agency," *Washington Post*, August 8, 2003, E1.

12. The amount increases every year according to a statutory formula.

13. Jonathan Weisman, "Pension Proposal Questioned," *Washington Post*, July 9, 2003, E1.

14. William H. Whyte, *The Organization Man* (New York: Simon & Schuster, 1956).

15. John Kenneth Galbraith, *The New Industrial State*, 4th ed. (Boston: Houghton Mifflin, 1985).

16. John Leland, "Putting All the Nest Eggs in the Company Basket," *New York Times*, April, 11, 2004, sec. 1, 21. See also Theo Francis, "Company Stock Fills

Many Retirement Plans Despite the Potential Risks to Employees," *Wall Street Journal*, September 11, 2001, C1.

17. Donald L. Barlett and James B. Steele, "The Broken Promise," *Time*, October 31, 2005, 36.

18. Barlett and Steele, "The Broken Promise," 36.

19. Mary Williams Walsh, "Many Companies Fight Shortfalls in Pension Funds," *New York Times*, January, 13, 2003, A1.

20. Congressional Budget Office, *A Guide to Understanding the Pension Benefit Guarantee Corporation* (Washington, D.C.: September 2005), 12.

21. Mary Williams Walsh and Michael Cooper, "New York Gets Sobering Look at Its Pensions," *New York Times*, August 20, 2006, sec. 1, 1.

22. Barlett and Steele, "The Broken Promise." See also Mary Williams Walsh, "Public Pension Plans Face Billions in Shortages," *New York Times*, August 8, 2006, A1.

23. "State of West Virginia Retirement Plans," at www.wvretirement.com/Plan %20Statistics.pdf (accessed March 8, 2008).

24. See Mary Williams Walsh, "Once Safe, Public Pensions Are Now Facing Cuts," *New York Times*, November 11, 2006, A1; Mary Williams Walsh, "Voters Release Houston from Pension Law," *New York Times*, May 17, 2004, C2.

25. Orlo Nichols, Michael Clingman, and Alice Wade, "Internal Real Rates of Return under the OASDI Program for Hypothetical Workers," Actuarial Note 2004.5, Social Security Administration, Office of the Chief Actuary, March 2005, at www.ssa.gov/OACT/NOTES/ran5/an2004-5.html (accessed March 3, 2008).

26. Board of Trustees, *2007 Annual Report*, 184.

27. Congressional Budget Office, *Is Social Security Progressive?* Economic and Budget Issue Brief (Washington, D.C.: December 15, 2006).

28. Congressional Budget Office, *Is Social Security Progressive?*

29. Eugene Steuerle and Jon M. Bakija, *Retooling Social Security for the 21st Century: Right and Wrong Approaches to Reform* (Washington, D.C.: Urban Institute Press, 1994), 119.

30. Don Fullerton and Brent Mast, *Income Redistribution from Social Security* (Washington, D.C.: AEI Press, 2005), 64.

31. Ben S. Bernanke, "The Global Saving Glut and the U.S. Current Account Deficit," Homer Jones Lecture, St. Louis, Mo., April 14, 2005, at www .federalreserve.gov/boarddocs/speeches/2005/20050414/default.htm (accessed March 8, 2008).

32. Martin Feldstein, "Social Security, Induced Retirement and Aggregate Capital Accumulation," *Journal of Political Economy* 82, no. 5 (September–October 1974): 905–26. See, generally, Peter J. Ferrara, *Social Security: The Inherent Contradiction* (Washington, D.C.: Cato Institute, 1980), 76–104.

33. Eduardo Porter, "Inherit the Wind: There's Little Else Left," *New York Times*, March 26, 2006, sec. 4, 1.

34. Seth Mydans, "A Tribunal to Get Neglected Parents Smiling Again," *New York Times*, December 27, 1996, A4.

35. Gene Epstein, "The Great American Savings Myth," *Barron's*, May 29, 2007, 1; Charles Steindel, "How Worrisome Is a Negative Saving Rate?" *Current Issues*, Federal Reserve Bank of New York 13, no. 4 (May 2007), at www.newyorkfed.org/research/current_issues/ci13-4.html (accessed April 18, 2008); William G. Gale and John Sabelhaus, "The Savings Crisis: In the Eye of the Beholder?" *Milken Institute Review* (Third Quarter, 1999): 46–56.

36. Office of Management and Budget, *Budget of the United States Government: Fiscal Year 2008, Analytical Perspectives* (Washington, D.C.: Government Printing Office, 2007), 289.

37. Congressional Budget Office, *Utilization of Tax Incentives for Retirement Saving: Update to 2003*, background paper (Washington, D.C.: March 2007).

CHAPTER 9

1. See Congressional Budget Office, *The Growth of Federal User Charges: An Update* (Washington, D.C.: October 1995).

2. See, for example, K. J. Meier and M. J. Licari, "The Effect of Cigarette Taxes on Cigarette Consumption, 1955 through 1994," *American Journal of Public Health* 87, no. 7 (July 1997): 1126–30.

3. Vernon W. Ruttan, *Technology, Growth, and Development: An Induced Innovation Perspective* (New York: Oxford University Press, 2001).

4. Martin Feldstein, "Avoidance and the Deadweight Loss of the Income Tax," National Bureau of Economic Research Working Paper No. 5055, Cambridge, Mass., March 1995.

5. Joel Slemrod and Jon Bakija, *Taxing Ourselves: A Citizen's Guide to the Debate over Taxes*, 3rd ed. (Cambridge, Mass.: MIT Press, 2004), 4.

6. Slemrod and Bakija, *Taxing Ourselves*, 4.

7. Berkshire Hathaway Inc., "2006 Annual Report," 2007, 20, at www.berkshirehathaway.com/2006ar/2006ar.pdf (accessed April 22, 2008).

8. See Consumer Federation of America and National Consumer Law Center, "Refund Anticipation Loans: Updated Facts and Figures," Joint Fact Sheet, January 17, 2006, at www.consumerfed.org/pdfs/RAL_2006_Early_info.pdf (accessed March 9, 2008).

9. C. Eugene Steuerle, *Contemporary U.S. Tax Policy* (Washington, D.C.: Urban Institute Press, 2004), x.

10. Steuerle, *Contemporary U.S. Tax Policy*, 2.

11. Steuerle, *Contemporary U.S. Tax Policy*, 2.

12. Slemrod and Bakija, *Taxing Ourselves*, 172–80.

13. Slemrod and Bakija, *Taxing Ourselves*, 35.

14. Slemrod and Bakija, *Taxing Ourselves*, 35.

15. Slemrod and Bakija, *Taxing Ourselves*, 6.

16. Steuerle, *Contemporary U.S. Tax Policy*, 6.

17. Congressional Budget Office, *Utilization of Tax Incentives for Retirement Saving: Update to 2003*, background paper (Washington, D.C.: March 2007).

18. Ray Kurzweil, *The Singularity Is Near: When Humans Transcend Biology* (New York: Viking Adult, 2005).

19. Bjorn Lomborg, ed., *Global Crises, Global Solutions* (Cambridge, UK: Cambridge University Press, 2004).

CHAPTER 10

1. *Fleming v. Nestor*, 363 U.S. 603 (1960).

2. National Center for Health Statistics, *Vital Statistics of the United States 2002: Volume I, Natality*, table 1-1, at www.cdc.gov/nchs/data/statab/natfinal2002.annvol1 _01.pdf (accessed March 9, 2008).

3. Congressional Budget Office, *The Budget and Economic Outlook: Fiscal Years 2008–2017* (Washington, D.C.: January 2007), 10–11.

4. Congressional Budget Office, *The Long-Term Outlook for Health Care Spending* (Washington, D.C.: November 2007), 5.

5. C. Eugene Steuerle, *Contemporary U.S. Tax Policy* (Washington, D.C.: Urban Institute Press, 2004), 8.

6. Mancur Olson, *The Logic of Collective Action: Public Goods and the Theory of Groups* (Cambridge, Mass.: Harvard University Press, 1965).

7. General Accounting Office, *Sugar Program: Supporting Sugar Prices Has Increased Users' Costs While Benefiting Producers*, GAO/RCED-00-126 (Washington, D.C.: July 2000), 5. GAO estimated that 70 percent of these benefits went to sugarbeet farmers. The U.S. Department of Agriculture estimates there were approximately seven thousand farms in 1997. Stephen Haley and Mir Ali, *Sugar Backgrounder*, Report SSS-249-01, Economic Research Service, U.S. Department of Agriculture, July 2007, 9.

8. General Accounting Office, *Sugar Program*, 5.

9. Dan Morgan, "Sugar Industry Expands Influence," *Washington Post*, November 3, 2007, A1.

10. Lee Hockstader, "Landrieu Beats GOP Challenge in Louisiana," *Washington Post*, December 8, 2002, A1.

11. Dan Morgan, Sarah Cohen, and Gilbert M. Gaul, "Dairy Industry Crushed Innovator Who Bested Price-Control System," *Washington Post*, December 10, 2006, A1.

12. Derrick Cain, "Data Show 10 Percent of Subsidy Recipients Took 66 Percent of Federal Farm Payments," *BNA Daily Report for Executives*, June 13, 2007, A-12.

13. William Yardley, "Alaskan Bridge Projects Resist Earmarks Purge," *New York Times*, March 6, 2007, A13.

14. *Congressional Record*, 103rd Cong., 1st Sess., vol. 139, January 6, 1993, 346.

15. Stewart Brand, "Environmental Heresies," *Technology Review*, May 2005.

16. Thomas W. Hazlett, "'Universal Service' Telephone Subsidies: What Does $7 Billion Buy?" June 2006, at www.senior.org/Documents/USF.Master.6.13.06.pdf (accessed March 1, 2008); Vince Vasquez, *Digital Welfare: The Failure of the Universal Service System* (San Francisco: Pacific Research Institute, 2006).

17. Board of Trustees of the Federal Old-Age and Survivors Insurance and Federal Disability Insurance Trust Funds, *2007 Annual Report* (Washington, D.C.: Government Printing Office, 2007), 2.

CONCLUSION

1. Mancur Olson, *The Rise and Decline of Nations: Economic Growth, Stagflation, and Social Rigidities* (New Haven, Conn.: Yale University Press, 1982).

2. Richard A. Easterlin, "The Economics of Happiness," *Dædalus* (Spring 2004): 26–33.

3. Bruno S. Frey and Alois Stutzer, *Happiness and Economics: How the Economy and Institutions Affect Human Well-Being* (Princeton, N.J.: Princeton University Press, 2002), 11–12.

4. F. Scott Fitzgerald, *The Crack-Up*, ed. Edmund Wilson (New York: New Directions, 1956), 69.

5. Alasdair MacIntyre, *After Virtue*, 2nd ed. (Notre Dame, Ind.: University of Notre Dame Press, 1984), 251.

6. See Christopher Hitchens, *God Is Not Great: How Religion Poisons Everything* (New York: Twelve Books, Hatchet Book Group, 2007); Richard Dawkins, *The God Delusion* (New York: Houghton Mifflin, 2006).

BIBLIOGRAPHY

Aldonas, Grant D., Robert Z. Lawrence, and Matthew J. Slaughter. "Succeeding in the Global Economy: A New Policy Agenda for the American Workers." Financial Services Forum, Washington, D.C., June 26, 2007.

Allen, Greg. "Medicare Fraud Acute in South Florida." National Public Radio Broadcast, October 11, 2007. www.npr.org/templates/story/story.php?storyId =15178883 (accessed March 7, 2008).

American Pet Products Manufacturers Association. "Pet Pampering and Pet Health Insurance Drive Pet Industry Sales to Another All Time High." Press release, February 11, 2008. www.appma.org/press_releasedetail.asp?id=118 (accessed February 29, 2008).

Anderson, Martin. *Welfare: The Political Economy of Welfare Reform in the United States.* Stanford, Calif.: Hoover Institution Press, 1978.

Antos, Joseph R., and Alice M. Rivlin. "Rising Health Care Spending—Federal and National." In *Restoring Fiscal Sanity 2007: The Health Spending Challenge*, edited by Alice M. Rivlin and Joseph R. Antos, 13–28. Washington, D.C.: Brookings Institution Press, 2007.

———. "Strategies for Slowing the Growth of Health Spending." In *Restoring Fiscal Sanity 2007: The Health Spending Challenge*, edited by Alice M. Rivlin and Joseph R. Antos, 29–79. Washington, D.C.: Brookings Institution Press, 2007.

Arias, Elizabeth. *United States Life Tables, 2003.* National Vital Statistics Reports. Washington, D.C.: Centers for Disease Control and Prevention, April 19, 2006.

Aronovitz, Leslie G. "Medicaid Integrity: Implementation of New Program Provides Opportunities for Federal Leadership to Combat Fraud, Waste, and Abuse." Statement before a hearing of the Subcommittee on Federal Financial Management, Government Information, and International Security, Committee on Homeland Security and Government Affairs, U.S. Senate, March 28, 2006, 1.

Arrow, Kenneth. *Social Choice and Individual Values.* 2nd ed. New Haven, Conn.: Yale University Press, 1963.

Aspden, Philip, et al., eds. *Preventing Medication Errors*. Washington, D.C.: Institute of Medicine, National Academies Press, 2006.

Barnes, Peter. *Capitalism 3.0: A Guide to Reclaiming the Commons*. San Francisco: Berrett Koehler Publishers, 2006.

Belsky, Jay, et al. "Are There Long-Term Effects of Early Child Care?" *Child Development* 78 (March/April 2007): 681–701.

Bennett, William J., ed. *The Book of Virtues: A Treasury of Great Moral Stories*. New York: Simon & Schuster, 1993.

Berkshire Hathaway Inc. "2006 Annual Report." 2007. www.berkshirehathaway .com/2006ar/2006ar.pdf (accessed April 22, 2008).

Bernanke, Ben S. "The Global Saving Glut and the U.S. Current Account Deficit." Homer Jones Lecture, St. Louis, Mo., April 14, 2005. www.federalreserve.gov/ boarddocs/speeches/2005/20050414/default.htm (accessed March 8, 2008).

———. "GSE Portfolios, Systematic Risk, and Affordable Housing." Speech before the Independent Community Bankers of America's Annual Convention and Techworld, Honolulu, Hawaii, March 6, 2007. www.federalreserve.gov/newsevents/ speech/bernanke20070306a.htm (accessed March 3, 2008).

Blank, Rebecca M. "Evaluating Welfare Reform in the United States." *Journal of Economic Literature* 40 (December 2002): 1105–66.

Blumberg, Linda J. "Who Pays for Employer-Sponsored Health Insurance?" *Health Affairs* 18, no. 6 (1999): 58–61.

Board of Trustees of the Federal Old-Age and Survivors Insurance and Federal Disability Insurance Trust Funds. *2007 Annual Report*. Washington, D.C.: Government Printing Office, 2007.

Bodenheimer, Thomas S., and Kevin Grumbach. *Understanding Health Policy: A Clinical Approach*. 4th ed. New York: McGraw-Hill, Lange Medical Books, 2005.

Boshara, Ray. "Every Baby a Trust Fund Baby." In *Ten Big Ideas for a New America*, 1–4. Washington, D.C.: New America Foundation, February 2007.

Bradley, Bill, Paul Jansen, and Les Silverman. "The Nonprofit Sector's $100 Billion Opportunity." *Harvard Business Review* (May 2003): 94–103.

Braun, Henry, Frank Jenkins, and Wendy Grigg. *Comparing Private Schools and Public Schools Using Hierarchical Linear Modeling* (NCES 2006-461), U.S. Department of Education, National Center for Education Statistics, Institute of Education Science. Washington, D.C.: Government Printing Office, 2006.

Brookings Institution. *From Poverty, Opportunity: Putting the Market to Work for Lower Income Families*. Washington, D.C.: Author, 2006.

Buchanan, James M. "A Hobbesian Interpretation of the Rawlsian Difference Principle." *Kyklos* 29, fasc. 1 (1976): 5–24.

Buchanan, James M., and Gordon Tullock. *The Calculus of Consent*. Ann Arbor: University of Michigan Press, 1962.

Bureau of National Affairs. "FTC, DOJ Support Continued Use of Nonlawyers to Do Real Estate Closings." *Daily Report for Executives*, April 3, 2002, A-27.

Burt, Martha. *Over the Edge: The Growth of Homelessness during the 1980s.* New York: Russell Sage Foundation, 1992.

Burtless, Gary. "The Work Response to a Guaranteed Income: A Survey of Experimental Evidence." In *Lessons from the Income Maintenance Experiments*, edited by Alicia H. Munnell, 22–52. Boston: Federal Reserve Bank of Boston, 1986.

Burtless, Gary, and Christopher Jencks. "American Inequality and Its Consequences." In *Agenda for a Nation*, edited by Henry J. Aaron, James M. Lindsay, and Pietro S. Nivola, 61–108. Washington, D.C.: Brookings Institution Press, 2003.

Cain, Glen G. "The Issues of Marital Stability and Family Composition and the Income Maintenance Experiments." In *Lessons from the Income Maintenance Experiments*, edited by Alicia H. Munnell, 60–93. Boston: Federal Reserve Bank of Boston, 1986.

Caplin, Andrew, et al. *Housing Partnerships: A New Approach to a Market at a Crossroads.* Cambridge, Mass.: MIT Press, 2007.

Card, David. "Is the New Immigration Really So Bad?" National Bureau of Economic Research Working Paper No. 11547, Cambridge, Mass., August 2005.

Catlin, Aaron, et al. "National Health Spending in 2005: The Slowdown Continues." *Health Affairs* (January/February 2007): 142–52.

Chakrabarti, Rajashri. "Can Increasing Private School Participation and Monetary Loss in a Voucher Program Affect Public School Performance? Evidence from Milwaukee." *Journal of Public Economics* (June 2008): 1371–1393.

Christensen, Clayton M., Richard Bohmer, and John Kenagy. "Will Disruptive Innovations Cure Health Care?" *Harvard Business Review* (September–October 2000): 102–12.

Ciotti, Paul. *Money and School Performance: Lessons from the Kansas City Desegregation Experiment.* Policy Analysis 298. Washington, D.C.: Cato Institute, March 16, 1998.

Cohen, Eric, and Yuval Levin. "Health Care in Three Acts." *Commentary* (February 2007): 46–52.

Cohen, Mark A. "Measuring the Costs and Benefits of Crime and Justice." In *Criminal Justice 2000, Volume 4: Measurement and Analysis of Crime and Justice*, edited by David Duffee, 263–325. Rockville, Md.: U.S. Department of Justice, National Institute of Justice, 2000.

Cohn, Jonathan. "Crash Course." *New Republic* (November 7, 2005): 22.

Committee for Economic Development. *Moving beyond the Employer-Based Health-Insurance System.* Washington, D.C.: October 2007.

Common Good. *Windows of Opportunity: State-Based Ideas for Improving Medical Injury Compensation and Enhancing Patient Safety.* Washington, D.C.: Author, 2006.

Congressional Budget Office. *The Budget and Economic Outlook: Fiscal Years 2008–2017.* Washington, D.C.: January 2007.

———. *The Growth of Federal User Charges: An Update.* Washington, D.C.: October 1995.

———. *A Guide to Understanding the Pension Benefit Guarantee Corporation.* Washington, D.C.: September 2005.

———. *Is Social Security Progressive?* Economic and Budget Issue Brief. Washington, D.C.: December 15, 2006.

———. *The Long-Term Budget Outlook.* Washington, D.C.: December 2005.

———. *The Long-Term Outlook for Health Care Spending.* Washington, D.C.: November 2007.

———. *Medical Malpractice Tort Limits and Health Care Spending.* Background paper. Washington, D.C.: April 2006.

———. *Updated Estimates of the Subsidies to the Housing GSEs.* Washington, D.C.: April 2004.

———. *Utilization of Tax Incentives for Retirement Saving: An Update.* Washington, D.C.: August 2003.

———. *Utilization of Tax Incentives for Retirement Saving: Update to 2003.* Background paper. Washington, D.C.: March 2007.

Congressional Record, 103rd Cong., 1st Sess., vol. 139, January 6, 1993.

Consumer Federation of America and National Consumer Law Center. "Refund Anticipation Loans: Updated Facts and Figures." Joint Fact Sheet. January 17, 2006. www.consumerfed.org/pdfs/RAL_2006_Early_info.pdf (accessed March 9, 2008).

Corrigan, Janet, Linda T. Kohn, and Molla S. Donaldson, eds. *To Err Is Human: Building a Safer Health System.* Washington, D.C.: Institutes of Medicine, National Academy Press, 2000.

Coulson, N. Edward. "Housing Policy and the Social Benefits of Homeownership." *Business Review,* Philadelphia Federal Reserve Bank (Second Quarter 2002): 7–16.

Coyle, Dennis J., and Aaron Wildavsky. "Social Experimentation in the Face of Formidable Fables." In *Lessons from the Income Maintenance Experiments,* edited by Alicia H. Munnell, 167–84. Boston: Federal Reserve Bank of Boston, 1986.

Current Population Survey. "Annual Demographic Survey." 2003. http://pubdb3.census.gov/macro/032004/pov/new29_100_01.htm (accessed March 2, 2008).

———. "Annual Social and Economic Supplement: Years of School Completed." 2006. http://pubdb3.census.gov/macro/032007/pov/new29_100_01.htm (accessed March 3, 2008).

———. "Annual Social and Economic Supplement: Educational Attainment." 2006. http://pubdb3.census.gov/macro/032007/perinc/new04_001.htm (accessed March 5, 2008).

Dawkins, Richard. *The God Delusion.* New York: Houghton Mifflin, 2006.

Drucker, Peter F. *Management: Tasks, Responsibilities, Practices.* New York: Harper Colophon, 1985.

———. *Managing the Non-Profit Organization: Principles and Practices.* New York: HarperCollins, 1990.

Easterlin, Richard A. "The Economics of Happiness." *Dædalus* (Spring 2004): 26–33.

Emanuel, Ezekiel J., and Victor R. Fuchs. "Health Care Vouchers—A Proposal for Universal Coverage." *New England Journal of Medicine* 352, no. 12 (March 24, 2005): 1255–60.

Entertainment Software Association. "Facts and Research: Top 10 Industry Facts." www.theesa.com/facts/top_10_facts.php (accessed February 29 2008).

Feldstein, Martin. "Avoidance and the Deadweight Loss of the Income Tax." National Bureau of Economic Research Working Paper No. 5055, Cambridge, Mass., March 1995.

———. "Social Security, Induced Retirement and Aggregate Capital Accumulation." *Journal of Political Economy* 82, no. 5 (September–October 1974): 905–26.

Ferrara, Peter J. *Social Security: The Inherent Contradiction*, Washington, D.C.: Cato Institute, 1980.

Fischel, William A. *Do Growth Controls Matter? A Review of Empirical Evidence on the Effectiveness and Efficiency of Local Government Land Use Regulation.* Cambridge, Mass.: Lincoln Institute of Land Policy, 1990.

———. *The Economics of Zoning Laws: A Property Rights Approach to American Land Use Controls.* Baltimore: John Hopkins University Press, 1985.

Fitzgerald, F. Scott. *The Crack-Up*, edited by Edmund Wilson. New York: New Directions, 1956.

Fleming v. Nestor. 363 U.S. 603 (1960).

Foster, William, and Jeffrey Bradach. "Should Nonprofits Seek Profits?" *Harvard Business Review* (January 2005): 92–100.

Frey, Bruno S., and Alois Stutzer. *Happiness and Economics: How the Economy and Institutions Affect Human Well-Being.* Princeton, N.J.: Princeton University Press, 2002.

Fullerton, Don, and Brent Mast. *Income Redistribution from Social Security*, 64. Washington, D.C.: AEI Press, 2005.

Galbraith, John Kenneth. *The New Industrial State.* 4th ed. Boston: Houghton Mifflin, 1985.

Gale, William G., and John Sabelhaus. "The Savings Crisis: In the Eye of the Beholder?" *Milken Institute Review* (Third Quarter, 1999): 46–56.

General Accounting Office. *Medicare Payment: CMS Methodology Adequate to Estimate National Error Rate.* GAO-06-300. Washington, D.C.: March 2006.

———. *Sugar Program: Supporting Sugar Prices Has Increased Users' Costs While Benefiting Producers.* GAO/RCED-00-126. Washington, D.C.: July 2000.

Glaeser, Edward L., Joseph Gyourko, and Raven Saks. "Why Have Housing Prices Gone Up?" *American Economic Review* 95 (May 2005): 329–33.

———. "Why Is Manhattan So Expensive? Regulation and the Rise in Housing Prices." *Journal of Law and Economics* 48, no. 2 (October 2005): 331–69.

Golden, Daniel. *The Price of Admission: How America's Ruling Class Buys Its Way into Elite Colleges—and Who Gets Left outside the Gates.* New York: Crown Publishers, 2006.

Goldratt, Eliyahu M., and Jeff Cox. *The Goal: A Process of Ongoing Improvement.* 2nd rev. ed. Great Barrington, Mass.: North River Press, 1992.

Gordon, Robert. "Class Struggle." *New Republic* (June 6/13, 2005): 24.

Greenspan, Alan. "Regulatory Reform of the Government-Sponsored Enterprises." Testimony before the Committee on Banking, Housing and Urban Affairs, U.S. Senate, April 6, 2005. www.federalreserve.gov/boarddocs/testimony/2005/20050406/default.htm (accessed March 3, 2008).

Haley, Stephen, and Mir Ali. *Sugar Backgrounder.* Report SSS-249-01, Economic Research Service, U.S. Department of Agriculture, July 2007.

Hayek, Friedrich A. *The Constitution of Liberty.* Chicago: University of Chicago Press, 1960.

———. *The Road to Serfdom.* Chicago: University of Chicago Press, 1944.

Hazlett, Thomas W. "'Universal Service' Telephone Subsidies: What Does $7 Billion Buy?" June 2006. www.senior.org/Documents/USF.Master.6.13.06.pdf (accessed March 1, 2008).

Henry, William A., III. *In Defense of Elitism.* New York: Doubleday, 1994.

Hirsch, E. D., Jr. *What Your Fifth Grader Needs to Know: Fundamentals of a Good Fifth-Grade Education.* New York: Dell Publishing, 1995.

Hitchens, Christopher. *God Is Not Great: How Religion Poisons Everything.* New York: Twelve Books, Hatchet Book Group, 2007.

Howard, Philip K. *The Death of Common Sense: How Law Is Suffocating America.* New York: Random House, 1994.

Hoxby, Caroline M. "School Choice and School Competition: Evidence from the United States." *Swedish Economic Policy Review* 10, no. 2 (2003). www.economics.harvard.edu/faculty/hoxby/papers/hoxby_2.pdf.

Hoynes, Hilary W., Marianne E. Page, and Ann Huff Stevens. "Poverty in America: Trends and Explanations." *Journal of Economic Perspectives* 20 (Winter 2006): 47–68.

International Consumer Electronics Show. "2006 Is the Year of DTV, Forecasts CEA." Press release, January 4, 2006. www.cesweb.org/press/news/rd_release_detail.asp?id=10913 (accessed February 29, 2008).

Karabel, Jerome. *The Chosen: The Hidden History of Admission and Exclusion at Harvard, Yale, and Princeton.* New York: Houghton Mifflin, 2005.

Katz, Lawrence F., Jeffrey R. Kling, and Jeffrey B. Liebman. "Moving to Opportunity in Boston: Early Results of a Randomized Mobility Experiment." *Quarterly Journal of Economics* 116, no. 2 (May 2001): 607–54.

Kendall, David B. *Fixing America's Health Care System.* Policy report. Washington, D.C.: Progressive Policy Institute, September 2005.

Kurzweil Ray. *The Singularity Is Near: When Humans Transcend Biology.* New York: Viking Adult, 2005.

Kurzweil, Ray, and Terry Grossman. *Fantastic Voyage: Live Long Enough to Live Forever.* Emmaus, Pa.: Rodale Books, 2004.

Lamb, Russell L. "The New Farm Economy." *Regulation* 26, no. 4 (Winter 2003–2004): 10–15.

Lerman, Robert I. "The Impact of Changing U.S. Family Structure on Child Poverty and Income Inequality." *Economica* 63 (Supplement 1993): S119–39.

Letts, Christine W., William Ryan, and Allen Grossman. "Virtuous Capital: What Foundations Can Learn from Venture Capitalists." *Harvard Business Review* (March–April 1997): 36–44.

Levine, Ned. "The Effects of Local Growth Controls on Regional Housing Production and Population Redistribution in California." *Urban Studies* 36, no. 12 (November 1999): 2047–68.

Levinson, Marc. *The Box: How the Shipping Container Made the World Smaller and the World Economy Bigger.* Princeton, N.J.: Princeton University Press, 2006.

Lomborg, Bjorn, ed. *Global Crises, Global Solutions.* Cambridge, UK: Cambridge University Press, 2004.

MacIntyre, Alasdair. *After Virtue.* 2nd ed. Notre Dame, Ind.: University of Notre Dame Press, 1984.

Malpezzi, Stephen, and Richard K. Green. "What Has Happened to the Bottom of the U.S. Housing Market?" *Urban Studies* 33, no. 10 (December 1996): 1807–20.

Marchwinski v. Howard. 60 Fed. Appx. 601, 2002 WL 1870916 (6th Cir., April 7, 2003).

Maslow, Abraham H. *Motivation and Personality.* 3rd ed. New York: Harper & Row, 1987.

Maynard, Rebecca, et al. "Changing Family Formation Behavior through Welfare Reform." In *Welfare, the Family, and Reproductive Behavior,* edited by Robert A. Moffitt, 134–76. Washington, D.C.: National Research Council, 1998.

McDonough, William, and Michael Braungart. *Cradle to Cradle: Remaking the Way We Make Things.* New York: North Point Press, 2002.

McLean, Bethany, and Peter Elkind. *The Smartest Guys in the Room: The Amazing Rise and Scandalous Fall of Enron.* New York: Portfolio, 2003.

Meier, K. J., and M. J. Licari. "The Effect of Cigarette Taxes on Cigarette Consumption, 1955 through 1994." *American Journal of Public Health* 87, no. 7 (July 1997): 1126–30.

Millennial Housing Commission. *Meeting Our Nation's Housing Challenges: Report of the Bipartisan Millennial Housing Commission.* Washington, D.C.: Government Printing Office, 2002.

Miller, Matthew. "Education: A Bold Experiment to Fix City Schools." *Atlantic Monthly* (July 1999): 15–31.

Miller, Ted R., Mark A. Cohen, and Brian Wiersema. *Victim Costs and Consequences: A New Look.* Research Report NCJ 155282. Washington, D.C.: U.S. Department of Justice, National Institute of Justice, January 1996.

Murray, Charles A. *Losing Ground: American Social Policy 1950–1980.* New York: Basic Books, 1984.

National Center for Health Statistics. *Vital Statistics of the United States 2002: Volume I, Natality,* table 1-1. www.cdc.gov/nchs/data/statab/natfinal2002.annvol1_01.pdf (accessed March 9, 2008).

National Commission on Excellence in Education. *A Nation at Risk*. Washington, D.C.: U.S. Department of Education, 1983.

National Research Council. *Rising Above the Gathering Storm: Energizing and Employing America for a Brighter Economic Future*. Washington, D.C.: National Academy Press, 2007.

Neumark, David, and William Wascher. "Minimum Wages and Employment: A Review of Evidence from the New Minimum Wage Research." National Bureau of Economic Research Working Paper No. 12663. Cambridge, Mass., November 2006.

Nichols, Orlo, Michael Clingman, and Alice Wade. "Internal Real Rates of Return under the OASDI Program for Hypothetical Workers." Actuarial Note 2004.5, Social Security Administration, Office of the Chief Actuary, March 2005. www.ssa.gov/OACT/NOTES/ran5/an2004-5.html (accessed March 3, 2008).

Niebuhr, Reinhold. *Moral Man and Immoral Society: A Study in Ethics and Politics*, Louisville, Ky.: Westminster John Knox Press, 1960.

Office of Management and Budget. *Budget of the United States Government: Fiscal Year 2008, Analytical Perspectives*. Washington, D.C.: Government Printing Office, 2007.

O'Flaherty, Brendon. *Making Room: The Economics of Homelessness*. Cambridge, Mass.: Harvard University Press, 1996.

Olasky, Marvin. *The Tragedy of American Compassion*. Washington, D.C.: Regnery Publishing, 1992.

Olson, Mancur. *The Logic of Collective Action: Public Goods and the Theory of Groups*. Cambridge, Mass.: Harvard University Press, 1965.

———. *The Rise and Decline of Nations: Economic Growth, Stagflation, and Social Rigidities*. New Haven, Conn.: Yale University Press, 1982.

O'Sullivan, Arthur. *Urban Economics*. 3rd ed. Chicago: Irwin McGraw-Hill, 1996.

Ottaviano, Gianmarco I. P., and Giovanni Peri. "Rethinking the Gains from Immigration." National Bureau of Economic Research Working Paper No. 11672, Cambridge, Mass., October 2005.

Passmore, Wayne. "The GSE Implicit Subsidy and Value of Government Ambiguity." Finance and Economic Discussion Series No. 2003-64, Board of Governors of the Federal Reserve System, December 2003.

Patterson, James T. *America's Struggle against Poverty in the Twentieth Century*. 4th rev. ed. Cambridge, Mass.: Harvard University Press, 2000.

Paul, Weiss, Rifkind, Wharton, & Garrison LLP and Huron Consulting Group Inc. *A Report to the Special Review Committee of the Board of Directors of Fannie Mae: Executive Summary*, http://download.fanniemae.com/execsum.pdf (accessed March 3, 2008).

Peters, Philip G. "Doctors and Juries." *University of Michigan Law Review* 105, no. 7 (May 2007): 1453–95.

Peterson, Paul E., and William G. Howell. *The Education Gap: Vouchers and Urban Schools*. Washington, D.C.: Brookings Institution Press, 2006.

Physicians' Working Group for Single-Payer National Health Insurance. "Proposal of the Physicians' Working Group for Single-Payer National Health Insurance." *Journal of the American Medical Association* 290, no. 6 (August 13, 2003): 798–805.

Pittet, Didier, et al. "Hand Hygiene among Physicians: Performance, Beliefs, and Perceptions." *Annals of Internal Medicine* 141 (July 2004): 1–8.

Posner, Richard A. *Economic Analysis of Law.* 6th ed. New York: Aspen Publishers, 2003.

Prahalad, C. K. *The Fortune at the Bottom of the Pyramid: Eradicating Poverty through Profits.* Upper Saddle River, N.J.: Wharton School Publishing, 2005.

President's Advisory Panel on Federal Tax Reform. *Simple, Fair, and Pro-Growth: Proposals to Fix America's Tax System.* Washington, D.C.: Government Printing Office, 2005.

Quigley, John M., and Steven Raphael. "Is Housing Unaffordable? Why Isn't It More Affordable?" *Journal of Economic Perspectives* 18 (Winter 2004): 191–214.

Rawls, John. *A Theory of Justice.* Cambridge, Mass.: Harvard University Press, 1971.

Reinsdorf, Marshall B. "Alternative Measures of Personal Saving." *Survey of Current Business* (February 2007): 7–13.

Rivoli, Pietra. *The Travels of a T-Shirt in the Global Economy: An Economist Examines the Markets, Power, and Politics of World Trade.* Hoboken, N.J.: John Wiley & Sons, 2005.

Rosen, Harvey S., Kenneth T. Rosen, and Douglas Holtz-Eakin. "Housing Tenure, Uncertainty, and Taxation." *Review of Economics and Statistics* 66, no. 3 (1984): 405–15.

Rossi, Peter H. *Down and Out in America: The Origins of Homelessness.* Chicago: University of Chicago Press, 1991.

Ruttan, Vernon W. *Technology, Growth, and Development: An Induced Innovation Perspective.* New York: Oxford University Press, 2001.

Ryan, William P. "The New Landscape for Nonprofits." *Harvard Business Review* (January–February 1999): 127–36.

Sabol, William J., Todd D. Minton, and Paige M. Harrison. "Prison and Jail Inmates at Midyear 2006." U.S. Department of Justice, Office of Justice Programs, Bureau of Justice Statistics, Bulletin NCJ 217675, June 2007.

Sawhill, Isabel. "Families at Risk." In *Setting National Priorities: The 2000 Election and Beyond,* edited by Henry J. Aaron and Robert D. Reischauer, 97–135. Washington, D.C.: Brookings Institution Press, 1999.

Schrag, Peter. "The Near-Myth of Our Failing Schools." *Atlantic Monthly* (October 1997): 72–80.

Sinai, Todd M., and Joel Waldfogel. *Do Low-Income Housing Subsidies Increase Housing Consumption?* National Bureau of Economic Research Working Paper No. W8709, Cambridge, Mass., January 2002.

Slemrod, Joel, and Jon Bakija. *Taxing Ourselves: A Citizen's Guide to the Debate over Taxes.* 3rd ed. Cambridge, Mass.: MIT Press, 2004.

Smith, Adam. *The Theory of Moral Sentiments,* edited by D. D. Raphael and A. L. Macfie. Indianapolis: Liberty Fund, 1982.

————. *The Wealth of Nations*. New York: Random House, 1994 [1776].

Spear, Steven J. "Fixing Health Care from the Inside, Today." *Harvard Business Review* (September 2005): 78–91.

Stanley, Marcus, Lawrence Katz, and Alan Krueger. "Developing Skills: What We Know about the Impacts of American Employment and Training Programs on Employment, Earnings, and Educational Outcomes." Unpublished paper, October 1998. www.economics.harvard.edu/faculty/katz/files/stanley_katz_krueger _98.pdf (accessed March 5, 2008).

"State of West Virginia Retirement Plans." www.wvretirement.com/Plan%20Statistics .pdf (accessed March 8, 2008).

Steindel, Charles. "How Worrisome Is a Negative Saving Rate?" *Current Issues*, Federal Reserve Bank of New York 13, no. 4 (May 2007), at www.newyorkfed .org/research/current_issues/ci13-4.html (accessed April 18, 2008).

Steuerle, C. Eugene. *Contemporary U.S. Tax Policy*. Washington, D.C.: Urban Institute Press, 2004.

Steuerle, Eugene, and Jon M. Bakija. *Retooling Social Security for the 21st Century: Right and Wrong Approaches to Reform*. Washington, D.C.: Urban Institute Press, 1994.

Stewart, James B. *Blind Eye: The Terrifying Story of a Doctor Who Got Away with Murder*. New York: Simon & Schuster, 2000.

Tax Foundation. *Putting a Face on America's Tax Returns*. Washington, D.C.: Author, 2005.

Taylor, Lori L. "Does the United States Still Overinvest in Housing?" *Economic Review*, Federal Reserve Bank of Dallas (Second Quarter 1998): 10–18.

Thorson, James A. "The Effects of Zoning on Housing Construction." *Journal of Housing Economics* 6, no. 1 (March 1997): 81–91.

Tinbergen, Jan. *Economic Policy: Principles and Design*. Amsterdam: North-Holland Publishing, 1956.

Tocqueville, Alexis de. *Democracy in America, Vol. II*. New York: Vintage Classics, 1990.

Tullock, Gordon. "The Welfare Costs of Tariffs, Monopolies, and Theft." *Western Economic Journal* 5 (March 1967): 224–32.

Unionstats. "Union Membership and Coverage Database from the CPS." February 8, 2008. www.unionstats.com/ (accessed March 3, 2008).

U.S. Bureau of Labor Statistics, U.S. Department of Labor. "Consumer Expenditures in 2005." February 2007, www.bls.gov/cex/csxann05.pdf (accessed May 25, 2008).

————. *The Employment Situation: September 2007*, Release USDL-07-1492, October 5, 2007.

U.S. Congress. House Ways and Means Committee. *The Social Security Bill*. Report on the 1935 Act, H.R. 7260, 74th Congress, 1st Sess., Report No. 615. www.ssa .gov/history/reports/35housereport.html (accessed March 8, 2008).

U.S. Department of Education. *A Test of Leadership: Charting the Future of U.S. Higher Education*. Washington, D.C.: 2006.

U.S. Department of Education, National Center for Education Evaluation and Regional Assistance. *Effectiveness of Reading and Mathematics Software Products: Findings from the First Student Cohort*. Washington, D.C.: Author, 2007.

U.S. Department of Housing and Urban Development. "HUD Data Shows Fannie Mae and Freddie Mac Have Trailed the Industry in Providing Affordable Housing in 44 States." News Release No. 04-066, July 6, 2004. www.hud.gov/news/release.cfm?content=pr04-066.cfm&CFID=1184198&CFTOKEN=48003960 (accessed March 3, 2008).

Vale, Lawrence J. *From the Puritans to the Projects: Public Housing and Public Neighbors*. Cambridge, Mass.: Harvard University Press, 2000.

Vasquez, Vince. *Digital Welfare: The Failure of the Universal Service System*. San Francisco: Pacific Research Institute, 2006.

Vedder, Richard. "Economic Growth, Economic Justice, and Public Policy." Testimony before the Joint Economic Committee of Congress, hearing on Ensuring our Economic Future by Promoting Middle-Class Prosperity, 110th Cong., 1st sess., January 31, 2007.

Wenglinsky, Harold. *Using Technology Wisely: The Keys to Success in Schools*. New York: Teachers College Press, 2005.

Whyte, William H. *The Organization Man*. New York: Simon & Schuster, 1956.

Wilson, James Q. *The Moral Sense*. New York: Free Press, 1993.

INDEX

ABOUT THE AUTHOR

Joseph V. Kennedy is an attorney and economist living in Arlington, Virginia. He has held several positions in the public and private sectors including Chief Economist of the U. S. Department of Commerce, General Counsel for the U. S. Senate Permanent Subcommittee on Investigations, Senior Economist with the Joint Economic Committee in Congress and over ten years as an economist and attorney with the Manufacturer's Alliance.